Praise for *Riding the Edge*

" **I** galloped through it. Couldn't help it. It was that good a read. It's beautifully written; my heart is flapping. The romance of adventure has never been so romantic or so adventurous. Michael and Deborah ride their bikes through Europe, and then the Middle East. On these pages you will find the heights of wisdom and introspection, food writing that rivals MFK Fisher's. The actual bike path is strewn with magnificent back road scenery and new friends, including the inspired and inspiring as well as the war devastated. But Michael and Deborah's life-changing encounter turns out to be, in fact, between themselves. Yes: to find one another is the real purpose of their journey."

> —**Risa Miller**, author of *Welcome to Heavenly Heights* and
> *My Before and After Life* and winner of the PEN Award
> for best first novel

" **A** t once, a shimmering travel memoir, spiritual quest, and pilgrimage into the heart of a relationship, *Riding the Edge* is one of the bravest books I've read this year. When a multicultural couple discards their successful careers and stagnant life to cycle through Europe and the Middle East, their journey takes them to deeper, darker, and ultimately higher places than anticipated.

"In captivating prose that captures epicurean delight as deftly as the terror of war, Michael Tobin shares a story of self-discovery, compassion, and divine providence that will have readers redefining the meaning of love and commitment."

> —**Milou Koenings**, *USA Today* best-selling author

"This is an unforgettable love story between a beautiful man and woman, two young people on an unforgettable physical and spiritual journey throughout Europe and the Middle East, seizing life courageously and appreciatively. It is a poem about the humanity of everyday people everywhere, but it is also a truthful and caring encounter with the complexity of the human soul, including the horrors of human destructiveness. The author succeeds in having us join in a celebration of life, even as he also conveys poignant sensitivity to the ultimate Holocaust that befell his people. A page turner you won't want to put down."

—**Prof. Israel W. Charny**, author of *The Genocide Contagion: How We Commit and Confront Holocaust and Genocide* (2016); *A Democratic Mind: Psychology and Psychiatry with Fewer Meds and More Soul* (2017); and *Psychotherapy for a Democratic Mind: Treating Intimacy, Tragedy, Violence, and Evil* (2018)

"Tobin is a very engaging writer with clear prose. Especially delightful are his passages on landscape, landmarks, and various regional cuisines. The chapters on Paris and Corfu are fascinating and memorable. Score 9 of 10."

—**Book Life/Publisher's Weekly Prize**

"Michael Tobin's *Riding the Edge: A Love Song to Deborah* is an extraordinary memoir of a bicycle odyssey in 1980 and how its unexpected and incredible encounters and experiences turned into a life-changing journey.

"Along their bicycle journey, they meet people who are survivors of WWII, devastated by the effects of the Holocaust in which their families were killed. This is what drew me into the memoir, these inner journeys. I loved the rich details of people, food, scenery, and weather! Those details brought the bicycle trip to life for me, giving depth to the emotional and spiritual impact of the journey. Michael Tobin's memoir is a beautifully written and profoundly personal story of love . . . it is also thought-provoking and inspiring."

—**Reader's Favorite Review**, Highest Rating 5 of 5

"There is not a sense that remains untouched by Michael Tobin's love song to Deborah and to their life together. One can smell and taste the forests and the rich and ethnic food, hear the cacophony of gripping personal stories, some painful, some filled with grace, along with the calls and whispers of animals and birds. One's mind's eye envisions the panoramic vistas, both the miraculously gorgeous and those assaulted by the horrors of war.

"The moistness of the soil, the coldness of the metals, the fabric of humanity, and the materials of their journey, both gentle and harsh, amid an unending search for resolution—all these create a full-heart and full-mind experience for the reader.

But most of all, this book moves the soul."

> —**Toby Klein Greenwald**, poet, journalist, award-win-
> ning theater director; recipient, American Jewish Press
> Association Simon Rockower Awards for Excellence in
> Jewish Journalism

"The author's love song to Deborah is written in tenderness and truth. It emerges from the depths of his being directly to the reader's temperament, and, to paraphrase Joseph Conrad, 'reaches the secret spring of our responsive emotions.' It is a perfect example of making art out of life. The power of this account persists long after the last word is read. *Riding the Edge* will shake you to the core, make you laugh, cry, and shout in outrage with the author at the suffering Deborah and he witnessed.

"This book is a game changer. It will challenge your assumptions, question your choices, and demand nothing less than a deep dive into the question of love and identity."

—**Daniel Chertoff**, author of *Palestine Posts: An Eyewitness Account of the Birth of Israel* (Toby Press, 2019)

"You have done a great job. And you have done something rare: I saw the story. I felt the story. It was palpable. The writing is gorgeous; I laughed, and I cried."

—**Marion Roach Smith**, author and renowned expert on memoir writing

"This is an intimate portrayal of two people who set out on a journey, sparked by longing and driven by a desire to discover their own history and purpose, a journey that takes you across the world and deep into themselves.

"Traveling through magnificent vistas and memorable moments, watch them be transformed. Simple meals become spiritual experiences, and chance encounters are serendipitous markers along the road directing them toward a deeper purpose.

"Peppered with anecdotes and philosophy, insightful musings and intriguing personas. Each place leaves its mark, each person its imprint. Through the Alps and litter, past castles and sea they travel. Across a traumatized Europe and a war-ravaged Middle East. They face the generational impact of war and the deep meaning of family. With each experience they uncover the humanness that connects us all and the way that love can change everything.

"Placed at the intersection of essence and memory, this book is at its very heart a gift, lovingly culled and magnificently rendered, given generously to you the reader so that you too can be swept away in the current of purpose and toward deep meaning.

"This inspirational memoir, written with an open heart, will change you."

—**Naama Heller**, author and food critic

"This work is utterly, utterly, infinitely, utterly brilliant. The depth of the author's thinking and breadth of descriptive powers are astounding."

—**Richard Shavei-Tzion**, published poet

"Reading this book was a privilege. The writing is brilliant. So vivid I could picture the scenery, taste the food, feel the emotions of pain, sadness, and terror. I cried, laughed, and felt enriched by the experience. I will tell everyone to read it."

—**Cheryl**, reader

"*Riding the Edge* is a compelling story that is beautifully written. It truly, truly is. And within its pages are lessons, thoughts, and experiences that will most definitely resonate with a wide range of readers. It is one of the highest quality pieces this reader has ever reviewed.

"The characters are vivid, often humorous, always compelling, and continually unique even as many share thematic stories of violence, either during the Holocaust, World War II, or in the chaos of Lebanon."

—**James Buchanan**, author, ghostwriter, literary critic

Riding the Edge
A Love Song to Deborah

MICHAEL TOBIN

This book is a memoir reflecting the author's present recollections of experiences over time. Its story and its words are the author's alone. Some names, details and characteristics may be changed, some events may be compressed, and some dialogue may be recreated.

Published by River Grove Books
Austin, TX
www.rivergrovebooks.com

Distributed by River Grove Books

Design and composition by Greenleaf Book Group and Gal Weizman
Cover design by Ben Herskowitz, Etc Studios

Publisher's Cataloging-in-Publication data is available.

Print ISBN: 978-1-63299-390-8

eBook ISBN: 978-1-63299-391-5

EAN: 0794712345077

First Edition

To Deborah: Who taught me how to listen

"No one ever travels so high
as he who knows not where he is going."

—Oliver Cromwell

Note to Readers

Dear Reader,

This is a book about truth and love.

My source materials included my extensive journal entries, letters to our respective families, and detailed maps on which we marked our route. Since my journal entries describe what happened in broad strokes, I added contextual details and re-created dialogues as I remember them.

All the encounters happened with real people in the manner in which I described. I searched extensively online to locate the individuals who had and continue to have such a profound impact on our lives. With one exception—Cathy, whom we met in Mykonos—I was unsuccessful in discovering anyone about whom I wrote. Therefore, I've changed names and, on occasion, other identifying data.

I share this story with you in the hope that the lessons we learned will inspire each of you to love with more passion, to take more risks for the truth, and to give of yourself to others as others gave to us.

With love,
Michael Tobin

Part 1
Leaving

In the longing
that starts one
on the path
is a kind of
homesickness.

Peter
Matthiessen,
The Snow Leopard

Middlebury, Vermont: Winter 1980

The endlessly ash-gray days hang over us like a heavy silent treatment—full of waiting, impossible to bear.

The weather's inescapable during the first eighteen days of January. The cold is so raw that each time you inhale, it's like a razor ripping at the back of your throat; pieces of your bare skin freeze to the metal it touches; and, if you're like me, your nose bleeds.

But it's the gray that makes your mind freeze up.

It destroys distinctions.

From our large bay window facing east toward the Green Mountains, I can barely make out the five apple trees that border our property and our neighbor's, a family of four that believes silence makes for cordial relationships.

Jim Mack, my usually taciturn auto mechanic, tells me weather like this can make "ah man's mind to seize up" like "crack up." I can picture it: Jim Mack and his buddies at the garage shaking their heads and saying, "Ain't it ah shame 'bout Lestah. The damn weathah got to him. His mind seized up like ah piston."

During these grim days, a mind can turn in on itself. Thoughts run amok, coming without sense or reason. For some, the only escape is alcohol or suicide, like my former client Bob, who graduated from multiple shots of Southern Comfort to a self-inflicted shotgun blast to his head.

And yet, as the Yaqui shaman, Don Juan, told Carlos Castaneda: *clarity blinds*. We don't grow from the illuminating light of certainty. When you have only answers, there are no questions. The shaman teaches us that the journey toward self-knowledge begins from confusion and doubt—those dark days when our minds struggle to find an exit.

You could say a mind that turns in on itself might discover the way out.

On the first Saturday in January, I convince Deborah to take a much-needed break from slaving over her dissertation to join me for breakfast at the Frog Hollow Café, a counterculture hangout for the spiritually restless.

We're halfway through our whole-wheat blueberry pancakes when we overhear a Paul Bunyan guy—long red beard, matching red ski hat, brown logger's shirt—complain, in a surprising Brooklyn accent, about his "damn pipes that froze."

Deborah and I give each other one of those knowing glances and laugh—a welcome relief. For a second, I wonder if my brilliant and beautiful Archimedes will explain to him about the ingenious hydraulic system she designed for our former home, a lakeside cabin, to keep the water flowing during those minus-twenty-five-degree days.

It's a revelation to see her smile. For the last two weeks she's been grinding her teeth, tensing every muscle from her stomach to her neck, and looking like she's ready to kill (me) over the slightest provocation. This "craziness" (my word)—this "understandable reaction" (her words)—began when the head of her doctoral committee called to inform her—for the fourth time—that she had to rewrite her thesis on psychotherapy and creativity.

It doesn't help that I received my doctorate six months earlier.

I gaze at her for a few long seconds. I love the way those intelligent contours of her face join to create striking geometric patterns. But it's the delicate curve of her cheeks, her sensual lips, and gentle eyes that soften her sharp, demanding features.

I long for her curves, our circuitous routes, and those serendipitous moments from our former life before ambition and career overshadowed the unexpected and elevated the shoulds and the have-tos to the position of command and control. Forget about those moments when our eyes lock, our breath quickens, and our bodies tingle. Now, our existence is stridently efficient, moving at linear velocity or Deborah's speed—the pace of a mind cluttered with case notes, research data, and arguments aimed at her doctoral committee.

This life is straight like Route 7, the two-way road that connects our five-bedroom home in Middlebury to Deborah's office in Rutland. In two days, dressed in a fashionable tweed pantsuit straight from her parents' exclusive boutique, she'll drive her lemon-colored Toyota at one minute per mile, a speed fast enough to risk yet another ticket. Twenty feet from her office, she'll take two deep breaths, adjust her professional mask, sit down in her black swivel chair, and confront her therapy clients for demanding too much of themselves.

Where is that wild siren?

The one who lit me up in the summer of '74 as she spun around the Antioch dance floor like a God-intoxicated whirling dervish, throwing off beams of light from an insane quantity of multicolored Third World jewelry she wore from head to toe.

I can't find her.

That siren without shame told me she had purchased those beads, stones, and crystals from a souk in Fez, Morocco, at an embarrassingly cheap price. And then like she was a goddammed improv actress, she pantomimed for me the scene with the merchant. Wordlessly, she showed how she bargained: Argue, flirt, feign disinterest, walk away, and then with a look of pained resignation, accept a price you tell the merchant is higher than any reasonable person ought to pay. Can't let him think, she told me, that a girl outsmarted him.

My top was spinning; my sense of equilibrium—gone.

On first impression, back in the summer of 1974, you might have thought I'd be exuberantly spontaneous—perhaps even passionate. I had a gypsy look about me with shoulder-length, black wavy hair, an abundant mustache, ruddy complexion, and piercing black eyes. Yet, despite my fiery Leo energy, I monitored the flame—especially in the wake left by my ex-wife, Susan.

But not this time.

The graceful power in Deborah's tall, lithe body created an immediate destabilizing effect in me. Her spiritual presence captivated me—kind of like a Native American priestess—the exact image of how I envisioned Pocahontas.

The first words I said to her were, "Excuse me, are you an American Indian?"

"Sorry to disappoint you," she answered, with a trace of a hillbilly accent. "I'm an American Arab."

"Oh . . . really . . . that's interesting," I said, trying to find someplace in my cerebral cortex where Arab with a twang works—maybe next to a rabbi with a long beard and side curls who plays quarterback for the New York Giants.

And then, like she was a mind reader, she asked, "Having trouble figuring out what box to put me in?"

"Yeah, you got me. No place in my brain for an Arab Dolly Parton. You got to help me out here."

Between dances, I found out she was a Lebanese Christian. All four of her grandparents were born in Lebanon and she was raised in the affluent Arab subculture of Charleston, West Virginia, a city she described as "cut off from the rest of humanity by the Appalachian Mountains and a thick yellow fog of Union Carbide pollutants."

Since graduating from Wellesley College, she had lived the last three years in France, Sweden, Italy, and Spain, and was fluent in each of those countries' languages. She was a teacher of Transcendental Meditation, and before coming to Antioch, had spent two of those three years in Italy and Spain meditating and working with Maharishi Mahesh Yogi, the founder of TM. Somewhere amid all this biographical material, she slipped in that her best friends from childhood and from Wellesley were all Jews. "What do you think that means?" she asked.

"I don't know," I answered. "My best friends were all non-Jews."

Lots of boxes. Lots of places to explore.

Five weeks later, on August 8, 1974, on the occasion of Richard Nixon's resignation, I invited Deborah to celebrate the long-awaited event with me.

As they say in social psychology, nothing can bring people closer together than a common enemy.

Sitting in front of a roaring fire at my friend Zandy's ski chalet, we drank a magnum of expensive champagne. At the precise instant that Nixon tearfully addressed the nation and said, ". . . therefore, I shall resign the Presidency, effective noon tomorrow," we tossed our glasses into the fire, kissed, and said good riddance to the man who taught us an old lesson: *You reap what you sow.*

By two in the morning, five weeks after first laying eyes on her, I showed my hand. The crazy thing was that my "I love you" was so unrehearsed, and so unlike me to express, that it had to be real—*terrifyingly so.* Like I'd just discovered the other half of my soul and come home. A lot scarier, in fact, because in a moment of health, you can always walk away from the madness of love. But how can you leave a part of yourself?

She cried. I loved her tears. Partly because of the power of her vulnerability—each drop contained a world of love, fear, joy, and sadness—feelings that matched my own. And, partly, because of the message I heard in those tears: *I don't need you to rescue me; I need to feel your presence.*

Over the next year, our relationship grew naturally without the need for assessment, definition, and that dreary work of searching under every emotional rock for that lost feeling of connection. So, in September 1975, we moved in together. No big decision, no terrifying sink-or-swim leap into the deep end of commitment. Merely the next evolutionary stage in a relationship that—as I saw it—was meant to be, like the rhythm of the tides and the phases of the moon. But back then when the river flowed by itself, I couldn't imagine that a gentle ripple contains a raging force and that the other side of the moon holds no light.

*   *   *

During those sullen days in January 1980, my psychotherapy clients' dreams and thoughts are heavy with death and loss.

Death, according to William James, is "the worm at the core," the basic fear from which none of us are free. Ernest Becker, in his Pulitzer Prize–winning book *The Denial of Death*, describes the fear of death as ever-present and all-consuming. Man, he says, can't reconcile the fact that "he's a god that shits . . . he sticks out of nature with a towering majesty and yet he goes back into the ground a few feet in order blindly and dumbly to rot and disappear forever."

Death doesn't frighten me; it's *not living* that scares the hell out of me. Like Dylan sang, "He not busy being born, is busy dying." I know about that. My father made a safe choice: He gave up the uncertainty of medical school for the security of selling tablecloths for his older brother, Lou. He hated himself for his cowardice but raged against my sister and me, as if the two of us were at fault.

For eighteen years, we watched him suffer the slow death of emptiness until my mother passed away from breast cancer, which was, for him, a kind of release. You can suffer forever and die, or you can decide to live. When my father got up from the seven-day shiva mourning period, he went into Lou's office and announced his retirement. At fifty-six, he disturbed his universe.

It's the slow inner death from meaninglessness—the one my father pulled away from at the last moment—that terrifies me.

"Imagine you're lying on your deathbed," I suggest to my clients as they drift into a deep state of relaxation, "and you're watching an instant replay of your life. What would you do differently? What choices would you have made or not made?"

I ask myself those same questions. What's missing? Our success brings us further from ourselves and each other. My sense of purpose is waning, my belief in what I am doing, weakening.

Our psychotherapeutic lifestyle is losing its luster, perhaps because we're living life vicariously, observing and listening more than participating. I want to touch and be touched by life again, to cry at someone's pain (even my own) rather than examine it clinically.

It's time for change—for a coup d'état of the spirit.

It's two p.m. on the last Sunday in January, and Deborah's been typing for five consecutive hours with no breaks for food or conversation. I feel restless. I have to get out, but there's nothing out there. A dense fog hovers low and thick over the dairy farms and mountains, absorbing everything in its wake.

"Weather's a circumstance," I tell myself. "Don't let it control you. Go for a long run." The temperature's an unseasonably warm thirty-seven degrees, close to perfect for a cold-weather runner. Surprisingly, Deborah agrees to accompany me on her bike.

Running and biking in Middlebury and beyond is usually a feast of moveable delights. Traversing meadows and woodlands, the undulating gravel roads connect the dairy farms and hamlets to Middlebury—although today, sadly, without those winter colors that I love: the contrasting shades of ivory crystals that hint at the snow's age; the old red-roofed Vermont farm houses, embraced by families of evergreens; Ben and Jerry's soon-to-be-famous black-and-white Holstein cows lingering in the pasture; and the Green Mountains, usually resplendent in emerald-colored pine and milk-white powder, are all swallowed by the fog into a no-man's-land of hazy distinctions.

We choose a smooth dirt road for a two-hour, fifteen-mile, round-trip bike-run from Middlebury to Weybridge. At three miles, I accelerate, running at a pace I call a "good tempo," quick but not furious, close to my competitive 10K speed. Deborah lags, making no effort to stay with me. After ten minutes, I reverse direction and return to her. Our eyes focus on one another. I have difficulty reading her.

"I wish you hadn't run ahead," she says. "I like being next to you."

"Really? I didn't think you'd notice."

"Why? Am I so difficult you have to run away from me?"

"I wasn't running away—just doing my thing. You should know

about that. It's not like you've been approachable. More like stay away or deal with your bitchiness."

"So why did you ask me to join you? Wouldn't a few hours away from the 'bitch' be exactly what you want: hassle-free, communing with nature and all that. You—"

Suddenly, the stirring in a bush to the left catches our attention. A large raccoon darts toward the frozen pond below an abandoned saw-mill. A flock of sparrows circles above. I watch their small gray bodies distinct against the leaden sky.

Why *did* I ask her to be with me?

I miss Deborah. We desperately need a change, a break from this cycle of resentment and distance. Moving together is a safe gamble, a way of keeping company without too much investment. We both like to move, and it's not too cold. At worst, we'll get more of the same: arguments and icy words, but I can always—literally—run away.

I turn toward her. "I asked you for the same reason you said yes. Because we want the same thing. We're just too afraid to make it happen, maybe too stubborn, or maybe both."

I notice Deborah's features softening, becoming more playful. "Michael," she commands, "come here!" She points to a spot one inch from her body—close enough to feel her heart beating and her warm breath on my cold cheeks. She puts her arms around me and draws me to her lips in an embrace more penetrating and appealing than words.

"Wow! What did I do to deserve that?" I ask, breathing heavily.

"For being you."

We pick up the pace, moving together side by side. The wind is stronger, and the temperature has dropped a few degrees. Deborah's face is red and moist. She smiles at me. I smile back. I'm breathing easily and effortlessly. The machine is working. Heart, muscles, lungs—the whole thumping, gasping, sweating, breathing organism working together, expressing the oneness of movement, taking you wherever it takes you, wherever you need to go.

With Deborah bicycling on my left side, we enter the Pulp Mill

Bridge, a 195-foot-long covered bridge spanning the Otter Creek, built in 1820 from red oak beams, constructed in an interlacing series of triangular lattices called trusses. Like all covered bridges, the Pulp Mill was designed to protect both itself and its travelers from the elements. Yet, it also provides an additional service: an intimate hideaway. Deep within its dark and warm interior where the moist air is rich with the aroma of rugged red oak, you can take your lover in your arms and steal a kiss, or make a life-changing decision . . .

"Michael," Deborah says, breaking the silence, "I love you, and I need you to be *with* me. We need more times like this to escape to ourselves and each other. Let's just keep going."

"Go where?" I ask.

"Anywhere. Everywhere!" she answers. "Bali. The Himalayas. The universe—wherever we want! Let's just stay on our bikes!

"Michael, just think about it. We could lie on a beach in Bali or trek in the Himalayas. Now is the time to do it. We don't have kids, we have enough money, and we have the skills and experience to start up again. Remember, you once told me you don't want to run your life like it's a mad dash from fear to security—like your father. We can make it something else."

For the next mile, we continue in silence. I run to the rhythm of the mantra: Escape. From what? To where? Anywhere far from this freezing grayness. Somewhere where the outcome is unknown and uncertain and where the path leads you wherever it's meant to lead you. Like a meditation—where surrender, not control, leads to depth.

For a few moments, my eyes follow the path of three star-like crystals as they drift to the ground. As we reach the outskirts of Middlebury, the snowfall grows heavier, blanketing the ground like a gentle eiderdown. But sadly, in a few hours, our world will become monochromatic. The gray will glow off the fresh snow like the light in old pictures. But with apologies to Robert Frost, a man who lived within a snowball's throw from our home—I'm not impressed.

After nine New England winters, the only thing this dazzling whiteness does is remind me that for the next four frigid months, I'll

be slipping and sliding on brown, crusty ice. As we approach our drive-
way, I think: "Right now it's *summer* in Bali."

Throughout the next week, we share our fears about leaving our practices, our concerns about having to begin again. But a deeper logic tells
us, "Trust yourselves. It's time to move on." We were meant to move on.
It's in our DNA to search, to feel uncomfortable with comfort. To not
let fear and security dictate our path in life.

My supervisor once told me to focus intently on the client's opening statement. "Listen carefully," he said. "The theme of the work is
embedded in that first sentence." Our first date and our first in-depth
conversation took place in Deborah's Antioch dorm room where we
pored over maps and dreamt of traveling east. Isn't East where the answers lie?

That night Deborah told me that for her the road to the Far East
passes through the Middle East, to Lebanon, her ancestral home, a
place where the tragic circumstance of civil war had prevented her
from becoming an exchange student. I remember her words well. "I
don't know why I feel like I must visit Lebanon, but I have to. Like I
have to complete something." Strangely, I thought at the time, that's
how I feel about Israel.

By the beginning of March, Deborah's committee accepts her thesis. By the end of March, we inform our clients that we'll be leaving in
two months. Despite our fears that it may be too hard for some, our clients seem more inspired than upset, more intrigued and curious than
crushed by the weight of abandonment.

Our expected date of departure is May 30, 1980. The plan is to
bicycle from Brussels to Athens, stopping for a month in Paris with
Deborah's friend from her student days at the Sorbonne, Alain, and
his girlfriend, Simone. From Athens, we'll set sail in a southeasterly
direction for the Aegean Islands until we reach Cyprus. From there,
we'll visit Deborah's relatives in Lebanon—assuming there's a break in
the fighting—return to Cyprus, and sail to Haifa. In Israel, we'll work
as kibbutz volunteers, sell our bikes, and fly to India, meditate with

Maharishi, go north to Nepal to trek in the Himalayas, and then travel overland across Southeast Asia.

The proposal looks good on paper, but a journey has a mind of its own and a heart that disrupts . . .

Part 2

Discovering

The personal
life deeply led
always expands
into truths
beyond itself.

ANAIS NIN

From Brussels to the French Border: May 31 to June 6

I want to live my life like Nietzsche: *Amor fati*—love your fate! Whatever life throws at you, embrace it. Own it. It's what you need to be you.

But not this.

Definitely not this.

Not my worst nightmare.

Not rats in the walls.

At least twenty, by the sound of their feet scurrying up and down, up and down, up and down. With a sense of smell a hundred times stronger than a human's, it's only a matter of time before their radar-like noses pick up the sweet scent of our half-eaten chocolate croissants and gnaw through this paper-thin plasterboard wall.

I'm terrified—the heart-pounding, palm-sweating, stammering kind of panic when your mind locks down and your vocal cords freeze, like in a dream where you can't escape your attacker.

This is my worst nightmare, the thing I fear above all else. When I was nine, an age when a mind is far too impressionable to distinguish between the literal and the literary, I encountered Winston Smith, the protagonist of Orwell's *1984*, who as a youth discovered a frenzied mob of rodents devouring his mother's murdered body.

Lying in bed one night, I entered Room 101 where a terrified Winston Smith, bound to a chair, faced two wire cages strapped to his face, holding starving rodents clawing at the metal to gorge on his nose, cheeks, and eyes. My nine-year-old mind pictured gaping holes in place of the features that made Winston—Winston.

And when I was ten, I read about a mob of crazed rodents that scratched right through the Sheetrock of a Harlem tenement until they reached a baby's crib and tore at the little four-month-old girl's flesh like it was a piece of cheese.

These images were far too terrifying for a prepubescent boy from a Long Island suburb to carry around in his head. To a child—at least this child—shadows in the corners became rats in the mind.

And now, in Brussels, Belgium, on the first night of an around-the-world odyssey, I'm facing the very real possibility that dozens of squealing rats, having picked up the sweet scent of our pastries, are about to end my trip—in the most final of ways—before it even begins.

I should have listened to myself and not given in so easily. I told Deborah that this repulsive Brussels hotel was fit for whores, winos, and bugs but not for two weary travelers who'd just spent seven hours in a plane and another five in the airport trying to assemble their bicycles. But she insisted, in her coy way, "Aren't you the same person who bragged about hitching across America, sleeping under bridges, not bathing for a week, and barely eating?"

At two in the morning, after we've been up for over twenty-four hours, she admits I was right, although her problem isn't the rats. It's the combined torture of bedsprings that dig into her lower back sending shooting pains down her right leg and the screeching sounds next door of a prostitute's fake orgasms that grate on the nerves like the shattering shrieks of two cats in heat.

This trip has not started well. The rats are just one piece—albeit a large one for me—of a ridiculous, messy beginning.

*   *   *

We landed in Brussels after flying seven hours on Capitol Air, a discount airline that Deborah's mother, the imperious Betty Mae Risk, demanded—no commanded—we not take. "The worst safety record in aviation history. You do remember, Deborah, that one of their planes missed the runway at the Charleston Airport and landed in a ditch."

What my not-quite-mother-in-law, the Queen of Misinformation, didn't realize was that two words that sound the same can be spelled differently. Like Capitol Air and Capital Airlines. Her Capital, a domestic-only airline, has a dismal record of crashes. Our Capitol flies to Brussels and lands safely.

I met Betty Mae for the first time in November 1975, two months after Deborah and I started living together. The encounter took place on the corner of Fifth Avenue and 52nd Street. Deborah's parents were in New York City on a buying trip for their clothing business and invited us to dinner at La Grenouille ("Frogs' Legs" in French), an upscale French restaurant. Places like that make me nervous, not so much because of the strange food. I love to eat, but I get confused by all those knives, spoons, and forks. Blame it on my father. To him, table manners were an anti-Semitic conspiracy to keep Jews out of the country clubs.

At the time, this is what I wrote in my journal about this memorable first meeting between me, the New York Jewish boyfriend, and Deborah's terrifying mother, the Lebanese queen with the hillbilly accent:

Two days before I meet her parents, Deborah insists I practice. She lays out the silverware like we're having a formal meal and gives me a lesson on when to use the small fork and spoon; how to chew ("Quietly, not with your mouth open and definitely not when you're talking"); when and how to wipe my mouth ("Not with the back of your hand"); how to use my knife—instead of my more reliable thumb—to push things like runaway peas back onto the fork ("If you use your thumb, I'll die of embarrassment and Betty Mae will hate you for life"); and what to do with my hands when I'm not eating ("How about if I play with myself?").

The evening of my test arrives. Turns out it's a multi-part exam. As we walk to La Grenouille, Betty Mae pulls me aside, puts her arm through mine like we're lovers in the 1940s. As her Parliament Light cigarette breath tickles the inside of my ear, she whispers, "You should know Deborah has a powerful need to be in control." I look up at Betty Mae, slightly shocked, but concealing it with my best poker face—direct eye contact, a conscientious effort not to blink, and a friendly, easy-going look—as if that statement is the most reasonable thing for a mother to say to her daughter's new boyfriend.

Betty Mae looks down to face me. Standing five feet ten inches in heels, she's an inch and a half taller than me, a position she clearly enjoys. She waits for my reaction. "Successful businesswoman" is written all over her. She's like a statue of a Lebanese queen: fiercely penetrating, deep-set, coal-dark eyes; regal nose; and sharply chiseled, angular face. Even to my inexperienced eye, I know that an exclusive New York hairstylist designed and shaped her severe jet-black hair with a few perfectly colored blonde streaks thrown in for effect.

A black pants suit and a white mink coat underscore the image of wealth and power. The message to me and to anyone else with whom she deigns to speak is clear: "I expect to be heard. I get what I want. I play in a man's world and I'm used to intimidating men."

Only one thing marks her as something other than she claims to be: her accent. Despite her best efforts at de-twanging, she can't hide her hill-billy roots. She's Cruella de Vil from the coal mining town of Bluefield, West Virginia.

"I appreciate you telling me this, Betty," I say, making strong eye contact, "because now—for the first time in my life—I finally have someone I trust to run my life."

She stares at me for a second, her Rolodex brain flipping for the right response, and then laughs and says, "You're the right one."

*   *   *

Despite Betty Mae's dire warnings about our choice of airlines, it wasn't our personal safety that concerned us. It was that of our bikes. We were determined to have them arrive undamaged, which is why we had gone to such great lengths to ensure that we packed and protected the bikes properly. We even enlisted the help of my bicycling aficionado, God-is-in-the-details brother-in-law, Bill (my sister's husband), a man who sounds positively born again when talking about the pros and cons of various brands of bubble wrap.

At the airport in Brussels, we grab the two boxes from the carousel. They appear to be intact—no wayward cardboard flaps, no bent or torn sides, no gaping holes from an angry hook. But sometimes—maybe often—things are not what they seem to be.

On further inspection, we discover Deborah's bike has arrived with two broken snaps that hold the pannier bags to the rear of her bike, and, after assembling mine, I hear a distinctive rubbing sound in tune to the rear wheel's rotation. The cause: a bent wheel guard. Deborah also notices that some important screws, washers, and bolts have disappeared, making the bike about as safe as a car with three missing lug nuts and a loose fourth one on the right front tire.

While we're attempting to unpack, diagnose, and repair our two Japanese bicycles, a flock of gawking, giggling Japanese tourists crowd around us. They go jingoistic because we own *their* bicycles. No different, I imagine, from waving the Stars and Stripes and singing "America the Beautiful" each time a customer leaves McDonald's on the Champs-Élysées with a Big Mac in his hand.

Meanwhile, three Belgian airport workers intervene. One of the three, a rather portly mustached Belgian in overalls, starts barking commands to Deborah in Flemish while gesturing fiercely with his hands that she should hand him the wrench she's been using to tighten the bolts.

Deborah asks him in French to bring her some screws and wire for a makeshift repair. The Belgian starts screaming in French that there are no screws in Europe to fit a Takara bike "because your General MacArthur forced the Japanese to adopt the American system."

Deborah turns to me and says, "He's an idiot. The Japanese use the metric system. The screws on our bikes fit a European bicycle." She asks one of the other workers if he can find some wire for her.

A few minutes later he returns with a spool and a cutter. In a matter of moments, Deborah has ingeniously secured the bicycles so we can now ride from the airport to our hotel. We quickly dress into our new bicycle shorts, shoes, and shirts, and pack our clothes and equipment into our panniers. We place the tent and sleeping bag on my bike and wheel our bicycles out of the airport into gale-force freezing rain, huge puddles, and heavy traffic. It's the worst combination for a cyclist, let alone two cyclists who've never ridden in traffic, in a foreign country, and with fully loaded bicycles held together by wire.

Good news: We find a bike shop on the way and replace the missing snaps, screws, bolts, and washers.

One hour later we arrive at our rat-infested hotel, drenched and blue with cold.

As the sixteenth-century English playwright John Heywood wrote, "A hard beginning makes a good ending."

It's now four a.m. and Deborah has drifted off to sleep. I lie in the bed terrorized by the repetitive pitter-patter scampering of rodents and by the periodic squeals of a rat leaking testosterone. I believe that there is something specific about a rat squeal that triggers our primitive fight/flight brains to send out instant distress signals. Terrified, I wait for the rats to breach the wall.

They don't.

Providence intervenes. No squeals, no scampering feet. Only Holy Silence. There is no other way to comprehend it—in an instant I achieve Grace.

It's pouring.

Viewed from the stained, cracked windows of our room, the rain is coming down in hard sheets, driven by strong southwesterly gusts. As the crow flies, Paris is in a straight, southwesterly direction from Brussels. Simple meaning: We're about to ride directly into a freezing downpour.

Andrew, the owner of the bike shop back in Vermont, warned us about the European rains. "You need mudguards, waterproof rain gear, and covers for your panniers. Know that brakes may not work effectively in a downpour, so ride slowly and carefully. Puddles can be your biggest enemy. They hide potholes, nails, glass, and other objects that can cause an immediate flat."

The wind renders umbrellas dangerously useless. There are no other cyclists on the road. The sky is mid-November Vermont gray— dark, foreboding, and unyielding. It's a day to sit by a fireplace, drink hot-buttered rum, read a Hermann Hesse novel, and fantasize about transformative experiences in exotic places. No one rides in this weather.

But we have one of those caught-between-a-rock-and-a-hard- place choices: Either stay with the rats or ride in the rain. For me, anything but the rats; for Deborah, anything but freezing rain.

Some things are not negotiable.

I'm the guy with the trauma. Another day of rats scurrying with- in the thin walls while I wait in terror for these four-legged devils to scratch and claw their way onto my bed is a fast-track to madness.

*   *   *

On our second date, Deborah and I take mescaline. Deborah suggests we dive into our deepest fears. We both land on rejection and failure. The rules of the game are: 1. Total transparency; 2. A willingness to explore worst-case scenarios like Deborah telling me she likes me only as a friend, or, for her, feeling like any relationship—even this promising one—will eventually fail, leaving her alone and depressed.

To heal from suffering, you embrace it fully. We go deeply into the pain of loss, rejection, and failure. We ask ourselves, "Would we reenter the game of love knowing the same outcome is likely to happen?" We both say yes. The alternative is living life defensively—to be hyperalert to the slightest chance of hurt. In a moment of clarity, we understand that avoid- ance of pain is the path of death. When you construct an impenetrable psychic wall to keep suffering at bay, you do so at the cost of destroying any chance of love, connection, and growth.

Under the influence of a psychedelic, we discover a partner to play with on the knife's edge between danger and growth. Until I met Deborah,

I had been unconsciously assessing every future relationship from the per-
spective of whether we'd challenge each other to seek growth over comfort.
After six hours in an altered state, I know I've found my soul mate and
fellow traveler. I sense—or is it hope?—Deborah feels the same.

*   *   *

Granted this sounds crazy, but when I raise my eyes in search of a sliver of sunlight in the heavy Belgian sky, I see a foreboding streak of gray clouds spreading across the length of the sky like a column of rats racing from west to east devouring everything before it.

I ask Deborah if she notices the column of rats. Her answer surprises me, "Rats? No. Elephants moving from west to east in a single file."

"We're going to do this?" she asks as she mounts her bike to lead us out of Brussels onto the isolated country roads we'll follow for the next ten days to Paris. Last night while I battled my rat fears, Deborah placed our 1:25,000 map on her bed and plotted and memorized our route out of the city. Thank God she's my traveling companion because when it comes to spatial intelligence—a right-brain function that enables you to comprehend a two-dimensional image such as a map and transpose it onto a three-dimensional object such as a winding, heavily trafficked road with shifts in the terrain and no clear signs to orient you—well, faced with that kind of challenge, my brain shuts down. I'm good at understanding concepts like Being and Nothingness, but that won't get us to Paris.

After four hours of slow riding in an unrelenting bitter downpour, we arrive soaked and bone-cold at an empty campsite on the outskirts of Hennuyères, a small village of three thousand residents. Admittedly, there's nothing purifying, transformative, or deeply satisfying about this first day on the road. We did what we had to do—we made our way through and about the dense Brussels traffic, maneuvering around puddles as if we were skiing between the poles of a giant slalom course, sometimes successfully and sometimes not. The drivers try their best to avoid splashing us, but in nonstop rain on roads with poor drainage, the back wheels of the cars shower us with a steady stream of ice water.

We assemble our two-person waterproof tent on a spot close to a barn where there's some protection from the rain and wind. Remarkably, the tent has remained dry because of Andrew's excellent advice about purchasing rain covers for our panniers and tent. I want to ask Deborah how she's doing, but cold and miserable as I am, I'm not sure I can muster up enough compassion to sympathize with what I anticipate will be a steady stream of complaints.

"Michael, how was that for you?" she asks.

"Awful, but we did it. And for you?"

"I hated every freezing moment. If the rain continues, let's take the train to Paris."

"I don't have a problem with that."

My response troubles me. No hesitation, not a moment to reflect whether getting off our bikes and onto a train is consistent with our decision to give up comfort for the physical hardships of the road. Granted, being bitterly cold, soaked, and wretched isn't anyone's idea of fun, but we succeeded in riding nearly forty miles in adverse conditions without falling, freezing, or quitting. Intense experiences like this force you to dig into yourself, to discover a level of mental toughness and resilience you didn't know you had. The stuff of heroes. And I'm feeling heroic as I lie in our dry tent in the warm comfort of my sleeping bag listening to the light rain tap on the roof of our tent. I turn toward Deborah and ask her how she's feeling.

"Better," she says. "We rode through a God-awful freezing downpour, but we did it. A few more experiences like this and I won't know who I am."

"Isn't that the idea?" I ask.

Where's the threshold? That perfect sweet spot where you challenge yourself to move beyond your limits? In yoga, they call it "playing the edge." To achieve the maximum benefit from a stretch you touch the point of pain and back off, ever so slightly. Is being soaked to the bone, hating every freezing moment, and pushing yourself to the precipice called playing the edge? I don't know. Maybe we're just being dramatic. Neither of us is sneezing, coughing, or wheezing; we exhibited remarkable physical and mental toughness; and our bikes and equipment met the test.

All true, but that was one day. Can we endure that level of misery tomorrow, the day after, and for days on end without breaking? A soldier on the first day of battle might feel a powerful adrenaline rush, but after thirty days of close combat, dead buddies, no sleep, and disgusting food, the only thing he experiences is fear, filth, and exhaustion.

Is the purpose of this odyssey to prove how tough we are, to show ourselves and our admirers that we're warriors? I hope not. I don't want this journey to be about self-esteem, about feeling tough, or brave, or in pursuit of any defining quality whether it's negative or positive. I want to learn, to discover, to be open to whatever comes our way, be it the good, the bad, or the ugly. I know that Deborah feels the same.

*   *   *

Fate smiles upon us. We awake to a dry azure sky free from the illusion of somber clouds marching across the skyline like a column of ashen-gray rats.

Our plan today is to ride forty miles on the narrow, tree-lined back roads to Maubeuge, France. According to the map, the route is flat with an occasional rolling hill to wake up complacent muscles. Deborah focuses on the map, memorizing the location of every crossroad, village, bump in the road, and monument to the fallen soldiers of both World Wars. She folds the map and puts it into her handlebar pack.

I go buy breakfast and lunch: soft white cheese, two baguettes, four apples, a salami (for me—Deborah's a vegetarian), four bars of Belgian chocolate, a small jar of otherworldly mayonnaise with Dijon mustard and truffles, and six eggs for boiling on our kerosene cook stove. After two hours of riding, we'll stop for a cappuccino and a croissant.

We move along at a gentle pace, maybe around twelve miles per hour. The road is flat, the effort easy, our breathing steady and calm. The way is narrow and undisturbed, lined with sturdy oak trees. An occasional car passes us, its driver and passengers gesturing with admiration. Our loaded bikes suggest a long-distance journey.

The mind follows the body. When the restless mind quiets, life unfolds at its own pace and rhythm. First, your body disappears, then your thoughts. You're empty: pain-free. You're pure movement, one with the rhythmic rotation of the bicycle as it moves effortlessly on the smooth surface of the newly tarred road.

You see differently. Your focus shifts to the surrounding landscape with its various shades of green, an occasional splash of red—and a small cottage encircled by a sea of trees next to a crystal pond. Something about it draws me. I motion to Deborah, trailing a hundred feet behind me, that I want to stop and explore the cabin and its environs.

Three of the cabin's walls are composed of large glass windows separated by wide wood frames. When we first arrive, it is hidden from the sun—the tiny cottage is dwarfed by the surrounding forest, which is rich with huge and magnificent trees. When we walk among the oaks, we see only their broad trunks until we raise our eyes upward to see the thick emerald foliage, and beyond that, the sun. It is a place you go to hide, to love, to write, to dream.

It's now three in the afternoon—late enough in the day for us to witness a dialogue of light between the pond, the cabin, and the sun. For much of the day, I would imagine the cabin is dark and still, a hibernating animal slumbering on the forest floor. But as the sun drops lower in the sky, amber-red light flows through the leaves and penetrates the glass, splashing onto the opposite walls, in undulating foliage-relief. The rendezvous of light creates the effect of mating gods, arriving quickly to take our breath away, and then . . . gone.

Deborah looks at me and says, "Thank God we're here."

We're seeing again—open to things. Our moving meditation has the effect of altering our consciousness so that each moment in time is discrete from the next, as if you were sitting by a riverbank observing the continuous flow of driftwood, each piece distinct in size and shape, floating downstream with the current. At those moments, there's no past or future, only an ongoing sense of a vivid present.

The gentle tempo of bike touring invites connection. The demands of a programmed life don't. How does a frenetic and overburdened mind notice the black-and-white Holsteins grazing in the emerald meadow that rises toward the foothills of the Green Mountains?

It doesn't.

But that was that mind and that life. This mind, in this life, notices the kids with their moms standing by the side of our quiet road calling out accolades in French. This mind, in this life, sees the fat Belgian milk cows lying in the bright green pasture adorned with an occasional yellow and blue wildflower. And this mind, in this life, can't help but notice the breathtaking field of mustard grass so dazzling that I fear gazing directly at its golden magnificence might burn the corneas as violently as staring into the sun's powerful rays.

We stop. It's not a choice. It's a necessity: a religious experience, a pilgrimage of gratitude to bless the Creator for His kindness, His divine artistry, and His use of sunlight to highlight the shades of yellow as varied as the golden, buttery strands of a natural blonde, her hair flowing down her shoulders on a gloriously sunny day.

Deborah breathes in the scene, closing her eyes on the inhalation and opening them on the out breath, a spontaneous, spiritual practice she invents for this godly occasion. Her edges have softened. That linear maleness that I recoil from has faded. Back in Vermont, she needed her aggression and drive to achieve. Now, I sense her letting go and connecting, like when she looks deeply into my eyes with love and the space between us melts.

I long for that feeling of oneness.

By five thirty, we arrive at the empty campground, tired and hungry. The site rests on a large grassy knoll with an occasional flat spot to pitch a tent. We set up our tent with a view of a majestic manor house, surrounded by a forest of pine and oak trees that tower over its four chimneys and gabled, red-tiled roof. Powerful oak doors emboldened with a coat of arms stand at the end of a black slate path, framed on either side by an honor guard of perfectly symmetrical manicured bushes.

The only sounds are the birds chanting their late afternoon melodies. The campground resides on a former estate, converted into a luxurious outdoor paradise, replete with hot showers and modern flush toilets with seats—not the squatting ones where if you lose your balance, you fall into a pile of excrement.

And then the owner of the campsite appears.

He materializes, ex nihilo, wearing a parrot on his right shoulder, a blue corduroy hat on his head, a red bandana around his neck, and a Fu Manchu mustache that doesn't quit. Dressed in bright orange overalls, the radiant color of a stunning Charleston sunset, he stands about six feet tall with the biceps, deltoids, pectoralis majors and minors of a twenty-five-year-old gymnast. He is sixty-five.

In French, he says, "I am Le Clown. Welcome to my campground." He approaches our bicycles, examines our panniers, and asks, "Where are you going? Ah, don't tell me. You are going around the world. Le Clown is right? Yes?"

"Yes," Deborah says in French. "How did you know?"

Le Clown points to the gold earring in my left ear, my black beard, and the red bandana covering my long, black, wavy hair and says, "*Il a un bandana rouge, une barbe noire et une boucle d'oreille. C'est un pirate. Vous êtes Barbe Noire, le pirate un homme aventureux et audacieux. C'est pourquoi je sais que vous faites le tour du monde.*"

"Can you translate that for me?" I ask Deborah.

Before she can answer, Le Clown turns to me and says in English with a musical French accent, "You are Blackbeard, the parrot with earring, beard, and bandana. You travel *le monde* for treasures."

I approach him, point to his parrot, and laughing, say, "He's a parrot; I'm a pirate."

"Ah, yes, but pirates have parrots," he replies with a wink.

"Indeed. We're both pirates," I say. "Le Clown wears a red bandana and a parrot on his shoulder. Michael—that's me—has a pierced ear and a bandana on his head. Has Le Clown traveled the globe looking for treasures?"

"Le Clown has discovered great treasures in many places in the world. Today I found you. You are my new pearls."

As he speaks, I'm asking myself why he calls himself Le Clown. Why in the third person, like Richard Nixon, who, after losing the California gubernatorial election whined, "You won't have Nixon to kick around anymore"?

Illeism is the term for addressing oneself in the third person. I learned it from scrabble. It's a common trait among egomaniacs like General MacArthur, who so deified himself that he referred to himself as "MacArthur."

But Le Clown doesn't fit into the box of a self-glorifying, adoration-seeking illeist. Everything about Le Clown—his mesmerizing blue eyes with laugh lines flowing from their outer corners, his ironic smile that communicates both an intimate familiarity with the absurd and the wisdom of experience, the attire of the fool whose persona masks his knowledge—all demand that we discover his story.

"Why do you call yourself Le Clown? Is that your only name?" I ask.

He gazes directly into my eyes, smiles, and says, "No. What parent would name their child Le Clown? My given name is Yves Draymond, but for many years now, I am known as Le Clown." He pauses and says, "I see you are curious. What would you like to ask me?"

"What's your story? Why do you speak about yourself like you're talking about another person?"

He looks at Deborah and asks, "You also want to hear my story? It interests you?" Deborah nods.

He begins by sharing a few details about growing up as the youngest of three brothers in rural Belgium on his family's sheep farm. The long periods of solitude tending the family's flock were when he discovered he could create imaginary worlds populated by heroes and demons, warriors and foes. While talking about his childhood, his whole body radiates with joy. And then, as he speaks about the War, his joy vanishes; his laugh lines harden; sorrow and suffering emanate from his eyes:

For five years, from the day the Nazis invaded Belgium, we only knew suffering. My Jewish friends disappeared or were shot for sport. My heart was black with hatred. I lived to kill Germans. It gave me deep pleasure. Don't let anyone tell you that revenge isn't sweet. It's more delicious than honey. I was good at it.

My nom de guerre was Le Saboteur. I was like an actor on the stage who becomes the character he plays. My part: revenge and death. To murder Germans, to blow up everything that had a swastika on it. We were mosquitoes to the Nazis: biting them, making them crazy with our buzzing, tasting Nazi blood in our mouths.

For Le Saboteur, the Germans had to die—no voice of conscience asking whether this was what God wanted. Le Saboteur knew what God wanted: Destroy evil, even if evil is an eighteen-year-old, scared German soldier who knows nothing. To Le Saboteur, the enemy was not human. Should you feel pity for vermin? No, you exterminate them.

But what I didn't know is that killing, even killing Nazis, comes at a big price. With every life you take, you cut out a piece of your soul until what's left is a machine that no longer feels love or joy.

That was me at the end of the war. Both my brothers were killed. My mother's heart was broken; she died right after the war. When we suffer, we think, "Only I suffer," but after the war who was not grieving? Who was not trying to find sense in madness?

Before the war, I was a magician and a part-time clown, performing at birthday parties. Post-war, the world was a sad place—no birthday parties, no circuses with bears and elephants, no clowns for forgetting your sorrows. We survivors forgot how to laugh. In 1945, when women dressed in black and children begged in the streets, joy and laughter went into hiding.

After the war, I had many frightful dreams—faces of dead Germans with terrified eyes, legs lying on the ground next to burnt bodies, children screaming. There were no psychiatrists to talk to about your nightmares;

no groups where you could cry together and confess the horrible things you'd done during the war. I became my psychiatrist. I learned that my terrifying dreams were the voice of my soul waking me from five years of living hell, five years of being Le Saboteur, the right part in the theater of madness . . .

You're both psychologists, so you know about imagination and the alter ego. To do what I did during the war, I had to create Le Saboteur. Le Saboteur was fearless. He had the heart, the mind, and the skills of a warrior. Le Saboteur acted his part as perfectly as Artur Rubinstein performs Chopin.

To create Le Saboteur, the Demand of Circumstance had to ignite the Power of Imagination. I never asked myself, "What should I do?" To Circumstance, I asked, "What is needed?" Imagination responded with the answer: The Alter Ego, Le Saboteur, a role the twenty-five-year-old Yves Draymond, a young man with gifted hands and a pirate's spirit, learned to play with enthusiasm and talent.

One day—I don't remember how many months after the war it was— I had that same feeling that Circumstance was demanding that I act, that I do what I must to make children laugh and smile again. So, I put on my clown costume, made my cheeks white, painted a funny smile on my face, and marched to the orphanage. The street kids started screaming in delight, and then as if God Himself willed it, they formed a single line and paraded behind me like I was the Pied Piper. I arrived at the orphanage with maybe twenty children, all dirty, in torn clothes, some without shoes, but all laughing and shouting, "Le Clown! Le Clown!"

On that day, I understood that Fate had brought me to the doorstep of the orphanage. Where Le Saboteur once lived, Le Clown would find his home.

Everything you can imagine is real. It's how I live my life.

I want to hug Le Clown and tell him, "I love you. You just gave us an amazing gift: the courage to be yourself. You had the conviction to be what circumstance demanded you be. You did what very few people do. You asked, 'If not me, then who?' And then you answered as Le Saboteur and as Le Clown."

But I don't. Some small part of me hesitates, a part that needs time to let the spirit of Le Clown infuse me, that needs to let go and just let my heart speak its mind.

I say this instead: "Thank you for your story, and thank you for being Le Saboteur and Le Clown. We won't forget you."

Deborah reaches out for Le Clown's hand and says, "Thank you. I love you."

"Yes," Le Clown says, "you're both my pearls."

*   *   *

Remember how hungry we were at five thirty? Well, by now, it's nearly seven. It's our last night in Belgium, and I'm insistent we sit down to a proper five-course meal in an excellent restaurant with a bottle of Pinot Noir.

My meal is awful.

If I knew the French words for rubbery, overcooked, tough, and inedible, I'd complain to the waiter. Proper restaurant etiquette would require the waiter to report my critique to the chef, who might have graciously apologized if I could speak French like the Lebanese Francophile sitting opposite me, the woman who studied French literature at the Sorbonne, can recite Dumas and Sartre without a trace of an accent, but refuses to complain on my behalf.

"Your problem; you deal with it."

Deborah, the vegetarian, ordered a cheese and onion omelet. From an aesthetic perspective alone, the omelet is a culinary masterpiece—sunshine yellow and perfectly rolled, garnished with a sprig of parsley and chives, with a scent of butter and the aroma of Gruyère.

"Amazing! You have no idea how good this is."

"So give me a bite."

"No, you're the meat-eater. Break your teeth on your dead flesh and leave my beautiful omelet alone."

When we first met, I told Deborah that I, too, was a vegetarian. I figured it would score some points with her. I was right. She immediately kissed me and said, "I'm thrilled to hear that." It wasn't completely true, but nor was it an outright lie. I was a vegetarian wannabe. So,

I thought, if you want to be with the person you love, why risk the chance of a premature rift at this delicate state in our relationship?

Morally ambiguous, no doubt; shameful and cowardly, indeed, but my distorted logic decided it would do no good for Deborah to know about my occasional tête-à-tête with a Big Mac or my secret rendezvous with a chicken breast. Therefore, whenever we were together, I ate what she ate: brown rice and vegetables, eggs, cheese, and whole-wheat everything.

Yet, there's a fundamental problem with pretending to be one thing as you sneak around being another. So, after weeks of wrestling with the pros and cons of confessing the truth, I decided that it was time to man up and come clean:

We're sitting in the airport restaurant drinking a cappuccino waiting to board our flight from Burlington, Vermont, to Charleston, West Virginia, to spend Christmas with her family.

"Wipe your mouth. You have coffee dripping from your mustache. Betty Mae would have a complete meltdown," Deborah says.

"Perfect, let her have her meltdown. It'll prove she's the Wicked Witch from the West."

I can tell she wants to laugh, but the mere mention of Betty Mae creates terror in Deborah. There are gangrenous wounds here that Deborah occasionally alludes to but are too painful to touch. From time to time, when the overwhelming experience of Betty Mae exceeds the prolific skill set of her emotionally intelligent daughter, I feel the hints of hatred oozing from those old infections. "Louise, the housekeeper, was the only real mother I had." Or, in a rare insight, she might say something like, "I hate her. She uses my success to brag about what an amazing mother she is. The only part I have in her pathetic drama is the role of the adoring daughter."

Deborah might not want to admit she hates her mother, but I have no problem. I hate that Betty Mae, the master manipulator, has trained Deborah to play the obsequious role of the parentified child, demanding she forfeit her needs to satisfy Betty Mae's insatiable appetite for adoration, attention, and validation.

"I know this trip makes you nervous. I got it. I'll be good. But you need to let go of your fear. You're stronger than her. She can't destroy you. Stop expecting her to love you. She can't."

"I know," she says, "you're right." A few moments later she goes to the bathroom. I call over the waitress and, at that instant, perhaps because I want to rid myself of the stench of Betty Mae's bullshit, I decide to end the lies and duplicity. I order a bacon, lettuce, and tomato sandwich.

The sandwich—crisp bacon protruding from all sides—arrives at the table moments before Deborah. She sits down and says nothing. She stares at the bacon, gazes directly in my eyes, briefly looks away, focuses again on me, returns to the bacon. Her cheeks flush; her lips quiver; her blink rate increases.

It would have been less painful if she had screamed at me, "You're a liar, a cheat, a worthless piece of shit!" or grabbed the BLT and thrown it at me. But she did none of the above. She cried briefly and quietly—no dramatic outbursts, no statements like, "How could you do this to me?"

"Did you really think I didn't know you were lying?" she asks. "You've been stuffing your Big Mac bags under the driver's seat. I knew which days you had chicken salad and when you were at McDonald's. You're a terrible cheat. I'm crying not because I'm sad, but because I'm relieved you finally ended this charade.

"Michael, I want you to promise me there'll be no more lies, no more pretending one thing and doing another. You're better than this. The person I love is not a guy who has a secret affair with a double cheeseburger. I'm not happy you're eating meat, but I can live with it. I can't live with lying."

CHAPTER 3

On the Road to Paris:
June 7 to June 12

O ne might assume bike touring is an escape from the daily
habits and schedules that structure our lives. Nothing could
be further from the truth.

As I write this, I've thought of skipping a discussion about the
tasks and habits of bike touring, but if I did, I might give the impression that routine is the antithesis of freedom, or that a journey into the
unknown frees one from the limitations of structure. It's not true, but I
understand why someone would see it that way.

I did.

Search a thesaurus for synonyms for the word "routine." You'll
find *monotonous, boring, dull, tedious, humdrum, mundane, predictable,* and *unchanging.* Words that I loathe. I'm passionate about what
I love and avoid what I don't. Wrong attitude when it comes to biking. Best to learn to love the routine of bike maintenance or you're one
small screw from deep shit.

Andrew, the staid owner of the pine-paneled ski and bike store,
must have sensed that I might need someone like him to lecture someone like me on the necessity of maintaining our beautifully crafted
road bikes. In retrospect, I'm glad he did.

"If you properly maintain your bikes," he said, staring directly at
me, "they will withstand thousands of miles of abuse through all kinds
of terrain and weather. That means you will need to lubricate your road
bike daily, true the spokes every few days, fix flats and change tires

34

as needed, and probably replace several minor parts like brake pads, cables, and a bolt here and there that you may accidentally strip if you use the wrong metric wrench. I don't want to give the impression that nothing could go wrong."

Andrew's right.

So why do I and so many others recoil from the necessity of bike maintenance? It's a question that occupies much of Robert Pirsig's *Zen and the Art of Motorcycle Maintenance*. His answer: We split the romance and adventure of bike touring from the machine itself, which demands technical care. I suppose we do the same with relationships when we separate the intense feeling of love from the small daily routines of keeping the relationship alive. Like children, we want our good feelings delivered free of charge.

It doesn't work for intimate connections and it doesn't work for bicycling.

If before setting out for the day, you don't go through the maintenance check Andrew suggested, there's a good chance your negligence will cause a simple hassle like a flat tire to become a major problem when you discover you ran out of patches.

Add to that ensuring that we have sufficient kerosene for our cookstove, and, when sunny, washing clothes and attaching the wet laundry to our bikes so between the wind and the sun our clothes will dry quickly. Beyond these tasks, we've added the daily practices of meditating every evening and morning for thirty minutes, along with another thirty minutes of morning yoga, and for me, evening journal writing.

But unlike the busyness of our previous life, in this one we can stop, notice, and appreciate a magnificent field of golden mustard grass.

The simplicity, certainty, and discipline of these daily tasks contrast the unpredictability and freedom of the road. An important takeaway is this: Without the daily structure that simplifies our lives, we might lose the opportunity for serendipitous encounters. We'd burn up too much energy repairing broken bikes that, with a bit of common sense and foresight, wouldn't have needed fixing.

In this spirit, I propose a new lexicon of synonyms for the word "routine" to include a vocabulary of self-mastery. I prefer words like *discipline, persistence, commitment, focus,* and *purpose.* Necessary qualities for a long-term relationship.

Over the next few days, we ride the narrow back roads to Paris, cutting through dense forests that at a whim might break to reveal a field of multicolored wildflowers, a red-roofed farmhouse, or a family of pigs frolicking in a pen littered with leftovers from the previous meal. In a blink, the window shuts, and the bright sun refracted by the thick foliage creates the effect of a thousand dancing Tinker Bells performing a ballet of flickering light.

Unlike the flat motorways of Belgium, the French country roads remind me of my Vermont running routes with their long, gentle slopes interspersed with short, steep climbs. I feel the edge as I challenge myself to push through the hills in the highest gear. My muscles, heart, and lungs strain to reach the crest. For a moment, I give into the sense of victory, and then, exhaling deeply, I let go and soar down the slope, hands-free and bellowing in delight. I'm the crazy guy in the lead car of the roller coaster.

Meanwhile, Deborah's gushing superlatives like a gooey-eyed teeny bopper at a Michael Jackson concert. "Did you see that light show? Wow! Amazing! I didn't think I could feel this way . . . I flew down that hill. I didn't brake once!" I'm thrilled to see her bragging about how she owns the road and rules her bike.

*   *   *

I've often wondered why there are so many nameless bit players appearing and then disappearing in the ongoing theatrical performance I call *My Life.* The cast is huge yet silent, seemingly contributing nothing more than the role of place fillers for an empty stage. Let's say I stop at a red light. An elderly, gray-haired lady ambles in front of my car. If I'm in a philosophical state of mind, I might ask myself, "Why is she a character in my drama? What purpose does she serve? What lesson can I learn from her?"

Probably nothing. There are no answers. The whole process is merely a speculative exercise—as meaningful as asking if God can kill Himself.

Unless . . . we are the one writing the script.

Here's how:

When a local appears on the side of the road, we stop and ask if we're on the right path to the next town. It's merely a convenient excuse to interact because Deborah's never lost. Although the numerical probability of bumping into someone as life changing as Le Clown is close to zero, there's 100 percent certainty that you'll never have a chance encounter with your next guru or friend if you don't stop. We stop, and most of the time we find out what we already know. We're headed in the right direction. But now and then, something like this happens:

Lianne, an attractive forty-something woman wearing jeans, sandals, and a white T-shirt emblazoned with the slogan War, What Is It Good For? stands by the side of the road. She holds a basket of wild raspberries. After telling us that we're on the right road to St. Quentin, she says, "No one stops at St. Quentin. It's an ugly place. So, where are you going after that?"

"Around the world," Deborah answers, and she then adds a few selective details, such as our encounter with Le Clown, the rats, and the weather.

Lianne turns to me, laughs, and says something like, "Really? You don't look like such a coward. What an amazing adventure!" she says. "I'm so envious." She looks at both of us with her large brown eyes and says, "Ah, if my husband agrees, can I join you?" Before either of us can answer, she says, "Don't worry, I won't leave my three kids." She pauses, turns her gaze downward, then makes direct eye contact with Deborah and asks, "Why Lebanon? Why a place of death?" Her eyes shut momentarily; her lips tighten. "I was a young child during the war. I still remember things I wish I could forget."

"I have family in Lebanon," Deborah says. "It's been my dream to visit them since I was a child. If it's too dangerous, we won't go. What can I say? I'm a Lebanese Christian American with a French and Swedish soul raised on hummus, kibbe, pizza, and hamburgers, and now I'm a vegetarian meditator. I'm trying to put the pieces together. Lebanon's a big part."

Lianne pauses for what appears to be a moment of decision making.

"Today's my lucky day," she says. "I rarely meet such interesting people. I won't let go of you guys so quickly. Come to my house in twenty minutes and have coffee and cake with me and my husband. My kids are with my mother, so we won't have any distractions. We're only five hundred meters from here. It's the red farmhouse on the right side. You can't miss it."

Then, as an afterthought, she says, "Fate's thrown us together. So let's break bread and figure out how to live in this crazy world."

She turns to me and in nearly flawless American English asks, "How's your French?"

"Much, much worse than your English."

"No problem. My husband and I speak English well. We lived in San Diego from 1972 until 1976. We learned to talk like Americans."

Lianne greets us at the door with an enormous smile and hugs us like we're old friends returning from a year in Tahiti with a memoir to share. She motions us inside. A well-preserved brown leather chair faces an ancient stone fireplace. I desperately want to collapse into its welcoming comfort and grab one of the English books on the shelves to the left. This is my kind of library: Steinbeck, Hemingway, a book of poetry from Gary Snyder, Carl Van Doren's biography of Benjamin Franklin, and even *Zen and the Art of Motorcycle Maintenance*.

"Did you read *Zen and the Art of Motorcycle Maintenance*?" I ask.

"No, my husband did. A voilà for him. A big yawn for me. Very un-French-like to hate philosophy—like an American falling asleep at your dreadful game of baseball."

"Yeah, something like that," I answer.

From the corner of my left eye, I notice Deborah in an animated conversation with Lianne's husband, Timothée. He's a touch over six feet, dark-haired, athletic-looking like Lianne, and about the same age, dressed in brown trekking pants and hiking boots. I have this theory about couples that if they look alike, they'll be good together. Not scientific but based on some fairly solid anecdotal research. From a physical perspective, they fit well.

Meanwhile, I join Lianne in the kitchen where she's tossing an endive salad dressed with a touch of olive oil and wine vinegar while educating me on U.S. foreign policy. "It's all about who has the biggest dick. Macho politics played out on the world stage. Look at what that asshole Carter did. Gets castrated by the Iranians and now he's the small boy with the little thing."

She tells Timothée and Deborah to join us at the table. Next to the salad bowl Lianne places a serving platter filled with soft and hard cheeses surrounded by a circle of ten thin slices of warm baguette. Somewhere between a discussion about the vapid American culture and a debate about the morality of Nagasaki and Hiroshima, we finish the salad, cheese, and baguette. Still arguing passionately against America's use of atomic weapons to end the war—a decision I believe was necessary and moral—Lianne prepares a gourmet vegetarian meal composed of a tomato-cheese quiche, *pommes frites*, and an asparagus souffle that she whips together at the same ferocious speed with which she delivers her arguments against the brutal and unnecessary use of force against "innocent Japanese civilians."

She's a trip. Turns out she's a freelance copywriter specializing in promo materials for nonprofits that support peace, ecology, social justice, and a host of humanitarian and left-wing political causes that range from saving the whales to defeating the current center-right government of Valéry Giscard d'Estaing and replacing it with the Socialist Party led by François Mitterrand.

While Lianne and I are in the throes of a fierce discussion riddled with frequent interruptions and rapid-fire arguments on the pros and cons of pacifism, a position she supports and I don't, Deborah's calmly discussing Transcendental Meditation with Timothée.

Timothée's about to follow Guru Deb into the metaphysical upper worlds of TM. My Deborah can sell anything. She broke all company-wide sales records peddling encyclopedias to the functionally illiterate living in the holler. If she could succeed at that morally ambivalent project, for which she carries a therapeutic level of guilt, I'm certain she can sell a product like TM to an eager customer like Timothée.

Time and intensity are inversely proportional. As the power and passion of each moment increase, the pace of the interactions decelerates as the conversation moves from the political and spiritual to the intimate. From ethical questions about war and peace, we transition to the reasons for our trip.

"I admire you guys," Lianne says. "Instead of making more money, you walk away from the bourgeois lifestyle. Takes courage."

"More like a necessary break than a walk-away," Deborah says. "Hopefully, we'll return wiser and more balanced."

We segue into a discussion about committed relationships. This is Deborah's turf, her intellectual and emotional comfort zone, and she guides us to questions of how a couple resolves competing needs; how they walk the line between excessive dependency—what I call a spaghetti relationship—and parallel play, where it's all about your own development at the expense of the connection.

"When I can't tell where I end and Timothée begins—like, you know, he sneezes and I wipe my nose—well, I make a fight over nothing. He withdraws and then we sort of work it out and get untangled," Lianne says.

We dance around the question of how to keep the thrill alive when the chores of the day overwhelm the heat of desire. Lianne dives right into that one. "A good screaming fight and a good makeup with lots of tears make for hot sex."

"Not us," Deborah says. "It's all about the connection. The stronger the bond, the better the sex."

"What's the bond have to do with sex?" I ask silently. A bond's a commitment, not a mood. My commitment to her hasn't wavered since that day on August 8, 1974, when Nixon resigned. What's she saying? "When I'm feeling committed to you, the sex is good but when I'm wavering, it's not"? I make a note to talk to her about what she meant but just as quickly dismiss it.

At any rate, by now, both Timothée and I are desperately in need of another topic. For intimate discussions of sex, even an open-minded American psychologist and an avant-garde Frenchman blush.

"Embarrassed, are we?" Lianne asks. "Deborah, I think we need to change the subject for these boys. Maybe we should talk about orgasms." Deborah laughs. Timothée and I squirm.

We drink two more bottles of excellent French table wine and dive into more wild discussions led by Lianne. "Let's screw convention and lie naked on a beach in Tahiti. Get away from this fucked-up world of deadlines and dickheads forever."

"No problem. When we get to Tahiti," I tell her, "I'll send you a postcard from a nude beach. If you're still up to it, you can join us. You never know. By then, we might be missing the deadlines and the dickheads."

The next morning, following a breakfast of cheese, yogurt, fresh fruit, croissants, a baguette each, and four cups of strong coffee, we say our goodbyes, exchange addresses, promise to remain in touch, yet know we won't because serendipitous encounters are best left as singular events shrouded in mystery and meaning. That way, when you write about how Fate or God brought you together for one sterling moment in eternity, you'll remember it in all its unique and shining glory.

Only a sadist could have invented a Michelin 1:250,000 topographical map with forty-four folds and creases. If my mathematical memory serves me correctly, this adds up to something like 3,000-plus possible ways to fold this map. Throw in the annoying wrinkle of folding it in the wind, and the number increases exponentially, assuming a gust hasn't blown the map off the picnic table into a puddle.

Deborah, though, folds as fast and as efficiently as she unfolds, nary a crease out of place. "What's the problem?" she asks.

"For you, none. You don't have a mashed-potato brain."

"Nonsense, that's just your father's critical voice. Let me show you." She does, and as expected, it's a flawless 360-degree triple salchow. Yet, for some puzzling reason, when I do what she does, the road from Brussels appears on the outside fold.

"Deborah, dear, I think I'm at my neurological edge. Promise me you'll never leave me. I won't know how to get home."

Neither Deborah nor I received a model for healthy relationships. My father vacillated between being a whiny, demanding husband and a loving caretaker when my mother was dying. My mother handled my father: She ran the show. He thought he did. My sister and I knew who had the power.

Deborah's mother, Betty Mae, was neither a stay-at-home mom nor a stay-at-home wife. She needed more excitement and more money than her simple Lebanese husband could provide. So, Deborah raised herself—and to some extent her two younger sisters—while Betty Mae performed her role as Charleston's Grande Dame of haute couture. To her credit, she did subcontract the job of parental love and care to Louise, a Black woman with a loving heart and street smarts.

Thanks to Deborah's parents and my father, we learned what not to do, but that's not enough.

During our first year living together—probably after a few glitches and misunderstandings—we got that we're wired differently and understood that's okay. What was really cool was that we naturally started doing chores based on our individual competencies and interests. Those chores had no connection to traditional male-female roles. More like: If you're good at it, do it, and if not, then learn how, or outsource it.

Here's how it plays out:

She fixes everything: rewires lamps, repairs broken pipes, restores furniture, keeps the locks from freezing when it's twenty-five below zero, and disassembles, cleans, and maintains our state-of-the-art bicycle gears, pedals, and handlebars.

I save us from starving: I buy and cook the food.

She keeps us connected.

I do as well.

She can't write well in English. Not her fault—she's from West Virginia.

I'm from New York. Miss Epstein and Mrs. Rosner, my seventh and eighth grade English teachers, inspired me to find my voice and create stories.

I show her how to express herself in writing because she believes she can't.

She reads and folds maps; I keep a chronicle of the journey.

She speaks fluent French, Swedish, Italian, and Spanish. I make small talk in pidgin French and eloquent hand gestures. I can speak to anyone.

I help her see the big picture; she pays attention to the details.

I see the absurd in everything; she sees the human.

I think first; she feels first.

We both laugh—usually at my jokes.

I turn her on to the pleasure and power of sweat; she encourages me to appreciate the gentle movement of yoga.

I pack her mind with ideas; she empties mine of noise.

I can't carry a tune; she sings beautifully.

She and I dance with passion, especially together. (I did mention we met on a dance floor.)

There's more, much more, but I'm hungry and it's my responsibility and delight to buy the bread, cheese, and croissants for breakfast.

The lovely, late spring days have an easy, laid-back feel to them like the rhythm of the billowy hills, the rolling green-yellow pastures, and white swirling clouds. Up at six thirty, on the road by eight thirty; ride for a few hours; break for coffee, cake, and conversation with a shop owner; back on the road; stop again to converse with the friendly farm folk who ask where we're going.

"*Nous allons à Jérusalem!*" ("On to Jerusalem!")

"*Extraordinaire!*" "*Impressionnant!*" "*Incroyable!*" "*Bonne chance!*"
Cheers and tributes for the two crusaders en route to the Holy Land.

As the distance to Paris shrinks, so does the space between the
red-tiled cottages that border our path to Paris. At our tempo, no faster
than an elite runner's, we inhale the pungent odor of cow manure com-
posting in sheds next to the bright red barns. The small farmhouses
and cottages that hug the road wear cloaks of creeping ivy that entwine
in an unruly pattern of quick turns and dives, and in a spectacular re-
versal of gravity, shoot toward the heavens. Window boxes overflowing
with a full spectrum of perennials, annuals, and herbs add a sense of
contrasting order and harmony to the chaotic stone walls covered with
wild green twines that seem driven by a mysterious string of proteins
encoded deep in their DNA.

Then, Deborah's derailleur, the mechanism that moves the bike's
chain from one sprocket to the next, falls off. Once held in place by a
small but significant screw, the derailleur is now as useful as a flat tire
minus a lug wrench.

We ask a farmer to direct us to the nearest bike shop. "It's only two
kilometers from here, in the town of Étrépilly. The owner's name is
René. Tell him Albert said to take good care of you."

"Merci, Albert."

We wheel our bikes to Étrépilly. Maybe I'm exaggerating, but no
fewer than ten cars stop to offer to drive us to the bike shop. We thank
them for their generosity, answer their questions about our travels,
graciously accept their accolades and words of encouragement, but decline their offers.

René's love handles pour from the sides of his greasy coveralls like an
avalanche plunging down an Alpine slope. I pray he can fix bikes because there's no way in hell he can ride one. I notice a picture of a tall
young man with the thin, wiry build of a serious bicyclist. With a tro-
phy raised high above his head, he grins from ear to ear. In another
picture, that same man stands on a podium; he receives a kiss from a

pretty girl. I ask Deborah to ask René if that's him in the picture.

Deborah translates and all three of us laugh.

"Yes, that's me in 1958 when I won two local races. Years before I fell in love with the pleasures of the palate."

René sure can fix bikes. In a heartbeat, he pulls out a close-fitting screw from a shaky wooden drawer that even an anarchist living on chaos and disorder would find disturbing. After measuring the aperture, he places the screw in a machine tool that calibrates, threads, and fits the screw to the exact size needed to hold the derailleur in place. The whole procedure takes thirty-five seconds. Bingo! The derailleur is now happily home, more secure than when it came off the assembly line in the Takara factory.

"Voilà, madame. With René's screw, you can ride around the world with no worries."

"Thank you so much. What do we owe you?"

"Nothing. This is a gift from me to you. You are beautiful people. I want to be part of your grand adventure. Remember me if you write a book."

We spend our last night before we take the shuttle to Paris packed like sardines in a rundown, crowded campground. Camped six inches from us are a drugged-out hippie couple from Holland, most likely friends of the devil, based on their dreadlocks and tattooed fingers with *hate* engraved on their left fingers and *love* on their right. From the dualities carved in their flesh, it could be they're Zoroastrians disguised as Satanists. Either way, they're seriously freaky. Together they can't weigh over two hundred pounds, but whether it's the crystal meth they're smoking or the coke they're snorting, they're humping and grinding all night long. And we can't sleep.

At one a.m., after being kept awake through four rounds of campground sex with no end in sight, I ask Deborah, "Is it the drugs?"

"Probably. Why don't you ask them? No, don't. They might ask us to join them."

By the seventh round, their tent becomes deathly silent. Could be they died from an overdose, exhaustion, or loss of body fluids. Good riddance—they give sex, Holland, and insanity a terrible name.

After three hours of fitful sleep, we disassemble our tent, skip yoga, meditation, and breakfast, and head for the train about ten kilometers from this campground from hell blessed by Satan himself and his rotten companions. We'll eat at the train station and meditate on the train. Yoga can wait until we arrive at Simone and Alain's apartment in Paris.

Paris: June 13 to July 10

P aris makes you smarter.
Could be it's the outdoor café with its intimate tables that beck-on us to huddle together, shoulder to shoulder and mind to mind, like Sartre and Camus and Hemingway and Fitzgerald. In this temple to intelligence, you merely close your eyes and imagine yourself at an adjacent table, eavesdropping on a high-spirited discussion about whether truth is fiction or fiction reveals truth.

Then again, there's something about the sophistication of French food that engages your mind and causes you to pause in wonder at the array of flavors that awaken your gustatory intelligence. French cuisine makes you think, demands discernment, and astonishes you with how a culinary genius can awaken the brilliant tastes in this simple onion soup and Caesar salad that we're currently waxing transcendent over:

Onion soup with a perfect layer of Gruyère resting on a slice of French bread that barely conceals the aromatic bouquet of sautéed onions, white wine, and beef broth.

Caesar salad with salty anchovies, fresh parmesan, and one beautiful egg a hair's breadth from hard nestled in a bed of fresh romaine. Oh, the croutons . . . crispy with a hint of garlic and lemon juice. And the pièce de résistance: Dijon dressing seasoned to perfection with freshly ground pepper and Worcestershire sauce.

A beautiful mind captivates. Age and experience are its friends. This Francophile Lebanese princess mesmerizes. She speaks French like a native, could go toe to toe with Simone de Beauvoir discussing existential feminism, and can speak with authority about French architecture and art. Deborah belongs in Paris. She discovered her French soul during her year as a Sweet Briar exchange student in 1969. Here in this Parisian café, eleven years later, at age thirty, she's aged perfectly.

"I was like Le Clown. I imagined my French personality. No accent, no American shoes, no blissed-out American girl in Paris. I fit in perfectly, with my Middle Eastern looks and French body type. No longer Debbie from West Virginia, I became *De-bo-rah*, the nineteen-year-old French girl studying literature and art history at the Sorbonne."

As we watch the ongoing parade of beautiful French men and women sauntering past our front-row seats in our outdoor *Théâtre Parisien*, we ask the question everyone asks—"How's it possible there are so many beautiful Parisians?" Even the plain ones look chic.

Sounding like a professor of French culture, Deborah says, "The French don't just live in a beautiful city; they are part of the aesthetic experience, just like the Arc de Triomphe and the Eiffel Tower. Paris turns unattractive into interesting, pretty into gorgeous, and lovely into magnificent. It's all about the clothes, the way they stroll down the street and move their lips and eyes. The French will themselves into being stunning."

"True, Professor. But don't forget the gene pool," I add. "Remember the French were Impressionists. They dabbled with lots of colors—especially the French colonialists who diddled with the locals. Look at the resulting genetic stew. You take the fine features of the North Africans, add the dark rich hue of the Congo, Cameroon, and Niger, and you get a lovely amalgam of great bones and chocolate-colored skin. Throw in spices from Indochina and Vietnam to the mix, and we have her."

A Eurasian woman—who probably has one parent of northern European extraction and the other Vietnamese—walks by dressed in a patterned skirt that falls somewhere between her knee and ankle. A high-collared white silk blouse rests on her slight frame. If I had the talent, I'd paint the entire package of light brown hair, almond-shaped eyes, and delicate Asian features and place it next to an exhibit of Paul Gauguin's Tahitian work.

I sense sparks of Deborah's Parisian soul emerging as she launches into a lyrical description of the layout and design of the French capital. She tells me that Parisian architecture, like the Parisians themselves, integrates multiple styles. Roman columns peacefully share space with Gothic arches. Renaissance mansions add an element of charm and grace to the wide, tree-lined boulevards designed by Baron Haussmann during the latter part of the nineteenth century. And, on either side of those wide boulevards, you notice the narrow cobblestone streets dating from the Middle Ages, when Paris was a crowded, diseased city.

"See the gargoyles on the building across from us? Do you know why they're part of the building?" Deborah asks. I don't. "Notice the nose. It's actually a spout designed to drain water from the roof away from the side of the building. Anywhere else in the world, they'd have an ugly metal drainpipe. Not the Parisians. Just another opportunity to create art."

Deborah tells me that the Paris before us didn't materialize in one Big Bang moment; it developed over time because of vision, persistence, and creativity—all human virtues. Yet once brought into being, these masterpieces of human ingenuity have their own unique power to influence and transform the individuals who reside in the buildings with their wrought-iron balconies, play boules in the magnificent parks and gardens of Paris, and pass the time in the neighborhood cafés discussing life, love, and soccer.

Our conversation about the human and architectural aesthetics of Paris continues for another hour.

And then.

"Michael, there's something I'd like to tell you." Deborah's demeanor is serious, a hint that what follows might darken the bright blue Parisian sky.

Something I'd like to tell you . . . such as *I have cancer*, or *I'm leaving you*, or *I'm pregnant*, or a thousand other fraught possibilities.

"I'm thinking about going to Sweden for a week or so. Maybe leaving next week."

I breathe. I feel the shock, the terror, and the anger burn. My body's tumbling down a hole. This is my most dreaded nightmare—Deborah abandoning me without warning—a repetition of what my ex-wife Susan did when she announced, "I'm leaving with Rich." And then she was gone . . . forever. That dishonesty, at least, made sense. We didn't love each other, and I was a lousy husband. But not this time—not with Deborah—not with the woman who is part of myself.

"I don't hear any 'us' or 'we,' or 'why' you want to go, only what you want. Excuse me—I'm jumping to conclusions. You didn't say 'I want,' or 'I decided.' Just an innocuous, 'I'm thinking.' I know you well, Deborah. 'I'm thinking' means 'I decided.'" I take a deep breath, exhale, and focus intently on Deborah. "When did you hatch up this plot to go without me? While we were talking about French architecture?"

"Obviously not. Right before we left. I tried to dismiss it. I knew it would be painful, and until I was positive that this was right for me . . . and for us—don't look so incredulous; yes, for us—I didn't want to discuss it. I needed to work things out first in my mind. I'm sorry to just dump this on you."

"So why are you going without me? Is it Niels?"

"I need to work something out, and yes, it involves Niels. I love you and I don't plan on leaving you. But I didn't expect to feel this attachment to Sweden. The farther we traveled from Vermont, the closer I felt to Sweden. If I can't let go, you and I might not have a future together."

"So, you're doing this for us? I guess I should be happy. How small-minded of me not to appreciate the sacrifice you're making . . . for us."

"I know this is a surprise. Can we table it until tomorrow? I'm sorry to dump this on you, but this is going in the wrong direction."

"What direction did you think it would go? Like I'd say, 'Deborah, I trust you; I bless you—do whatever you feel you must.'"

"No. I knew it would be hard. We need to talk more. Let's discuss this tomorrow after we've settled in and you're not in shock."

She reaches for my hand. "Michael, I love you. You're my life partner."

I'm not reassured. I feel betrayed and blindsided. More like how I felt thirty minutes after Susan announced she was leaving me. It was May 1971, and we were living in the married officers' quarters in Darmstadt, Germany. I was a captain in the 93rd Signal Battalion. I had just made love to my wife when my close friend Rich, the commanding general's son, arrived to tell me that he and Susan were in love and were leaving together that night. I looked at Susan in shock; she looked down and mumbled, "I love Rich." That was the last time I saw her.

We arrive at 65 Boulevard de Sébastopol. The 120-year-old building typifies Haussmann's classic architectural style—light gray stone facade, wrought-iron balconies, a ground floor designated for shopping and commerce, and upper floors reserved for residents. Most of the baron's structures don't exceed six floors. For a man known both for his no-nonsense approach to urban design and a partiality to straight lines, the poet in him found his true expression in his staircases. A flourish of curves, stone, and intricately crafted iron railings express the hidden soul of the standoffish Baron Haussmann.

The narrow, well-worn stairs glide upward in a snakelike fashion, creating something of a challenge for us. Thanks to the baron, our building is *sans ascenseur*—no elevator. As brilliant as he was, and as inspiring as his staircases might be, Haussmann's buildings have a fundamental design flaw—insufficient space for an elevator. To reach the third floor—fourth if you're from the U.S.—we have to carry our fully laden bikes up seventy uneven stone steps.

We knock on the door, red-faced and panting. Simone and Alain greet us.

The psychology of first impressions claims it takes one-tenth of a second to form a judgment that's at best 50 percent accurate. Nevertheless, we stick with that assessment, refusing to entertain the possibility there's a rich world behind an *abstract* persona.

Now I know that *abstract* is not a word we use to describe people, but it works here. Let's start with Simone: She has wispy light brown hair combed to the left side and held in place with one brown, unremarkable bobby pin, a pale complexion, and watery blue eyes. I would describe her body as nondescript—thin, no curves, about five feet five inches. Her black polyester pullover and black loose trousers reveal nothing about her personality unless this is how you dress to play the adult version of hide-and-seek.

Alain is Simone's double. Also clad in black from feet to neck, he wears a wool turtleneck sweater, pleated pants, black socks, and black loafers. Appearing to me like an emaciated painter of indoor still lifes, his pallor is ghost-like, his hair longish, straight, and dark, and his eyes—exactly like Simone's—are light blue and watery. Standing about six feet, he couldn't be an ounce over 130 pounds. A thin patrician nose augments the picture of the tortured artist.

The one thing I can say with absolute certainty is that if they experience any joy at all, it's not while outside riding their bikes on a warm sunny day. No, they're the type to be reading Simone de Beauvoir or Claude Lévi-Strauss under the artificial light of the living room lamp with the curtains closed.

In perfect Oxford English with a hint of a French lilt, Simone says, "Alain, you're blocking the doorway. Let them in."

"Oh, sorry," he says in a strong French accent, "please come in." He extends his hand to me. "I'm Alain, and this is Simone."

"He knows who we are," Simone says.

"Yes, of course he does," Alain answers.

"Nice to meet both of you," I interject. "Thank you so much for your hospitality."

Deborah dittos my sentiments in French and asks Alain if he's still in touch with Chantal, a mutual friend of theirs from the Sorbonne. Alain blushes and mumbles, "I haven't seen her in four years."

Simone interrupts and says to Deborah in English, "She was his old flame. We met when the embers were dying. Just as well, she wasn't his type. He needs someone melancholy and tortured like me."

I start laughing and say, "Sounds like we'll have a great time being miserable with you."

Simone looks at me for a few moments. Her demeanor appears

serious like a deadpan comedian and she says, "You're very American, aren't you?"

"Bingo! Baseball, hotdogs, and Jimi Hendrix are my thing."

Simone cracks a smile and says, "I'll see what I can do to cure you."

"Great! I'm game," I answer.

Simone again stares at me for a moment and asks, "You're Jewish. Aren't you?"

"Why? Are you an anti-Semite?"

I notice Deborah watching this game of verbal ping-pong. She looks bemused. Alain seems confused. I'm delighted to return Simone's shots. It's refreshing to converse with someone who says what she thinks when she thinks it.

She half smiles and says, "Hilarious. No, I'm not an anti-Semite. I'm one degree away from being Jewish enough for the Nazis. Though not sufficiently Jewish for my ex-boyfriend. My father's father was Jewish; my mother's pure French Catholic."

"That sounds like a story. I mean the boyfriend part." I wonder about this abrupt foray into the ethnic jungle. What crouching tigers lay in wait? My sense with Simone is that whatever is hidden won't re-main so for long. Something like go for the jugular or shut up.

"I'm sure we'll get around to it," she says. "I want to warn you. I know you Americans love small talk, but I don't. I have no patience for the weather or the news."

"So, what should we talk about?" I ask as I peer out the window and notice dark clouds blocking the sun. "It looks like rain."

"Quite the comedian," she replies. "Talk to Alain. He can talk about nothing or everything. He tells me I am artless when it comes to communicating. That I need to learn subtlety and indirectness."

"Perfect. So, if I got it right about you, I don't have to say 'excuse me' to end our conversation. I can just say, 'I'm tired,' or 'I need some time alone,' or 'I have nothing more to say,' or 'I find this conversation boring,' and that's okay with you?"

"Yes, I prefer it that way. You need to be more sensitive with Alain."

"Wonderful," I say. "I think we'll get along swimmingly."

"What's swimmingly?" she asks.

"Quite well."

The apartment's ceilings are high; the floors are polished oak with an occasional knot to add to the richness; the walls are white, adorned with Picasso, Monet, and Rousseau prints. The signature Haussmannian moldings, finely carved and painted, add a touch of elegance to the ceilings. The kitchen is small but functional. Apparently, a Frenchman doesn't need the large, extravagantly equipped kitchen of most middle-class American homes. The French pride themselves with getting more from less. A good cast-iron frying pan, copper cookware, a cheese grater, a whisk, Sabatier knives, and a few additional accoutrements are all a French cook needs to create a meal fit for a Louis.

Our bedroom has enough floor space for yoga and, as luck would have it, we can use the Persian rug that lies in front of our double bed as a rich man's yoga mat. Alain and Simone must have exchanged the French language books with English ones because the only authors on the mahogany shelves are Dickens, Melville, and Twain.

"Well, I see you charmed Simone. She seems quite taken by you," Deborah says as she removes her clothes from the pannier and places them in the top drawer of the antique dresser.

"I prefer being with people who are straight. They don't blindside you with their secrets."

Her lips tighten, her fingers clench. She releases a long breath like a cigarette smoker. And then she softens her features.

"Okay, tomorrow I'm inviting you for a date to discuss Sweden. Deal?" she asks. I grunt in response. "I'll take that as a yes."

An hour later, we join Alain and Simone in the salon where they're both reading and enjoying a glass of white wine.

Alain offers us wine. "If it's okay with you, we'll eat in an hour and a half, around eight. I must prepare the crêpes in thirty minutes. Would either of you like to learn how to make French crêpes?"

"Michael's the chef, not me," Deborah says. "He's very good. Food's not that important to me."

"Thank you, Alain. I'd love to learn to make a crêpe from a real French chef, not Julia Child."

"You mean that big woman with the funny voice? A wonderful ambassador for French cuisine. Her first 'divine' French meal was at a restaurant in Rouen. She called the oysters, sole meunière, and wine a 'revelation.' Maybe you'll find God in my crêpes?"

"Why not? I found God in a croissant, so no reason why I can't discover Him or Her in crêpes."

Simone actually laughs and says, "You and Alain should get along swimmingly. I've been telling Alain he needs a male friend. He's too much of a loner. So, you're a connoisseur of French cuisine?"

"No, I'm an epicurean. Most people eat to live. Not me. I live to eat. I can't distinguish a C-flat from a C-sharp, but blindfold me and give me a spoonful of—let's say—blended soup, and I can tell you what's in it, including the herbs and spices. I was raised and trained by a Francophile."

"Meaning?" she asks.

"When we were kids, my father would take us to French restaurants in New York City where he would teach us about French cuisine.

"I may have been the only American ten-year-old who could eat escargot, foie gras, and coq au vin without vomiting. My father was in love with everything French. He spoke French fluently and lived here, in Paris, on a boat moored at the Place de la Concorde marina from 1969 to 1978."

This is too tasty for Simone to pass by. She interrogates me about why my father lived on a boat, about our relationship, my background, and the impact he had and continues to have on me. She chews on my answers until she devours each one fully and then summarizes with a pithy and insightful comment disguised as a question. "I see. Your father is a restless man looking for something real, but searching in all the wrong places?

"Why is it that so many unhappy souls believe they'll find themselves in Paris?" she asks. "Funny, Alain and I have lived our entire lives here, and neither of us has figured out the Truth. Are you in Paris trying to finish what your father started? Very Oedipal. You think you'll find The Answer here?"

"Good chance with you interrogating me, I will. Maybe if Hemingway had you in his life, he wouldn't have killed himself."

"Very funny. Always the comedian, always deflecting."

"Simone," I say, "do you know the expression, 'What's good for the goose is good for the gander'?" She says yes. "Good, because the day will come when I get to put you on the stand."

"Excellent. I look forward to it."

The next hour with Alain provides a welcome interlude from the intensity of Simone's questions and commentaries. Alain instructs by example. He first demonstrates and then has me repeat his steps. He shows me how to whisk the egg whites so they're fluffy, and how to beat the batter of milk, yolks, flour, and vanilla sugar so that all the ingredients are totally mixed. "The pièce de résistance is the Calvados, an apple brandy produced in Normandy. It adds a sweet and tart flavor to the crêpe."

Over dinner, we learn the following about Simone: She's a thirty-three-year-old, bored government translator in her first month of a four-year course to become a lay psychoanalyst. She has an older sister to whom she hasn't spoken in nine years after a falling out related to their parents' divorce. Her father, a family physician, passed away from pancreatic cancer eight years ago. Her mother, a retired professor of French literature and now a part-time French tutor, had a Tunisian lover named Said during Simone's adolescence.

"Said was better suited for my mother than my father was. Unfortunately, she ended their affair when my father threatened divorce. My mother didn't cheat," Simone explains. "She told my father exactly what she was up to. He didn't care. What bothered him was that she had a lover before he did. They eventually divorced when I was twenty-three. I took my mother's side, my sister took my father's, and we haven't spoken since."

About Alain, we discover he's a thirty-one-year-old unemployed employment counselor specializing in placing middle-management employees in the financial area. "Kind of pathetic to be an unemployed employment counselor," he admits. "My agency folded, and I ended up on the streets with the rest of the staff."

He's the oldest of four—two brothers and one sister—from a conservative Catholic family from Dijon. His father is the owner of a modestly successful men's shoe store that he took over from his modestly successful father. His mother assists his father in the store but longs to be a *pâtissiere*.

"She's too scared to follow her heart. I'm afraid I'm like her. What I really want is to learn to program. I'm scared to take the entry exam for the corporate training program. The odds of making it are terrible. Only 10 percent pass."

Deborah prods him into acknowledging that he's no less intelligent than the 10 percent. She suggests he learn what those who passed did and see if he can do the same. He agrees.

Speaking of odds, at first glance, Alain and Simone as a couple seem like a roll of the dice—a long shot at best. Take a gentle soul like Alain and an angst-ridden control freak like Simone and I'd tell you it's a bad bet. But I'm wrong. Deborah asks them how they met.

"Three years ago, I attended a lecture by the rock-star French psychoanalyst Jacques Lacan," Alain says. "Simone was sitting next to me. Lacan made no sense to me, so I asked her if she understood his mirror stage of development. She looked smart, and from the way she was nodding, I figured she got him."

He laughs like a man who loves his lover's warts and says, "This is what she said: 'Do you expect me to give you a lesson about Lacan's theories while he's giving a lecture? If you're not too weird, I'll go out for a coffee—if you pay—and I'll give you a free class on Lacan's mirror stage.'"

Before he goes any further, Simone interrupts and says, "Don't say a word about our sex life or you're out of the room and on the couch."

*   *   *

I awaken from a dream feeling distraught. I turn on the night light, find my journal and pen, and jot it down:

Black ominous waters break violently against the stone embankments flanking the road that leads us toward the border of Sweden. Ahead is a land that's pure white—a passionless, ethereal innocence in stark contrast to the power, darkness, and fury of the rough seas on either side of us. We approach the land on bikes. Deborah stops to talk to a woman, first in French and then in Swedish. As she talks, her face exudes joy, her voice deepens, her whole being overflows with love. She crosses the border on foot, leaving me behind. My soul disappears like a vanishing cloud . . .

The dream hangs over me like a disturbing question. Why are Sweden and Niels this well-guarded secret that Deborah won't share? Yes, she's taken me to the Swedish border—metaphorically—by having told me many times about her love affair with Sweden and her relationship with Niels. But in the dream, she's in a state of ecstatic joy as she's about to cross into the ethereal stillness of Sweden, while I wait on the opposite side alone, surrounded by turbulent waters. Is the dream revealing more than my terror? Is there truth to it? Am I the unwanted intruder who Deborah believes will spoil the spiritual purity that Sweden and Niels symbolize for her? Troubling questions that undermine my sense of equilibrium. Thoughts of losing Deborah blacken my mood like the heavy cloud cover that envelops Paris this morning.

"Michael, when would you like to go out for our date?" she asks.

"Now. Let's go to the café on Sébastopol."

After a few moments of stilted small talk, she says, "I never told you this: When I first met you, I was still in love with Niels. My plan was to finish at Antioch, return to Sweden, and then Niels and I would go to the TM center in Spain, where I'd work as a school counselor. I didn't expect or want to get involved in a new relationship. I had Niels and I couldn't imagine I'd ever find someone I could love more.

"Then you came along, and the universe suddenly became messy.

You were nothing like Niels. He's a gentle, lyrical soul who walks to the beat of his own compositions. He's pure creative energy. He touched me in a very deep way . . . Different from you.

"You're funny, street smart, and have a brain without boundaries. You helped me to appreciate the absurd and to be physically and mentally tough. You're the first guy Betty Mae can't intimidate. You're my brave knight; you protect me from the Dragon Lady. You understood me in a way that Niels couldn't.

"I'm not leaving you. But my heart isn't 100 percent with you. I can't get there without seeing Niels and walking away for the last time. I know it's risky . . . But it's what I have to do."

"Of course you're leaving me," I say. "Doesn't matter if it's for a week or forever, you're still leaving. As far as I see it, you've been having a secret affair in your mind and now that you're about to make it real, you tell me."

"I'm sorry. I was wrong. I should have told you as soon as I began thinking about going to Sweden. I was afraid, and I couldn't make sense of why I wanted to go. At first, I kept thinking, 'Are you crazy? You love Michael. It's unfair to hurt him. He's your life partner.' But no matter how hard I tried to talk myself out of it, I couldn't."

The waiter brings our two cheese omelets, a croissant each, a baguette, and cappuccinos. The warm, crispy taste of the fresh baguette creates a fleeting interruption in the intensity of our interaction. I survey the café, and for the first time see couples huddled together engaged in animated conversations. A woman to my far right speaks in subdued tones; the man remains silent. An edgy interlude to an otherwise wonderful relationship? The last heartbeat to a dying connection? A café serves food, but it serves another function as well, as a therapeutic setting in which couples ignite the spark between them, attempt to extinguish the raging fire, or acknowledge the embers are dying.

If only I had the inner certainty and strength to say, "Go and I'm gone," or "Go. Do what you must. I believe in you." But I'm neither a tough guy nor a saint. If I'm supposed to feel clarity, I don't. I remain silent, caught in a web of competing voices.

"Michael, talk to me. What's going on?"

"What do you want me to say? You made yourself clear. I get that Niels is the itch you've got to scratch, but you're tearing into my flesh. You're putting me through one goddamn test—asking me to trust when I feel betrayed."

Perhaps the café trains the waiters in the subtle art of diffusion and distraction. Noticing a couple at the brink of losing all control and publicly embarrassing themselves, the skillful waiter, pushing a cart laden with a colorful assortment of cakes, pies, and tarts, intervenes and asks, "Madame and sir, may I suggest the dessert special for the day, a cherry plum tart?"

The couple disengage, turn to focus on the cart. She asks the waiter, "Would you suggest the cherry plum tart over the other cakes and pies?"

He replies, "Yes, madame, you won't be disappointed." During that brief interlude, the couple compose themselves, sense the pulse of love still beats beneath the bitterness and pain, and decide to lower the intensity to a level that might facilitate mutual understanding.

I can see that Deborah wants to take my hand in hers. I hold back. Her face is taut, her eyes are red and moist. She swallows back her tears. "I know I'm hurting you deeply, but I have to go to Sweden for me—to know I can move on, that there's no hidden longing inside of me that separates us. And maybe I'm going for no other reason than I feel I must, to scratch that so-called itch that won't disappear. It's not just scary for you. It's also terrifying for me."

It's not terrified that I feel right now. It's betrayed and blindsided. But for the sake of my sanity and our relationship, I'll tell myself, "She's not abandoning me. She's not running away. She's seeking truth and resolution." I'll remind myself while Deborah is gone that this is the price you pay when you fall in love with a woman with many doors to her soul, with parts that I can't reach.

"I hope for both of our sakes I can do it," I say. "We're on a slippery slope right now and I don't know where we'll land. I'll work on letting go and trusting you because anything less would be terrible for me and a disaster for us. I love you, but right now that feels more difficult than summitting Everest without oxygen."

Around the same time that the psychologist and purveyor of eschatological truths, Sheldon Kopp, asserted, "You can't have anything unless you first let go of it," Janice Joplin, the heart-piercing singer of hope and despair, reminded us in her song "Me and Bobby McGee" that we're free when we stop holding on to the way we think things should be.

Their words loop around in my mind like the circular movement of a child's locomotive. The message is obvious: There's a time to hold a position fiercely like a dog with a bone, and there's a time to let go, move on, and trust. This is the time to accept, to understand that neither impeccable logic nor agonizing exhortations can change what's meant to be. Deborah's going to Sweden. Accept it.

I accept.

Castaneda teaches us that the warrior excels on one field of battle—on the frontline of uncertainty; a bleak terrain containing all possibility.

Uncertainty terrifies—these final days in Paris could be our last. Yet not knowing liberates the artist in us. The breadth of our imagination, the skill in which we manage the circumstances, and the choices we make will determine whether love or resentment will be the outcome.

We can play out the drama, create the screeching sounds of suffering, and feel the intense discomfort of an imprisoned soul, or decide, in part, like a cancer patient with six more lucid days left, to make every moment count. We choose love over fear.

For the next six days, we create a Paris state of mind. Call it the art of deflection over an excess of reality:

1. We find a super cool café on the Left Bank close to the iconic bookstore Shakespeare and Company.

2. She finds a table, sits alone, and I approach her as if this is our first encounter.

3. I say, "I see you're alone. Are you waiting for someone?" (She replies no. I detect a slight smile. A green light? I make my move.) "Would you mind if I join you?"

4. She hesitates and then replies, "Why not?"

5. "I'm Michael, and you are?"

6. "Deborah." She waits; the tension builds. The ball is in my court. Do I begin with a compliment, a question, or with the unexpected sleight of hand? In the subtle dance between the sexes, you don't want your first step to be the one that lands on her foot. So I ask, "What's the one line I can say that will knock your socks off?"

7. She laughs and says, "You may have just said it." (We pass the first hurdle. We're attuned, open to what may be . . .)

8. A French moment ripe with possibility and romance? A spark, ready to ignite? A pleasant glow, about to turn into a warmer fire? A few shared details provide context and color—call it the oxygen needed to keep the flame alive. Both of us travel solo—more freedom to be with or to be alone. Appealing and Challenging.

Appealing: The hunt is far more alluring when the pursued is quicker and less vulnerable.

Challenging: The so-called pursued does a one-eighty, gazes directly into the black piercing eyes of the pursuer, and asks, "So why me?"

"Because you're beautiful in a smart, powerful way . . . Because we're in the City of Light and Love and I don't want to lose the moment . . . Because I feel this magnetic pull toward you . . . Because . . . You want me to keep going? I have more."

"Flattering . . . let's save it for later. Let's spend the day together."

She plays a deft hand. Cool, direct—waiting to discover where Fate might lead us. For now, just where we are, across from one another in a crowded Left Bank café, sipping cappuccinos and munching on lemon tarts. The conversation has a life of its own as it meanders through recollections and impressions from the road.

Ah, yes, the venue: A café in the heart of the Latin Quarter, a minute's stroll to Shakespeare and Company, where you can let your imagination soar and travel with Anaïs Nin to the crowded souks of Marrakesh or sail with Lawrence Durrell on the azure waters of the Aegean to discover the magic and poetry of the Greek Islands.

Is there a more perfect setting for a Parisian state of mind? The slow pace of the café lends itself to the cultivation of a uniquely French philosophy. Hard to imagine a Parisian mindset absent a convincing outlook on love, sex, aesthetics, and the usual troubling questions about meaning and purpose.

"What's more important to you," she asks, "being in love or being free?"

"Both. Like now. We created this."

She reaches for my hand and says, "Michael, look at me. I mean, really look at me."

I feel naked—like my soul is on display, like I once heard someone say, "You want to know if someone really loves you? Tell me if you feel seen."

"I love you," she says. "We'll figure it out."

CHAPTER 5

Paris: Part 2

There's this thing the Parisians do that's called *flâner*: A hard word to translate because it describes a behavior specific to the Parisian culture. But since I'm writing about Paris in English— at the risk of misinterpretation—*flâner* means to stroll, to amble aimlessly.

Meaning?

No have-tos, no to-do list to check off, no schedule to follow— merely experience the moment and connect to the beautiful woman walking hand in hand by your side. You're in a *flâner* state of mind. You meander, letting your eyes roam, perhaps noticing an antique shop displaying an especially lovely mahogany clock you estimate to be from the nineteenth century. You share your observation with your lover.

She might suggest you enter the old antique shop for a closer examination of the clock. You don't notice that thirty minutes fly by as the shopkeeper with the droopy mustache and stained vest gives you a tour of his store, pointing out various items dated from the time of Louis XIV. Both of you know you have no intention of buying anything. No matter, he's most likely of a mixed mind about parting with his old friends. You move on.

She draws your attention to a street juggler—first four balls, then five. He adds a flaming torch, discards the balls, juggles five fiery torches, and then, as if that's not impressive enough, picks up a foot-long sword and thrusts it down his mouth, where it seems to arrive somewhere close to his upper intestine.

Eventually, you will have "*flânéd*" yourselves to your destination—a dusty old bookstore dripping with nostalgia and the lingering odor of nicotine exhaled over the years by a long line of chain-smoking literary giants. Pay homage: At the Shakespeare and Company bookstore, you're about to enter a holy temple where F. Scott Fitzgerald, Ernest Hemingway, and James Joyce read, conversed, and argued. Forget about Shakespeare, he was stuck across the channel in Stratford-upon-Avon; it's the Company we're most interested in.

I don't have a watch, but I'd guess two hours pass. I'm upstairs folded inside a dusty, oversized chair as relaxed as a hibernating bear snoozing away the dark days of winter. Deborah's a foot from me engrossed in a book by Iyengar on Hatha Yoga, curled inside her oversized and ragged sofa-chair like a pearl nestled in a shell.

I'm reading a thin book I discovered in the section entitled Religion and Spirituality called *Basic Judaism* by Milton Steinberg, a peculiar choice considering I was on a direct path to *The Tibetan Book of the Dead*.

"Why a book on Judaism? I've known you for nearly six years. You've shown no interest in anything Jewish," she says. "Are you having a secret roots experience you'd like to share?"

"Very cute. But since you asked, no special reason. It caught my eye, and that's it. Actually, seems like there's more to Judaism than I realized."

"I get it. Just another one of your fleeting intellectual pursuits. Like the history of the Visigoths or the life of Willie Mays."

It's a mile and a half from Shakespeare and Company to the Rodin Museum. We walk, hand in hand, along Boulevard Saint-Germain and Rue de Varenne, pausing in astonishment to breathe in the tantalizing aroma of fresh pastries, warm French bread, and the pungent odors of Camembert, Roquefort, and Brie. We pass a crowded market displaying vegetables like pieces of art: onions the size of softballs and blood-red tomatoes begging to fulfill their higher purpose in a *tarte à la moutarde*. Yes, Mr. Hemingway, Paris is a "moveable feast."

Rodin compels, excites, and challenges. He animates the

inanimate—almost like what God Himself did when he created the first man. Like the Creator, he finds the soul embedded in the white stone and black metal and exhales his life force into the inert objects. Ergo: *The Kiss*.

Two nudes, male and female—bodies intertwined—embrace in a kiss. His right hand caresses her left thigh; her left hand folds around his neck, drawing his lips to hers. Their right knees touch one another; her right elbow leans on his left hand. He sits erect and strong as if he's invulnerable; she finds his tenderness and pulls him toward her. It's uncertain if the kiss is the aperitif that precedes the entrée or the nightcap that follows.

In either case, I feel like a voyeur who accidentally stumbles upon two lovers during a moment of profound intimacy and sensuality. I want to turn away, but how can I? The raw sexuality of *The Kiss* lures me into its erotic web like a fly trapped in the steel threads of a spider's snare. I can't get loose. I remain fixed where I stand—only a hand's length from the lovers—until my liberator arrives.

"Michael, it's nearly closing time. We should leave."

It's a three-mile walk from Musée Rodin back to Simone and Alain's apartment. A mile-plus stretch runs parallel to the Seine, and at a point close to Place de la Concorde, we pass the marina where my father moored his boat, *Circe*, from 1969 to 1978. Positive memories of my father are as rare and precious as a black opal; the times he and I spent on his thirty-eight-foot yacht getting high on hashish are the rare gems.

When I was a college student at NYU, I made a surprising discovery: A few tokes on a joint could transform my father—an angry, aggressive male—into a delightful conversationalist and a deep thinker. So, every time I'd travel from Darmstadt, Germany, where I was stationed, I'd smuggle a few grams of hashish into France and we'd get stoned. One special memory occurred a few days after Susan left me for her lover Rich. After I pulled a few strings, the alcoholic battalion commander granted me a week's leave from my meaningless job as the training officer for the Ninety-Third Signal Battalion:

On the Circe, *my father and I smoke bowls of hash, eat some amazing French food, and talk about life until Paris is silent. As brilliant as my father is, when it comes to emotional intelligence, he's usually clueless. Not that week on the boat. He pays attention, interjects appropriately, and figures out the right measure of space and support. I love him—not so much like a son to a father but as an older friend, and, for one week, a wise mentor.*

As I stare at the long wooden houseboat in the space where he once docked *Circe*, Deborah draws me close to her and strokes my hair. No need for her to ask what's going on; she knows the story well.

Over wine and cheese, we share the experiences of the day with Simone and Alain. Because she can't help herself, Simone probes, interrogates, and interprets. When we reach the part where Deborah tells her I bought a book about Judaism, she's like a bloodhound.

"Tell me. Why a book on Judaism?" she asks.

"No special reason," I answer. "It was next to a book on Buddhism and it caught my eye. Why the question? Something to do with your Jewish ex-boyfriend?"

"Always deflecting. I assure you there's more to your decision than a perceptual happenstance. Answer these questions and I'll prove it to you."

"Go for it, Sherlock. Probe away." By now, Deborah's sitting on the edge of her seat almost like Simone's doing her bidding by uncovering my confused Jewish psyche.

Deborah has firsthand experience of my bizarre reaction to the Christmas bush she wanted to place in our house. But that pales in comparison to my escape from the Yom Kippur service that she once pressured me to attend. "It's the holiest day of the Jewish calendar," she told me. "Let's experience it together."

Crazy as this might sound, my Lebanese Christian shiksa stayed for the entire six-hour service while I split. That evening, after she berated me for not sticking it out, she said, "I didn't understand a thing, but something about the service touched me deeply."

Not me. What was profound for Deborah was agony for me—like the noise of a dentist's drill deep inside a cavity.

Simone leans toward me, fixes her gaze, and asks, "Where were you when Israel declared victory at the end of the Six-Day War?"

"What does that have to do with anything?"

"It has everything to do with everything," she says. "If you answer the question, you'll understand where I'm going."

"At the Montreal World's Fair," I answer.

"Of course you remember where you were. Just like you know where you were when Kennedy was assassinated. Every Jew, even a pork-eating Jew like you, knows where he was when Israel won the war. I'm certain you followed the news religiously. Yes?"

"Can I plead the Fifth?"

"I don't understand what that means," she says. "Just answer the question."

"Glued to the news during the war. What does that prove?"

"If Deborah wanted to have a Christmas tree in your house, would you agree?" What is she—a goddamn mind-reading witch? I look in Deborah's direction—for what, I don't know. I have no illusions I'll find support from that corner.

"Did you and Deborah talk about this behind my back? What other secrets has she shared with you?" Deborah laughs. Simone is undeterred.

"Again, you use every diversion to avoid answering. Why are you so afraid of the truth?"

"No, I would not and did not agree to the Christmas tree. You got me. I couldn't care less about celebrating Hanukkah, but a Christmas tree was too much even for a pork-eating Jew like me."

"Isn't it strange that you have a non-Jewish girlfriend, eat foods your religion forbids, and up until today, you've shown no interest in anything Jewish, yet you won't allow a meaningless symbol in your house? If Deborah insisted on having a tree, would you end your relationship?"

"It wouldn't come to that. We'd figure a compromise."

"Like what? Stockings over the fireplace or mistletoe?" she asks.

Deborah intervenes and says, "No, he didn't agree to that either. I backed off. Christmas makes him cuckoo, and it's not that important to me. At any rate, we go to my parents' home in West Virginia for Christmas, where Michael is more than happy to receive generous gifts from my mother and eat ham, shrimp, and bacon along with all the other goyim."

"So, now that we've established your feelings are rather ambivalent about the Jewish subject," Simone continues, "let's understand why you bought a book on Judaism."

"You tell me, Professor Lacan. You seem to have all the answers."

"Very well. You bought the book because you're a Jew, and like most Jews, you can never run away from your Jewish roots. There will always be a reminder like a Christmas tree or a book that suddenly catches your attention. You won't know why, nor will you ask the right questions. You'll merely dismiss it as happenstance, a coincidence lacking any deeper meaning. Well, you're wrong and you'll discover that when you arrive in Israel."

"Simone, I'm not your ex-boyfriend and Deborah's not you."

"Write to me from Israel and tell me if my assumptions were incorrect."

We sense, at least temporarily, that we've taken this subject as far as we can. At Simone's initiative, we make a seamless pivot to a discussion about boorish Americans, present company excluded; the stupidity of the anti-collectivist American paradigm of the rugged individual—think Davy Crockett, the Lone Ranger, James Dean. An optimistic, can-do attitude that lacks an intellectual and moral foundation, i.e., progress for progress's sake, etc., etc., etc.

"Simone, remember who got you out of deep shit in World War II? None other than the can-do, optimistic American GI who risked his ass to save the brave French, who—do I also need to remind you—handed the keys to their beloved Paris to none other than Satan himself, Adolf Hitler. Well done, France. You guys are exceptional at sitting in *cafés* and discussing points beyond infinity, but you're total losers when you have to defend your country."

Just as she is about to launch a counterattack, Alain enters stage left, announcing that the dinner of steaks, salad, *frites*, and an omelet for Deborah is now ready. I have the impression the French leave their arguments in the salon. Fierce disagreements can upset one's digestion.

One day gone, four more to go before Deborah leaves for Sweden . . .

* * *

Cole Porter may claim to "*love Paris when it drizzles*," but it's nonsense. A myth. Paris sucks in the rain. Cross the street and a damn Parisian driver will splash sewer water on your shoes and pants. Try to maneuver around impatient Frenchmen and see if they don't stab you with their umbrellas, and then tell me if you love Paris when it's raining. Forget about doing the *flâner* in a downpour.

It's Metro time.

A pulsating press of French flesh of every shape and color push and shove to get underground. But wait! The Metro is so much more than a ticket to ride.

It's showtime.

Get your front-row spot at the subterranean concert. What's your pleasure? Rock? Folk? Classical? Indian? Doesn't matter. You'll find something you love 150 feet below ground at the world's greatest live musical festival. No tickets needed. If you wish, toss a franc or a dollar into the hat and let the good times roll. Ready to be surprised?

A Rastafarian—dreadlocks, beard, rainbow-colored beret, a Richie Havens vibe about him—hits some crazy notes on the sax. Could be he's playing "Bess, You Is My Woman Now" from *Porgy and Bess*. Deep underground, the vibrating pitch of his sax reverberates like a fast-moving ball leaping from wall to wall. The effect is a mesmerizing acoustic illusion: Five saxophones—perfectly attuned. One moment their pitch ascends and at the next descends to improvise an otherworldly (no, actually, an underworldly) musical phenomenon, a breakthrough sound.

Deborah gestures it's time to go. We're off to the Louvre where, once again, we get to elbow our way through a mass of humanity. Only this time, it's not French flesh we'll press, but the beefier American variety along with the bonier Japanese as people jostle, slide, and push their way to get close to the elusive *Mona Lisa*.

Let's bypass thousands of years of art history and hop to the first floor of the Louvre where we'll find her, center stage between a row of Italian and French paintings. You can't miss her because middle-aged, balding Frank from Topeka is circling the enigmatic Italian lady like she's a Cadillac in a showroom. The significant difference for Frank between the shiny black Cadillac and the *Mona Lisa* is that, in the scene before us, he pushes and shoves himself around the mysterious black-haired lady from Italy while shouting repeatedly to his wife, the plump woman wearing Adidas sneakers and a St. Louis Cardinals baseball cap, "She's still staring at me!" Of course she is, Frank. The world's most famous lady only has eyes for you.

But let's not get hung up on the hundreds of Franks and the scores of Japanese with their Minoltas and Nikons mounted on tripods. In fact, let's make them all disappear and imagine an intimate encounter with Lisa Gherardini, the reluctant wife of the wealthy slave trader Francesco del Giocondo.

It's my fourth pilgrimage to the Florentine beauty and Deborah's 150th—more or less.

I stand only a yard from the *Mona Lisa* and concentrate on this secretive woman whose eyes lock with mine. We can speculate; we can imagine; we can project, but whatever lies behind that baffling mien and those dark brown eyes that say, *I see things I can't disclose,* will remain concealed within the stillness of her mind. I feel her silence; I sense her quiet reserve protects and confuses, and I want to tell her: *Don't speak. Don't disclose. Your power lies in your restraint. Remain elusive and indefinable. Your enemies can't possess what they can't define.*

What I admire in the *Mona Lisa* terrifies me in Deborah.

*   *   *

We dash from the Louvre, jumping over puddles and running between the raindrops, so to speak. Five minutes of sprinting brings us to the

Metro where we warm ourselves to the lovely sounds of a string ensemble—a soothing classical piece for a violin, a viola, and a cello.

We arrive at the apartment around seven p.m., and this time, we kids get to let ourselves in. This morning, as we were about to embark for our day at the Louvre, Simone handed a key to Deborah and said, "This way neither of us depends on one another." To Simone, a key is not merely a simple metallic device designed to unlock a door. Truth lies on the level of abstraction—a key symbolizes liberation from the tyranny of mutually obsequious relationships. I guess she's not worried we'll pinch her heirloom silverware engraved with the letter *L* for Laberge.

In fact, four sets of those silver knives, forks, and spoons rest on the dining room table along with light blue dinner plates and crystal wine glasses. The settings lay on an elegant white linen tablecloth, embroidered with an elaborate floral design—the kind of tablecloth your average American family would cover with a disposable plastic sheet. I'm with the French on this one.

"What's the occasion?" I ask.

"Such an American question. The only sit-down occasions you Americans understand are the obligatory ones—Thanksgiving and Christmas. You eat on the run, catch your breath on Thanksgiving, and then sprint to Christmas. Learn from the French. Spend an evening with friends, enjoy fine food and wine, and create a memorable event. That's exactly what Alain suggested we do for you this evening—surprise you with a lovely French meal.

"He's such a sweet man. You must wonder why we're together, a gentle soul like Alain and a difficult neurotic like me. He doesn't just accept my neuroses, he loves them. He calls them my delightful quirks and idiosyncrasies. He's so good to me, I may have to kill him in self-defense. He's putting me at risk of becoming happy. How would a troubled philosopher with a tortured past cope with such bourgeois sentiments of love and happiness?"

Simone presents me with quite a challenge. Do I take the American bait and confront her sweeping generalizations—which to be honest aren't all that off the mark? True confession: We haven't had one leisurely evening at home with friends in the last three years.

Okay, so let's forget about defending the American lifestyle and just respond to Simone's self-deprecating monologue. Radical for a neurotic. They're usually too wrapped up in their suffering to laugh at themselves—too attached to being miserable to get that unhappiness is a choice. No neurotic wants to surrender that trump card. But Simone gives me an opening here. She's teasing her "tortured philosopher." So, I make my move.

"Shame on you, Simone. What self-respecting tormented soul murders her lover for making her feel good? You—not Alain—are responsible for these bourgeois sentiments. Any true existentialist worth her weight in misery knows that. Suicide, not murder, is how one rids oneself of this disease of happiness." I hum a few verses from the theme song of M*A*S*H, "Suicide Is Painless."

Simone laughs.

No polite giggles or subdued chuckles, but a genuine belly laugh. This seems so unusual for Simone that Alain darts from the kitchen in concern until he realizes his neurotic girlfriend is having a moment, and he, being the wonderful man that he is, puts his arm around her, gives her a kiss, and asks me with a smile, "Are you responsible for this?"

"No. More like Laurel and Hardy and Abbott and Costello. We take our cues from one another."

For such an occasion, you need to be properly attired. For us around-the-world bicyclists, this could pose quite a challenge. You don't pack a complete wardrobe of fine clothes in a pannier. You take the bare necessities, wash the life out of them, and then replace them with whatever fits. For this formal dinner, I choose a white shirt—my only white shirt—that at first glance looks like a cheap version of the tablecloth. Deborah, as usual, looks lovely in her light blue cotton dress that perfectly matches the dinner plates.

I find Alain in the kitchen stirring sauces and whisking dressings. "I hope the meal will live up to your expectations," he says.

"I'm certain it will exceed them," I reply.

It does.

Granted, I've never experienced the gastronomic artistry of a three-star Michelin restaurant. However, I doubt there's a chef, living or dead, who put more love into his stuffed mushrooms with truffles; blended more tenderness into his sweet potato soup with saffron-infused cream; added more attention to his fillets of sole meunière; sculpted more delight into his intermezzo, a beet sorbet; and invested more of himself into the tender chateaubriand and the souffle he prepared especially for Deborah.

I bow in pleasure to this modest chef with the big heart!

Following my exchange with Simone there was an immediate change in her demeanor. Her hardness melted, her skin tone brightened, and her voice took on a pleasant—almost girlish—lilt. At the risk of being hyperbolic, I would say that by the start of the meal, she was on the edge of happiness—remarkable, considering how a few hours earlier, she had moved through life wrapped in a shroud of melancholy.

A conversation has many fits and starts, sharp turns, and steep climbs, but sometimes, you lock on a direction and you stay the course. Somewhere around the time Alain serves the end-of-meal espresso, Deborah asks Simone about her childhood experience growing up in post-war France.

Simone was born the same year as I, 1946, six months after Germany surrendered. Deborah's innocent question, under the influence of wine, the safe company of two friends, and the absence of melancholy (which for some is a defense against trauma), triggers a reaction that none of us expect.

Simone bursts out crying. Her tears fall like torrents. Alain strokes her hand and then draws her closer to him. He knows her tears.

"I'm sorry, I didn't expect this. I don't want to ruin our evening." Simone glances at Deborah.

"You won't," Deborah says, her voice warm and compassionate. "You'd turn over heaven and earth to be there for us. We can do the same for you."

Simone swallows back sobs. Deep furrows line her pale cheeks, and pallid circles materialize under her watery blue eyes. Her eyes clamp tight; she retreats inside. I imagine her whirling downward into a blind cave where memories like crouching beasts hide within the crevices, ready to attack, about to overwhelm. I want to tell her, "Scream! Vomit! Do whatever you must to release this horror." She remains silent, frozen in terror. Alain gently strokes her hair and says, "Let Deborah and Michael be there for you. It's what you need."

"Ghosts," she whispers, her voice shaking. "My two brothers burned to death . . . from a British bomb that landed on my parents' house. This was my childhood. Nightmares and ghosts."

I notice the color has drained from Deborah's face. I suspect she'd say the same about me. Neither of us shocks easily, but I sense we're about to enter a dimension of trauma far beyond our imagination and experience. Far beyond the healing power of words.

"At night, I'd lie in bed terrified, unable to shut out my father's nightmares. Each one was a fragment of horror that over time told a story. When the bomb hit my parents' home, Andre and Michel were playing in the basement. My father tried to save them, but fire separated him from his sons. They screamed until they became silent.

"He watched their flesh roast until the only thing that remained of my brothers was ash. Ash that he scooped up and preserved in a jar he kept in his office." She stops, looks down momentarily, then says in a voice heavy with bitterness and grief, "My father saved Jews from the ovens. His reward: His sons turned to dust by British bombs. A burnt offering to the God of Nothingness.

"My father's life ended with the death of my brothers. He never forgave himself for failing to rescue them. He raged against us like we had no right to live in the same world that took his sons.

"This was the world I was born into—a childhood burdened with suffering. If you smiled, you were disloyal to the memory of Andre and Michel. When the boys died, joy and happiness died with them. My sister and I felt guilty for being children. We didn't cry. We didn't play. We read books and tiptoed around my father."

She falls silent.

Deborah, Alain, and I are still. Yet my guts want to scream out against the silent God who allowed this. I ache for Simone and her family: her father, a principled man traumatized for life by an event of horrific proportions; the two terrified boys trapped in a burning inferno; Simone, an innocent child born into tragedy and raised in an atmosphere of rage and despair; her mother and sister, scarred for life by the sinister hand of fate—all of them victims of hate and violence.

Deborah gives Simone a hug and kisses her on the forehead. "Simone, I have no words for you other than I love you and I'm here for you."

Simone looks directly at Deborah and then me and says, "Thank you."

I reach for my seventh chocolate truffle and try to find something to say. Nothing comes. It is Alain who breaks the ice with the eighth course—heart-shaped cookies made with almond flour and clarified butter.

Two days gone, three to go until Deborah leaves for Sweden . . .

* * *

A leopard doesn't change spots that quickly. The following morning, Simone tells us, "You're going to the Pompidou Center today, to a photographic exhibit of the Holocaust. I reserved tickets for you. Pick them up at the ticket counter." It doesn't matter that we have plans to go to the Impressionist Museum and then to a vegetarian restaurant. Simone commands, we obey.

"By the way," Deborah says, "I didn't tell you that in three days I'm going to Sweden for a week."

Ten years ago, when Deborah hung out with Alain, she must have mentioned to him that she had been an exchange student in Sweden, because he asks, "Are you going to visit the family you lived with, way up north?"

"No, I'm visiting a friend who lives outside of Stockholm. We were together for two years with Maharishi in Italy and Spain. After that, we opened a leather shop in Stockholm together."

I can sense Simone is picking up the scent. She turns to me. "You don't want to go with Deborah?"

I tense my jaw; my stomach tightens. I choose to dodge rather than reveal. "It's complicated. Deborah needs some alone time with her friend."

"And this friend is a male or a female?"

Deborah answers, "A male."

We're at a crossroads. I could jump in and offer more information. I don't. Simone's surprisingly quiet and reflective. She knows she's on to something. Multilevel conversations dripping with subtext and multiple meanings may be her playing ground, but from his fidgeting, I can tell Alain would rather be back in the kitchen. I know Deborah won't say more unless she gets a green light from me, and I'm deliberately not signaling anything. Let her deal with it.

I wait for Simone to make her move. By her own admission, subtleties and indirection are not her forte, so I assume Simone will take the straight path and say something like, "Michael, are you okay with this?" Or to Deborah, "I gather there's a story here. Why are you visiting him?"

I'm wrong.

Instead, she says, "He must be an important person for you. I hope whatever you need to work out, you will. You and Michael are beautiful together; I know you'll deal with whatever you have to."

* * *

The first thing we notice when we enter the exhibit hall is the parallel rows of ropes and posts. The rope on the right side separates the viewer from the wall of photos by approximately a yard. The left-sided cord and stanchions act as a barricade to ensure that the crowd walks in single file. These parallel barriers define a path about one and a half yards in width, narrow enough to maintain a solemn pace, yet wide enough to pass.

We wait for our turn to begin the exhibit. A long row of silent visitors walks counterclockwise—at a slow and deliberate speed. No one smiles. Some wipe tears with a handkerchief. An elderly woman sobs. A young woman, perhaps her granddaughter, steadies her. A middle-aged man turns to the woman behind him and points to a black-and-white photo displaying a mound of worn shoes. I sense there's a terrifying memory hidden somewhere in that pile. The woman covers her mouth as if she's trying to stifle a scream. My eyes focus on a distinguished gentleman—gray beard, appears to be in his midfifties, wearing the black yarmulke of an Orthodox Jew. I notice his lips move as if he's praying; I wonder if he's reciting Kaddish, the Jewish prayer for the dead.

In the first stage of the exhibit, the Nazi cartoonists characterize the Jew as a disease-bearing organism. A grotesque image portrays the Jew as a rat with a hooked nose, thick lips, and skullcap. The images before us tell the story of how the Nazi propaganda machine brainwashed the German public. Represent the individual Jew as a rodent, a snake, or a poisonous spider and he becomes a dangerous predator that must be exterminated. Picture the entire Jewish nation as a swarm of locusts or a plague of rats, and genocide becomes a moral imperative.

We progress at a somber pace, past a timeline of horrors that begins with photographs of the Nazi occupation of Europe in 1939 and '40.

Six tall SS storm troopers surround a small, bent rabbi. Contempt drips from their lips; hatred leaches from their pores. The Nazi sadists aim their weapons at the defenseless old Jew.

The graphic chronology of the destruction of European Jewry resumes with the deportation of the Jews to the ghettos and transit stations.

Nazi soldiers, using their rifles like cattle prods, shove and push Jews of all stripes and ages to the edge of a platform. Yellow six-pointed stars stitched to their chests brand them as contaminated pariahs. In their hands, the condemned Jews carry satchels containing the last of their possessions. Like obedient soldiers at attention, empty cattle cars stand by, duty bound to transport their cargo to its ultimate destination.

The photomontage moves on to the Final Solution. Like mourners at a funeral, we file past image after image of living cadavers with dead expressions.

Lifeless eyes stare—without purpose—from within deep empty sockets. Filthy striped pajamas—the uniform of the near-dead—drape bony shoulders and emaciated, broken bodies. Freezing skeletons hover together—bone to bone—inside wooden sleeping compartments.

How is it possible that a spark of life still flickers within the hearts of these barely alive prisoners?

Deborah pauses before a photograph of a ten-foot-high mound of ashes—the cremated remains of gassed inmates. Underneath the photo is a description of the Nazis' extermination procedures:

First, the unsuspecting prisoners disrobe in front of their SS escorts, who order them to shower and be deloused before presumably being assigned to the barracks. In single file, the Nazis march the ill-fated victims to the gas chambers. To create the maximum space, the SS command the victims to raise their arms, enabling as many prisoners as possible to fit into one gas chamber. Auschwitz's three largest chambers could gas 2,000 people in five minutes.

The Sonderkommandos—Jewish prisoners picked to perform extermination duties—carry the bodies from the gas chambers to an antechamber where they remove the hair, gold teeth, and metal fillings from the corpses. Once they collect the recyclables, the Sonderkommandos burn the bodies in ovens and pyres, gather the ashes, and shovel them into large piles. The Nazis recycle the remains—an amorphous collection of once identifiable individuals possessing names, personalities, and families—and use the ashes of murdered Jews, gypsies, and other undesirables to fertilize their rose bushes, rhododendrons, and crops. The German polluters dump what they don't recycle into the surrounding rivers and streams—the same source that provides drinking water for the locals.

Deborah's crying. Deep loss is etched in her face. I envy her ability to mourn. She stands before a photo of cremated bodies and, I know for her, each handful of ash contains the remnant of a unique soul. I'm numb—frozen in rage, demanding vengeance. I imagine in my mind

how I would torture the obese storm trooper in the photo to the right
of the ashes:

*He holds a Luger in his right hand and stands over a dead Jew lying
at his feet. His face radiates satisfaction and pride as if he feels worthy of
a medal for heroism.*

I want to saw off his penis with a serrated knife and stuff it in his
mouth. And, while he still has life in him, I'll cut into his abundant
flesh and gut him organ by organ. I want to hear him beg for mercy and
scream in agony. Let him know this is the price for sadistic pleasure.

A man in front of Deborah stands before a picture of starving prisoners sitting by the entrance of a wooden barrack. He stares intently
at one prisoner and then turns to Deborah and says in English, "Come
closer. I want to show you something." He is an attractive, well-dressed
gentleman in his early sixties. He points to a young man—a living skel-
eton—and says, "This is me, days before the Russians liberated us."
Deborah gazes intently at the photo and then back at the man as if
she's trying to place what he said in some logical corner of her mind.

My mind goes into overdrive. A million questions flood my brain.
He's an eyewitness to the worst of man's inhumanity, a protagonist in a
tragic tale he seems to want to share and that I need to hear.

Within moments, we are sitting in the café listening to his story. Jacob
tells us his family traces its roots to Toledo, Spain. In the mid-sixteenth
century, his ancestors immigrated to Holland from Portugal and established themselves in Amsterdam, where they lived—more or less
peacefully—until the German occupation in 1940.

"The Nazis, along with their Dutch collaborators, murdered
108,000 Dutch Jews—including two of my grandparents, both of my
parents, my two brothers, and my sister. I am the one survivor from an
extended family of fifty."

He tightens his facial muscles, shakes his head from side to side,
and breathes out slowly. How can a human heart contain so much
grief? How can a human mind comprehend the extermination of an
entire family?

"I'm sorry, I'm getting ahead of myself." Jacob notices that Deborah is close to tears and asks, "Should I stop? I don't want to upset you, dear."

Deborah says, "Don't worry about me. I'll be okay."

He takes her hand and says, "You're a very kind girl." He resumes his story:

During 1941, the Germans and their Dutch collaborators tightened the noose around the Jewish community. Like the rest of the European Jews, we were stripped of our rights and confined to a ghetto. Yet, compared to what happened next, it was survivable.

The roundup and deportation began in June 1942. Jews were sent to a transit camp called Westerbork in the northeastern part of Holland. From there, the Germans transported us to Auschwitz, Sobibor, Bergen-Belsen, and Theresienstadt. The picture you saw of me was at Theresienstadt.

By the end of 1942, we were still in our apartment—the only Jews among eight non-Jewish families. For me, the waiting was torture. I thought about suicide, but I didn't have the courage. The illusion of hope didn't last. On December 15, 1942, the guillotine fell. Six armed Dutch policemen stormed our apartment and gave us fifteen minutes to gather a bag each. It was almost a relief. I was already a dead man, so whatever happened, I'd deal with it.

Two weeks after arriving at Westerbork, the Germans transported my parents and sister to Auschwitz and sent both my brothers to Sobibor. After the war, I discovered that my parents and sister went directly from the train to the gas chamber. I never discovered how the Nazis murdered my brothers. Please God, they died killing Germans during the Sobibor uprising.

The Nazis gave the Westerbork Jewish Committee the authority to play God—to choose which Jew to send to the death camps and who would stay behind. For the next eleven months, I remained unselected, assigned to a work detail repairing leaks and building structures. On January 18, 1944, the Committee deported me to Theresienstadt, a camp seventy kilometers (forty-two miles) north of Prague.

I sense Jacob is in a distant place, far from this modern café with its avant-garde steel chairs and tables and walls adorned with Impressionist prints. He's the man with the lifeless eyes sitting before the Theresienstadt barracks. I can feel the weight of his grief penetrating my damp eyes, pressing like a yoke on my shoulders, and pulsating in my veins like a furious current. I don't know whether to sob for his suffering or to rage against the beasts that caused it.

Deborah's tears awaken him to the present. "I'm so sorry to cause you so much discomfort. I should stop."

"No," Deborah says. "Absolutely not. Please don't worry about me. You were about to talk about Theresienstadt. Please continue."

Theresienstadt was a hybrid camp—a ghetto administered by Jews appointed by the Nazis. For the Nazis, it was their "humane showcase"—an illusion they'd roll out to dupe naïve Red Cross inspectors. That's why they selected me for Theresienstadt—to build a foolproof dummy camp. It worked. The camp orchestra played a recital of Brahms and the "kindly guards" smiled and acted chummy with their hand-picked group of recently fattened-up, well-dressed, and immaculately groomed prisoners.

All an inspector needed to do was raise the thin curtain, and he'd find the real Theresienstadt. Starvation. Disease. Vermin. And the ever-present sadism. Thirty-three thousand prisoners died in Theresienstadt, mostly from disease and malnutrition. Everyone was sick—coughing blood, open sores all over the body with puss oozing from every infected wound, and always, always scratching. The lice, fleas, and mites made you insane. You couldn't sleep at night; you just wanted to tear your flesh right to the bone. And then there was the constant hunger. Our rations for the day were under a thousand calories—mostly watery soup made from rotten vegetables and an occasional treat of stale bread. Grown men would fight over a moldy roll. I witnessed a man catch a rat that was trying to snatch a piece of bread from his pocket. In a state of total madness, he grabbed the rat by the tail and smashed it against a rock over and over again, screaming, "Don't steal my bread."

The Nazis had an insatiable appetite for cruelty. They had a favorite game: They'd line up a group of prisoners—maybe five or six of us—and they'd dangle rats by their tails, wave them in front of our faces, and then drop them down our drawers. We had to stand at attention while the squealing rats nibbled at our privates.

This is too much for me. It's straight out of 1984—only far worse. At least a closed cage separated the rat from Winston Smith's nose. Jacob notices what I imagine must be an expression of total horror. "Michael, are you okay?"

"No, but continue," I answer.

By the beginning of 1945, I weighed around thirty-seven kilos (eighty-five pounds). I had lost 40 percent of my body weight. I could hardly walk. From head to toe, I was covered with open wounds that drew flies like a magnet. The Nazis stopped transporting Jews to the death camps. We were either going to die in Theresienstadt or hang on until the Russians liberated us.

You can't ask a dead man if he has a will to live. It's merely a matter of fate. Neither life nor death had any meaning for me. At least, that's what I thought until the Angel of Death stared right into my eyes. In May, the Nazis abandoned the camp, leaving us near dead to fend for ourselves. A group of us starving inmates broke into a grain bin and stuffed handfuls of raw barley and wheat berries into our mouths.

We were crazed animals at the doorstep of death following some instinct for survival. My stomach swelled up. The pain was unbearable, like I was about to explode. I did something I hadn't done since the war began: I prayed. I begged God to let me defecate. I told him, "I've gone this far. Please don't let me die." I recited our holiest prayer, the Shema: Shema Yisroel Adonai Eloheinu, Adonai Ehad—"Hear, O Israel, the Lord Our God, the Lord Is One." And then it all came out—all the undigested grains. I sobbed and sobbed.

Deborah and I are both crying. The three of us sit quietly for a moment. Through her tears, Deborah tells Jacob, "I don't know why you chose us to share your story; I feel honored that you did. Your story will live on with us."

Eventually, Jacob returned to Holland, married a survivor, raised a family, developed a successful business, and learned to laugh again.

In the Metro, on the way to Simone and Alain's, Deborah says to me, "You're silent. What's going on with you?"

"I keep hearing this voice in my head saying, 'They would have murdered you for an identity you've rejected.' I don't know what it means, and I don't know what to do with it."

Deborah turns away for a moment and then focuses on me. She strokes my hand and says, "I know you'll figure it out . . . we'll figure it out."

Three days gone, two to go . . .

Paris: Part 3

The rain is relentless.

Simone and Alain are in Dijon for two days to visit his family. Deborah and I cuddle, fool around a bit, and read, and then repeat the cycle—until we get hungry, and I run down three flights, buy some cheese from the *fromagerie*, a baguette from the boulangerie, a pear tart from the patisserie, and dash back up to enjoy a lovely meal in our Parisian apartment with the pitter-patter of rain tapping on the windows.

Simone and Alain will return just when Deborah leaves. *When Deborah leaves.* So much intensity over the last few days that I've almost managed to put *It* on the back burner, to place *It* in a steel safe, to stuff *It* in the rear of the hall closet. I'm my mother's son—don't whine, beg, or act out. I don't even know if I'm allowed to suffer in silence.

I have a sudden memory of my mother.

I'm twelve and I come home all upset and I tell my mother that the music teacher, Mr. Farago, hit me. (In 1958, a teacher could still whack a kid.)

"What did you do to bother him?" she asked.

"Nothing. I swear!" No drama, not a bleep on the radar. She picks up the phone and dials Mr. Farago. This is what I hear my mother say:

"Ah, I see. Yes, I understand. I'm sorry." It doesn't sound good for my team. My mother approaches me, raises her right hand, and slaps me across the face—the first and only time she ever hit me. In a voice so filled with truth that I can still hear it resonating in my brain, she says,

"This will be the last time you shame a Holocaust survivor. Apologize to him right now and tell him you will never act out in his class again. Do you understand?"

And then, later, she gave me a reading list of Holocaust-related literature: Leon Uris's *Exodus* and Elie Wiesel's *Night*. Perhaps the seeds my mother planted twenty-one years ago are now sprouting.

Four days gone, one to go . . .

My internal chronometer tells me it's around six thirty a.m.—just when you'd expect those first waves of summer sunlight to pour through your east-facing window and flood your room with light.

Deborah wakes up and mumbles, "What are we doing today?"

"Look out the window. You want to go out in this weather?"

"I guess not." No problem. Just follow the natural rhythm of things. Simple. On an inside day, you go inside. Read—a bit of Dickens's *A Tale of Two Cities*. ("It was the best of times, it was the worst of times, it was the age of wisdom, it was the age of foolishness.") Write about Jacob, struggle to find the words. Meditate—a wordless hour of pure bliss. Fool around—tenderly, no rush. Stretch—thirty slow minutes of easy yoga. Nap—let the body do what the body needs. Reflect—on Jacob, on being Jewish, on Sweden.

At around four in the afternoon, Deborah says, "We need to talk about the elephant in the room. You haven't said a word about my leaving. You know I'm flying out tomorrow."

"Yes, five p.m. direct flight from Charles de Gaulle Airport to Arlanda Airport Stockholm."

"Very cute. Nothing to add—no more insights or feelings?"

"What do you want me to say? I've already told you how I feel. You want a detailed list of all my fears and resentments? If I begged you to stay, would you?"

"No. You won't beg, and I won't stay," she says. "How about if we're just real with each other?"

"Fine, be real. What would you like to tell me?"

"First, I love you. These last few days together have been amazing.

You've been amazing. I dropped a bombshell on you. I hurt you deeply. Anyone else would have created a big drama."

"Thank my mother. All credit goes to her. Is that all you want to tell me?"

"No. Tell me how you feel."

"Why? So you can nurture me—give me some warm female support? Forget it. The one inflicting the pain doesn't get to be the caretaker. At least not to me."

"I hear. So I won't give you emotional support. But I want this from you: I want you to live by the same convictions with me that you do with yourself. You listen to your inner voice, you trust it, and it guides you. Don't make this about betrayal. It's about finding my truth. Sorry, but we didn't sign up for easy. This is the path we chose."

Five days gone. Tomorrow, Sweden . . .

* * *

Alain and Simone return at eleven thirty a.m. Deborah takes the train to the airport at one p.m.

I lie down on my bed at one thirty p.m. and let myself experience the worst-case scenario: Deborah decides to remain in Sweden. If I can handle this, I can handle anything. I ask myself, "Will life go on?"

Yes, life will go on, or I will get on with life, even if the dreaded becomes the actual. The pain will be unbearable, the emptiness and loss excruciating. Not feeling her touch, not being challenged to discover the best of who I am, not having my soul mate and life partner by my side—the thought of it feels like pieces of my flesh being ripped from me. And yes, I'll find the warrior in me. I'll have no choice. I'll suffer, accept what is, and move on.

So, let's move on to life in Paris with Simone, Alain, and Martina, a new friend of Simone's and a recent resident of the apartment building. The nightly scene usually begins around seven p.m. when Alain, Simone, and I sit down for our evening meal and discussion—either a dialogue between Simone and me or a monologue from Simone directed at me.

Alain makes sure that the food and wine flow. On most nights, Martina joins us around eleven p.m.

I'll begin with Simone's comments about Deborah and Niels, then her story about what happened to her and her Jewish boyfriend, and then move on to Martina, or, more aptly, my dilemma with Martina.

Simone on Deborah: "She's smart, beautiful, and complex, and, like most men, you want to own all of her. It won't work. She has parts of her personality that you can't reach, and she can't share. I know you're scared. You deserve credit. You're different from most men. You don't play games to control her. You're smart enough to realize that if you did, she'd walk away."

She adds, "I can tell you're proud of Deborah. You admire her abilities and her strengths. But be careful you don't ignore her vulnerabilities. We women need a man who gives us the space to be ourselves, who's not afraid of who we are, yet understands our pain and our need to feel safe. Alain's that man for me. I hope you're that man for Deborah."

Simone tells me that three days earlier, while I was asleep, she and Deborah had a lengthy conversation about Sweden and Niels. Her take on Niels: "Ask yourself who this Swedish guy is to her. Why is she willing to risk everything to be with him?"

Simone doesn't wait for the answers I don't have. She continues.

"He's your shadow, your opposite—he's Deborah's muse. He can reach the musician and artist in her. You can't. You're smart, clever, and sensitive—wonderful qualities for a relationship, but you'll never share that part of her.

"Niels is Deborah's ticket away from the expected and the familiar. She says he's not like us—no struggles, no worries. He doesn't plan, make goals, or follow a career path. He trusts the Universe will show him his way. Your Deborah is American, ambitious, and psychologically complex. Her Swedish self is uncomplicated. The struggle isn't between you and Niels. It's within Deborah. It's about deciding who she is and who she wants to be."

Simone's prediction: "Don't worry; she'll come back to you. You protect her from her mother; Niels can't, and that's everything."

"Why is that everything?" I ask.

"Because a woman who can't separate from her mother will never be whole. Niels might bring out parts of her you can't, but she'll never achieve her potential without 'killing off' her mother. She needs a warrior by her side—not a muse. You're it. You're the brave soldier who protects her from the dark female spirit. Niels is a perfect partner if you want to live in a cave, meditate, and play music. But that's not where you live. You're both psychologists; you two don't run from ugliness.

"And if I'm wrong and Deborah makes a terrible choice, I'll introduce you to a lot of sexy French women who'd be thrilled to be with a guy like you."

Turns out I don't have to interrogate Simone about her Jewish ex. She volunteers the information: "I was the only non-Jew among all the kibbutz volunteers. I didn't fit in. My boyfriend pulled away from me. He told me he felt like a traitor to his people—like being with me would be continuing Hitler's work. He remained in Israel, and I returned bitter and brokenhearted."

Now Martina, Simone and Alain's friend and neighbor.

What can I say? The girl is drop-dead gorgeous—long, light brown hair, green eyes, and an irresistible smile. And from the neck down . . . Don't ask. Believe me—she's delightful.

Martina is Argentinian—twenty-five, effervescent, flirtatious, and a virtuoso in the art of seduction: a touch here, a smile there, a bit of male-female ping-pong to enliven the conversation. One moment she looks deeply into my eyes like I'm her lover; the next she throws her head back and laughs, only to follow up with a challenging comment about some idea I've expressed. The woman gets what turns me on.

I've been out of the game since September 1975, but the bicycle analogy holds. I still know how to maintain balance and shift gears. The problem is that I'm not sure whether I should get off the bike or keep riding. And there's this nagging thought at the back of my mind: While I'm debating with myself, my dear girlfriend may very well be in the arms of her Swedish lover.

Pure libido? Sweet revenge?

First, more on Martina: From 1976, a vicious military dictatorship headed by General Jorge Rafael Videla Redondo takes over Argentina. It is in this oppressive climate that Martina, a student at the National University of the Arts in Buenos Aires, leaves her family and moves to Paris in 1978 to study at the National School of Fine Arts.

In July 1980, the Junta still rules. For reasons Martina won't reveal, she hasn't spoken or written to her parents and two older sisters since late 1979. I ask her about life under the Junta and she replies in her charming Spanish-French accent, "Michael, no talk—please—of sad things. Only what makes us smile."

"What makes you smile?"

"You make me smile. You say funny things and you say smart things. And you know how to listen."

In another, less complicated lifetime, I would know exactly how to play this hand. But in this life—right now—facing this beautiful woman, I can't find my game face. I try telling myself, *she's flashing you a green light, make your move. Look into her eyes—with confidence—and tell her, "I'm happy I make you feel good."*

That response doesn't flow. I try to break my resistance by reminding myself that I wouldn't be in this dilemma if Deborah hadn't gone to Sweden. Nothing doing. As much as it's flattering to have the full attention of a beautiful woman, something in me doesn't want this to happen. I don't know if I'm a coward, afraid of disappointing a passionate woman, or a fool hiding behind a warped sense of loyalty and commitment.

Martina has been watching me, as if my thoughts have been playing across my face. I feel her kindness and warmth.

"Oh, I see that scares you," she says. "Why? Are you not used to a woman saying what she feels?"

"No, quite the opposite. I worry when a woman doesn't tell me how she feels. Better to know where I stand than to play mind games."

Throughout this interaction, Martina and I are curled up on the couch facing one another. Our positions mirror one another: She leans her right elbow on the back of the couch; I rest my left. Our knees are six inches from touching, our lips—only centimeters apart. The tension is unbearable.

"Did Simone tell you about Deborah?"

"Yes. She called her a special soul—beautiful and deep. She told me why she's in Sweden. You love her very much, don't you? Is she the reason for the sudden change?"

"I suppose so. I don't know why it should matter. She's with another man right now. The only contract we have is unwritten and we seem to have different interpretations. Frankly, my reaction doesn't make sense."

"Does everything have to be so logical and worked out? You need to go deeper to understand. Would you like me to help you?"

Another Martina is emerging. She's now the gentle guide, the oracle, and the wise witch, and our knees are nearly touching.

"Yes. I need a helping hand. And yours is the one closest to mine." She laughs. "True confession," I say. "You scare me."

"Martina, you know who you are. You know the effect you have on men. You're beautiful, sexy, and genuinely kind and attentive. That's an irresistible combination I'm trying to resist. Your passion terrifies me. I'd have to let go of every thread of the performer in me to be with you. I'm not sure I could do that."

She leans forward, studying me with her blue-green X-ray eyes like she's probing for the truth behind my words.

"Michael, that's not your problem. You're not a performer. If we got together, we'd figure it out. But we won't be because your heart won't let you. Don't you realize that?"

"I do and I don't. I don't understand this part in me that says no, especially since Deborah said yes to what she wants."

"Let's say there are two kinds of men. One lives for passion and the other for connection. Which one are you?"

"Connection. Not that I have anything against passion. Does it have to be either-or?"

"I would think so. Passion needs separation and death. Zero attachment. You must feel it's your last moment together and then let go, like the Tibetan priest who creates an intricate sand mandala and then destroys it. Connection is different. It's slow, deep, and transformative. You need to release parts of yourself to make room for another. You need to see yourself as part of something beyond your own needs and desires. That your true self includes another.

"What is Deborah seeking—passion or connection?" she asks.

"Connection. Perhaps to herself first—which may be why she's in Sweden. Losing my connection to her would be like death for me. Not a passionate death that inspires love poems. No, a part of myself would die—consciously or unconsciously, I don't believe I'd ever stop mourning. I'd get on with life, yes, but the emptiness would remain."

I feel a wave of emotions wash over me. Sadness. Anger. Confusion. If it's not betrayal, then why do I feel my guts ripping?

"Now you understand your resistance to me," she says softly. "She's with you whether she's in Sweden with another man or in Paris next to you. She needs to discover what you already know. If you're meant to be together, she'll let go of Sweden and all that it means to her to be with you. If not, your time together was merely a few chapters in a larger story.

"May I give you advice?" she asks. "Be courageous and trust your heart. Like now. Your instincts told you we shouldn't be lovers. You knew you needed a friend, not a one-night stand."

She's right, but a doubt still lingers. Maybe for one night, I should have traded connection for passion.

On Friday evening, July 4, Deborah returns. I'm not sure what to expect. An amorous rendezvous between reunited lovers? A sad ending to a love story? A tender moment between two deeply connected souls? Whatever I expected or imagined, this is not it. It's far worse. She's ice, colder than a Swedish winter—a distant stranger.

She's seated in the kitchen drinking coffee and talking to Simone. She has a tense, somber look on her face. I walk toward her to give her a hug; she remains seated and offers me a perfunctory hello. I return her greeting with a similar version of my own—purposefully lifeless and lacking an ounce of enthusiasm. I exit the kitchen, return, and this time say in a pseudo-cheerful voice, "Hello, Deborah, come and give your beloved a hug!"

She stands up, approaches me, and gives me a hug you'd expect from your sixty-year-old virgin aunt. "I'm sorry, Michael, I'm just not in the mood for jokes right now. I'm tired and I need to sleep. We'll talk in the morning." And she leaves the kitchen to go to bed.

I turn to Simone. "Do you know what's going on?"

"She's here with you. Just give her time and don't pressure her."

"In other words, let her be a bitch and keep my mouth shut. What did she tell you about Sweden?"

"She had a wonderful time, and she felt connected to a part of herself she hasn't experienced since she was last in Sweden five years ago."

"It's déjà vu all over again," I say. "We traveled this same path five years ago when she last returned from Sweden. It was brutal then. It will be worse now. Five years ago, she had her career to distract her. Now, she has plenty of time to think and few distractions."

"Don't forget—she's here because her life is with you. She may act like her real self is in Sweden and you're to blame for forcing her to return. Be patient. She'll remember why she's back."

Knowing what I know makes our last five days in Paris bearable. I wouldn't call Deborah unpleasant. More like distant in a kind of I'm-working-something-out sort of way. I don't ask for information; she doesn't volunteer much more than, "I'm sorry; I know I'm hard to be with right now. When I'm ready, we'll talk."

For now, I'll give her space. It's the smart thing to do.

We dodge the rain, do some museum hopping, eat out a bit, and hang out with Alain and Simone. Martina drops by a few times; she and Deborah hit it off. I'm impressed by how Deborah switches between Spanish and French, especially considering she's just come off a week of speaking Swedish. Martina catches me alone for a moment and says, "I understand now. Deborah's great. You deserve each other."

At nine a.m., Thursday, July 10, after expressing our tearful good-byes, we board the train from Paris heading east. We'll disembark at Coulommiers and start riding in a southeasterly direction.

The rain pours down in sheets.

CHAPTER 7

From Paris to Italy: July 10 to August 10

The rain burns our eyes, stiffens our muscles, and makes mold in the moist, murky regions of our bodies. Nothing protects us from moisture—not our expensive rain gear with the manufacturer's guarantee that not a drop of water will penetrate its finely sewn fabric, nor our waterproof tent that drips, drips, drips throughout the night like a Chinese water torture. Water is insidious—far more devious than the most paranoid mind can conjure. Like an interrogator probing for weaknesses, rain discovers the slightest cracks, the tiny tears, and the imperceptible holes, to reach the skin where it infiltrates to our bones, leaving us shivering and miserable.

For ninety-six consecutive hours, the rain is unrelenting. To be fair, not for every one of those 5,760 minutes does the rain descend with the torrential power of a waterfall. There are moments when we ride through dense clouds of mist that are like a mere spray of light moisture—refreshing if you're running a marathon on a hot day. At other times, the wind blows northwesterly as we ride southeasterly, driving the rain into our eyes, stinging our skin, and slapping our faces like an angry parent. Then, following a logic known only to God and Her weather angels, the wind will quiet, the downpour will cease, the sky will lighten, and a gentle rain will fall. We're sure the sun is only a cloud away—a desperate delusion. In a blink, a furious downpour descends, driving hope to its knees and despair to our souls.

Over these four days, we ride from Louan-Villegruis-Fontaine to

Romilly-sur-Seine, from Romilly-sur-Seine to Troyes, from Troyes to Châtillon-sur-Seine, and from Châtillon-sur-Seine to Chanceaux—where at this moment, we attempt to warm ourselves inside our relatively dry sleeping bags that lie on the damp tent floor we've pitched on wet, muddy grass—the driest spot we found in the empty campground.

I can't describe the landscape we've passed, nor the hills we've climbed, nor the people we didn't see because only a madman or a masochist would be outside in this weather. The only humans we notice on the road are the ones in their cars, waving at us and giving us a thumbs up for being brave, or stupid, or both. The encouragement makes me feel heroic, but that passes as quickly as the person offering the cheer. Misery is as constant as the depressing weather, while a pleasant feeling is as fleeting as a wave of light.

I do what I usually do when faced with obstacles—I just push ahead and focus on getting to the goal. I play games in my head: I fix on an object—like a tree or a building—as far as I can see, and ride there. And then I pick another distant destination. I remember when I was in basic training and we were on a twenty-five-mile march in the boiling Kentucky heat. The sergeant screamed, "If you can't walk fast, walk slow. And if you can't walk slow, crawl on your knees. And if you can't crawl on your knees, crawl on your belly. Just move."

We just move—sometimes fast, sometimes slow—but never with pleasure. We move forward to our next campground and the possibility of a hot meal in a warm restaurant, sitting at a table next to a blazing fire in an old stone fireplace. It keeps us going, and what we imagine usually materializes. Doesn't matter if the food is as ordinary as the country diner that you stumble upon on the back roads of Tennessee. Because inside these rustic French restaurants, like in a Tennessee diner, it's always warm and dry.

And warm and dry feels delicious.

Deborah complains—nonstop at every stop. She's in a state so far beyond discomfort that she longs for an easy death or a painless escape from this reality, a quick exit to a place on the globe where it never rains in the summer and the temperature is always in the high seventies.

"Ibiza's that place." She tries to convince me we should store our bikes and fly to the hip island off the coast of Spain, where the sun shines all summer and the temperatures are temperate.

In 1972, she spent the summer living in a hundred-year-old adobe *finca* with Katja, a German artist and former partisan, and her husband Karl, a tour guide and survivor of Auschwitz. Every day, she'd ride Katja's Schwinn bicycle with a basket in the front on the narrow road from the house to the hamlet where she'd pick up fresh produce and bread for Karl and Katja. It was during that summer that Deborah, twenty-two years old, first learned about the horrors of the Holocaust and the courage of the Resistance.

Right here and now, on this cold, rainy day in Chanceaux, France, close to Dijon, Ibiza pulls at us like the aroma of fresh-baked bread lures a starving man. We're hungry for blue skies, the warmth of the sun on our faces, and a dry place—free from the incessant dripping of drop after drop of condensed moisture—to lie down and fall into a deep, dreamless sleep. I agree with Deborah. "Let's follow the sun and take a vacation in Ibiza until the insane French weather decides it's summer."

We try calling Karl and Katja in Ibiza. No answer. We send them a telegram. No reply. We wait a day, eat slow meals at the local restaurants, call multiple times without success, send more telegrams. Nothing.

We can't wait any longer, so we venture out in pouring rain for the forty-mile journey to Dijon. Deborah comments as we mount our bikes that right now it's probably warm and dry in Stockholm. Not a weather report unless she's comparing her current frigid temperature to the warmth and comfort she felt two weeks ago in sunny Sweden. I hold back from responding to the subtext at the risk I might lose it and say something ugly, like *stop whining and fly to Sweden if that's what you want.*

Until Deborah's "innocuous" reference to the weather there, Sweden's been a tabled subject since we left Paris. Blame it on the weather or the power of denial—we've spoken nary a word on the issue. Of the various emotional responses possible in this situation, I've opted for patience. Based on the advice of two women whom I respect—Simone and Martina—I'm playing the long game. Deborah voted with her feet—she's back, which gives her the freedom to yearn for Sweden and all that it represents while still having me. Confronting her ambivalence might force her to make the "courageous" decision that she thinks her heart wants, even if her head tells her otherwise. Plus, she's too waterlogged right now to think rationally. The wise path for the time being remains restraint and forbearance. I'll wait to see if she initiates a conversation instead of tossing out emotionally charged references.

After another unpleasant day of riding through persistent puddles in unending rain, we arrive at a campground outside of Dijon, edgy, soaked, and one wrong comment from losing it. The minute we enter the campground, Deborah dashes to call Karl and Katja. Once again, there's no answer. Deborah can be tense. She does moody; she has her bitchy moments. Yet, for her, anger is an emotion she rarely feels and almost never expresses.

Not this time. She's way beyond irritability, somewhere on the border between frenzy and madness—itching for a fight, about to stomp her feet and flail her arms. A string of expletives like impatient thoroughbreds poised at the starting gate hover at the edge of her lips about to burst from her mouth at the first provocation.

Be smart. Don't react; don't joke; don't confront, I tell myself. *She's hormonal. Take nothing she says personally.* She may tell me she hates me. She might say she's quitting the bike trip and leaving this very moment for Sweden. Or, she could say, "I can't."

"You can't what?" I would respond.

"I just can't."

And I'll feign empathy and act as if I understand what she means. Or she might just break down sobbing and say, "It's too hard. I can't go one more day in the rain." I can deal with that—it's not too far from where I'm holding.

But then Deborah, being Deborah, does a one-eighty. "We're not letting this fucking rain stop us. We're continuing until the sun shines or we die from exposure."

That's my girl! A millimeter from insanity, and she finds her inner warrior. On the brink of a breakdown, the survivor in her says, "Fuck this. I'll be damned if I'll give up." This close to deafening her soul with the incessant echoes of self-pity and victimhood, she proclaims, "Not me. Not now. Never." She's my hero. My inspiration.

That night, as we snuggle together for the first time since we left Paris, she talks about Sweden and Niels. "I'm sorry for what I put you through. You've been amazing. Many times, I've thought that I don't deserve you. It's taken me awhile to realize that not Sweden, not Niels, not anything will pull us apart."

For the first time since we departed Paris, the wetness flowing down my cheeks emanates from my emotions rather than from the heavens—as if each teardrop contains a bucketful of pain waiting for its cathartic moment. Now is that moment—the one Simone said would come if I didn't push for it. I hear Deborah crying and we embrace. There is a force so much greater than the two of us that keeps our minds and bodies intertwined as one—not entangled like a fishing line, but as two intrinsic parts of a whole, separate yet connected.

The next morning, we awake to silence. Not a whisper of rain tapping on the canvas roof, no billowing walls snapping in and out from gusts of wind, no gurgling sounds rising from the floor of our tent caused by oversaturated ground. I open the door to the tent: The dove has returned with an olive branch—the rain has ceased. I look upward at the sky—not yet clear. Light gray with a touch of blue that hints at the possibility of sunshine by late morning. One can only hope for a brighter day.

By eight thirty, we're on the road headed for St. Georges. By eleven a.m., the sun makes an appearance; by noon, the clouds have disappeared. The sky is as blue as a topaz. The temperature is delightful—probably in the midseventies.

*   *   *

I'm feeling optimistic, as though we're entering the sunny side of the cycle when caterpillars metamorphize into multicolored butterflies, when lightning bugs glow on and off like miniature flashlights, and when a warm summer breeze gently caresses our bodies as we sit shoulder to shoulder, enjoying a late-night snack and a cup of tea. The sky is dark. The stars are bright. A crescent moon rests at the far end of the western sky.

Life feels wonderful, as if we're part of a larger cycle of change invisibly powered by a counterplay of opposites: darkness and light, war and peace, cruelty and kindness—Niels and me. At one moment, the cycle of life seems to pause at one pole, while at the next it appears to stop at its polar opposite—an apparent dialectic in which a period of struggle and pain metamorphizes into a blessing of serenity and peace, not opposites at all, but essential parts of a larger whole. Yet, the further we travel from the truth, the more fractured the whole appears to be, until the only "truth" that remains is the lie that life is nothing more than irreconcilable opposites and random connections.

CHAPTER 8

From Paris to Italy: Part 2

W e awaken at the break of dawn to the crowing of a rooster. I inhale the pungent odor of manure, an aroma that triggers immediate positive associations. Long runs on the dirt roads around Middlebury, past dairy farms. Pastures filled with fat milk cows grazing in the summer sun.

I open the flap of the tent and stick my head out to check the weather.

The blazing red sun suspended in the eastern sky burns through the morning haze. Mist, like steam, rises from the damp emerald grass where it meets the warm, early rays of the sun and then disappears, absorbed in the heat and light. On the northern edge of the campground, a flock of sheep grazes on a grassy slope. To the east, I can see the stone needle of a church spire pointing to the heavens.

What we have is a perfect summer day for riding the narrow roads from Nuits-Saint-Georges to Ouroux-sur-Saône—almost heavenly. No, wrong analogy. It doesn't quite get the feeling of sun after nearly five weeks of rain. More like *The Wizard of Oz*'s transition from its black-and-white opening to the over-the-rainbow technicolor explosion upon landing in Oz. Even Dorothy's sepia-toned dress morphs into bright blue gingham.

Life looks so much better—is so much better—in color than in black and white.

We true our spokes, put air in our tires, tighten everything we can, and fasten as much of our damp clothes as possible on the back of our bikes to let them dry in the warm sun. And then we take off in a southeasterly direction with the glorious rays of the sun beating on our faces. So much better to be red from sun and sweat than from freezing rain and fierce winds. *This* is the around-the-world bike trip we fantasized about five months ago when we decided to exchange the upwardly mobile world of success for the leisurely freedom of human-powered movement.

The country roads roll like the rhythm of waves—up and down, up and down, punctuated by an occasional steep incline and a fast descent. On our right side, a continuous row of stone walls defines the border between the road and the adjacent fields and farmhouses. On the side of a distant hill, I notice clusters of dark grapes, two months shy from being harvested. The sky is an unbroken sea of blue without a hint of haze or a filtering of light. The sun spreads its rays, illuminating every blade of grass, each rustle of a leaf, the singular purple flower that leans its delicate stem toward the weather-beaten wood fence.

I glance at Deborah, who's about twenty yards behind me. Her face is taut; her body is tense; she's battling pain. I stop and wait for her to come to me. She tells me she's suffering terribly from a urinary or bladder infection.

"Can you make it to Ouroux-sur-Saône?" I ask. "Probably another two hours. They should have a doctor there."

"What choice do I have?"

Two and a half hours later, punctuated by frequent stops so that Deborah can dismount and relieve the pressure from the saddle pressing against her bladder, we arrive in Ouroux-sur-Saône. In a town of twenty-five hundred residents, it's easy to locate the single doctor at the only clinic, which is attached to his house. Everyone in town knows the "kind, young doctor," Dr. Claude (his first name), and "his lovely wife, Nicole," and their "adorable three-month-old daughter, Helene."

"His lovely wife, Nicole" greets us at the clinic and tells us that the doctor will be with us shortly. She's thin like Deborah, and about the same height and age, with short, light brown hair, intelligent blue eyes, and a warm smile. In French, she asks us where we've been and where we're going. She notices I say and appear to understand nothing, so she asks, in perfect English, if I speak French.

"Only when ordering food," I answer.

She smiles and says, "Too bad you're in a medical clinic instead of a restaurant." She asks us about our trip, our professions, and our plans when we return to the U.S.

Dr. Claude appears and beckons Deborah into his office. He is my height and probably around my age, black hair, slightly balding, a bit soft in the middle with a round cherubic face—those pinchable cheeks my aunt Molly could never resist. The locals who directed us here got it right: he looks kind and lovable—a person you immediately trust and like. He speaks to me in French, which his wife translates.

"Don't worry, I'll take excellent care of her."

Twenty minutes later Deborah exits the doctor's office holding a box of antibiotics for a urinary tract infection. The doctor accompanies us to our bikes and suggests we spend an extra day in town while the antibiotics take effect. He tells us where to find an excellent restaurant and campground.

As we are about to ride there, both he and his wife reappear and tell us, "Don't go yet."

"I apologize for being so rude," Dr. Claude says. "Fortunately, my wife has more sense than me. When I returned to the office, Nicole asked me if I had invited you for dinner. When I told her no, she said, 'An interesting couple visits Ouroux-sur-Saône and you just let them slip away? Shame on you.' So, please join us for dinner around seven thirty."

Nicole whispers something to Claude and then adds in English, "No need to check into the campground. Please spend the next two nights in our home. We'd be delighted to have you as our guests."

"How generous. We'll accept," Deborah says.

I turn to Deborah and say to her, "Your urinary tract infection has turned out to be quite a blessing for us." Nicole, Claude, and Deborah laugh. It turns out Claude speaks English well.

*   *   *

Nicole and Claude's modern, eight-room, stone-and-wood home stands at the epicenter of a sizeable property, surrounded by equal parcels of land on all sides. Four tall oak-wood columns, their arms extended in victory like they just finished the Boston Marathon, connect to the wooden molding beneath the sloped, slate roof. Facing the house, a casual array of garden chairs, tables, and umbrellas—configured in intimate pairs and relaxed, conversational circles—reflects the easy, open vibe of its gracious owners.

The friendly feeling extends to the interior of their home, where the living and dining room walls display photos of what appear to be large extended families on both sides—lots of happy little ones, grinning teens, and proud parents and grandparents.

Our room is warm and inviting, like Nicole and Claude. From pillow to base, a stuffed St. Bernard lies sprawled on our double bed. He looks so real, I almost expect to discover a puddle of drool where his cloth tongue touches the turquoise bedspread. The walls are painted in a soothing shade of lavender, and, like the living and dining rooms, there are more photos of both Nicole and Claude's families. One picture, in particular, catches my attention. It's a photo of an athletic-looking teenage Claude wrestling on the grass with his near double—either a fraternal twin or a brother close in age. Both boys grin, seeming to enjoy this friendly competition.

Everything's perfect.

In a heartbeat, you'd trade your messy family, with all its petty jealousies and nasty secrets, for this picture of love and harmony. For God's sake, the fake dog is so real, I might take it for a walk or just curl up inside its cozy body and experience unconditional love for the first time. In Nicole and Claude's haven of love and connection, there's no angst, no nagging feeling of emptiness nibbling at the core, demanding answers. This much comfort terrifies me. When the tank's full, you don't search; you just breathe in easy love—not the hard kind, where the love you get is earned, not granted.

Deborah interrupts my mini meditation on the perils of love and serenity and asks, "What are you thinking about?"

"About the dangers of too much love and not enough struggle."

"Is that your impression of the good doctor and his kind wife? Their loving home disturbs you?"

"Yeah. I'm afraid it will be all smiles, good cheer, and forgettable."

"Maybe you should check your suffering at the door and experience their kindness and generosity. Not every encounter needs to turn your brain inside out. Maybe they'll surprise you."

I laugh and say, "Sharp as always." I draw her body close to mine, kiss her deeply, and say, "Did I ever tell you that you have one sexy brain?"

"Yes, many times. So do you."

At eight p.m., the sun's one red ball above the western horizon. The not-quite half-moon rises high in the eastern sky; the waning rays of the sun illuminate the western clouds in brilliant hues of orange and red, while the clouds to the east glow like cotton balls dyed with blue and indigo. The lightning bugs practice their final dress rehearsal before the curtain rises around nine thirty. The round outdoor table is set for four. An uncorked bottle of wine rests on the table waiting to share its rich bounty.

I understand, now, how clarity obscures light, how the certainty of an assumption blinds us from truth, how the solidity of an opinion blocks the flow of knowledge, how so much of what we perceive to be real is a projection of our imagination.

I'm guilty on all accounts. Nicole and Claude surprise. They shatter the pretty box I put them in. They dazzle the palate and challenge the mind.

It turns out that Nicole and Claude are vegans—no meat, fish, eggs, or dairy—a blessing for Deborah, a bit of a yawn for me. No matter. I'm a foodie and I can sink my teeth into a plate of tofu nearly as fast as into a porterhouse.

Speaking of tofu, the evening begins with a lentil and grilled tofu salad. Artistry. Taste buds flash and sparkle. The culinary equivalent of Mikhail Baryshnikov pirouetting flawlessly on your tongue. "An aphrodisiac," Deborah whispers in my ear.

Nicole and Claude grew up in Lyon, where he studied medicine and she, French literature and creative writing. A poet by avocation and vocation, she focuses on the sunny side with an occasional downward turn toward the melancholy. "I am French after all."

She tells us about her hippie brother, lost somewhere between Goa and Burma. "My parents don't sleep. They're convinced he's dead—overdosed on heroin. In their lighter moments, he's a barefoot siddhi in filthy orange robes begging for food." I don't know if I'm relieved or intrigued to discover that appearances deceive—that the story of this family contains hidden subplots that photos don't reveal.

Her father's a product of the war, traumatized by the loss of his best friend and his family—all gassed to death in Auschwitz. "From the little he's told us, he worked for the Resistance. The Butcher of Lyon, Klaus Barbie, would have personally tortured him by skinning him alive and pouring ammonia on his body. He specialized in children. At fifteen, I learned why my father has moods."

Claude serves the second course: blended sweet potato and carrot soup with cinnamon, ginger, and coconut milk. The color of sunset, the aroma of India, an offering to the Auspicious One, Shiva.

From the age of two, Claude knew he'd be a doctor. "My father was a doctor, his father was a doctor, my mother's father was a doctor, and her grandfather was a doctor—a powerful message that the men in my family are destined to be doctors. By the time I was ten, I could identify every organ in the body and name all the major muscle groups, arteries, and veins." *Is there choice under the weight of so much destiny?*

We share a few vignettes from the trip—Simone and Jacob's stories, Le Clown, the scenery, and riding in rough weather. Claude asks us, "What have you learned so far from the trip?"

We wait while Nicole serves ratatouille made with eggplants, red peppers, tomatoes, zucchini, and squash scented with herbs—all from Nicole's organic garden. It's food you admire for its radiance and then savor as a total sensory experience.

"It's strange," Deborah answers. "It's like we're protagonists in a story we're writing and one that's been written for us. Like we have the illusion of freedom, but a force greater than us calls the shots.

"We chose to leave the U.S., but we didn't choose to be here with you. It happened—magically. Like it did with Jacob and with Le Clown. The journey has a mind of its own. We know the next town but not the adventure that may await us. Like why do we keep on encountering stories of war and survival? Why us and what are they supposed to teach us?"

This time both Nicole and Claude minister the main course: tempeh and mushroom bourguignon with red peppers, carrots, onions, and red wine. Deborah moans in delight, then whispers, "You brag about your sophisticated palate. Isn't this so much better than all the dead flesh you've eaten?"

"Amazing," Nicole says. "In poetry, we describe a paradox as something that on the surface is contradictory, but at its depth, reflects a deeper meaning and truth. When you were talking, I pictured verses of a poem being written in some distant corner in my mind—also a paradox. When I write a poem, I feel like I'm the instrument that reveals the poem. So, who really writes the poem? Who engineers the encounters?"

"What Deborah said is true for me," I say. "It's a crazy contradiction between feeling powerful and self-directed on the one hand and like an innocent kid being led on the other. Here's the paradox: Our minds can reach galaxies beyond galaxies, and our bodies are food for worms. Gods that shit. That's us.

"I've thought a lot about the meaning of death in my life—with all its manifestations. Take us for example. I feel this intense connection right now. Yet, tomorrow it will be over, and we'll say our goodbyes. As much as we'll promise to be in touch, we won't. We'll move on and remember this as a few wonderful hours. A brief and shining encounter we'll need to let go of.

"A woman I met in Paris compared passion with death. Knowing something will end makes the time so much more meaningful. I think that's why we keep on encountering death—to remind us to live."

Speaking of death, you could die for the dessert: delicately thin whole-wheat crêpes made with vanilla-bean paste, almond milk, and coconut oil, filled with roasted cashews and wild berries. I may never want to leave. Their kindness is staggering.

"As I listen to you both," Claude says, "I've been asking myself if I chose to be a doctor or was that choice made for me? That I'm a doctor by circumstance and expectation is okay. In my world, destiny plays a powerful role. You both would probably say, 'Then embrace your destiny; make it your own.' I think I have. Now, for sure, I will. Thank you. I don't think you realize the gift you've given me."

At one thirty a.m., we fall into bed and awake around eight. Deborah's feeling great. We decide to head out after breakfast. Both Nicole and Claude are visibly disappointed but make their best effort to be supportive. Deborah and Nicole embrace. Through her tears, Nicole tells us, "We're different from you both. Leaving is hard for us. I don't want to let you go, like you're two angels that came with a message and then departed. You're our friends. I wish we could share the rest of our lives. You may forget us, but I won't. Now and then, I'll send you a message of love wherever you may be."

We hug, say our goodbyes, and then we ride out of town.

I wonder if there'll be a time when saying goodbye will be painful.

CHAPTER 9

From Paris to Italy: Part 3

From Nicole and Claude's home, we head southeast to Montrevel-en-Bresse, a leisurely forty-three-mile ride on flat back roads past vineyards and dairy farms. The weather is perfect for bike touring—high seventies, no wind, zero precipitation. Billowy white clouds like puffs of smoke hang motionless in the air until—like puffs of smoke—they disappear into the bright blue sky.

Many bends ahead, we see a small stone church surrounded by a three-foot-high wall constructed from boulders, with pebbles and rocks to secure the roughhewn blocks in place.

The open doors of the little church beckon us inside to sit and meditate on one of the many empty benches. A quiet, friendly church such as this provides a perfect setting for deep meditation. The sweet aroma of burning incense along with a primitive painting of a radiant Jesus preaching to the masses serve as excellent accoutrements for the practice of Transcendental Meditation.

When Deborah initiated me into the practice of TM, I had as much interest in meditation as I did in vegetarianism. It was part of my plan to soften the heart of the woman who hadn't yet understood that we were meant to be together. To my surprise—unlike swearing off beef, chicken, and fish—I embraced the twice-daily, twenty-minute discipline with total commitment, no less so than brushing teeth. Since that holy day, August 28, 1974, when Deborah guided me through the puja ceremony—flowers, fruit, incense, and my personal never-to-be-spoken-out-loud Sanskrit mantra—I haven't missed a meditation.

We sit side by side on a wooden pew—in deep, meditative

silence—experiencing an inner universe where time stands still. The mind is pure space—empty of thoughts, images, and sounds except for the subtle, subvocal vibrations of the mantra that the focused mind senses as acutely as a distant sound detected by a wolf. The mantra appears and then disappears in harmony with the rhythm of the breath. In breath: The mind senses then focuses on the subtle sound of the mantra. Out breath: The mantra exits slowly with the exhalation, emptying the mind.

One hour later—yes, our meditations are now one hour a day, twice a day—we're back on the road, riding past verdant cow pasture after pasture, vineyard after vineyard, local after local—always waving and sometimes motioning us to stop so they can inquire where we're headed as if they long for the vicarious thrill of our adventure. I sense we're tapping into some faraway youthful travel fantasy—dreams long forgotten or discarded as unrealistic in an adult world of responsibilities and commitments.

At seven p.m., we arrive at our modest campground in Montrevel-en-Bresse. Two tents down on the north side, there's a couple about our age, with loaded bikes standing next to their two-person tent. She's Asian—possibly Filipino, short, cute, athletic, looks approachable. He's six feet, thin, and, from his blond hair and Nordic features, most likely Northern European—less approachable, only because many Northern Europeans give off a kind of formal vibe.

Deborah approaches the couple and starts an animated conversation. I join them and she introduces me to Louisa and Julian, who are on a two-week bicycle tour throughout Burgundy.

"This is our third glorious day," Louisa says. We find out she's originally from some remote atoll in the Philippines—one of the few populated islands among that archipelago. They're married and live in his hometown of Amsterdam where he works as a freelance civil engineer, she as a choreographer for a small modern dance ensemble. We set a date for dinner in an hour at a local restaurant.

We arrive there to find Louisa and Julian seated with menus in hand. Neither of them speaks French well, so Deborah translates.

Louisa's radiant. Petite, with long black hair tied in the back. Her soft skin is the color of light chocolate, her face round and friendly. Her large brown eyes light up with every smile and laugh. Yet it's her voice that carries me to her faraway atoll—lyrical, light, and flowing, without the hard tones you often hear when Western women express themselves. Like pure femininity, untouched by the confusion of Western values—a perfect blend of soft and strong, confident and yielding, grounded and curious.

Until eighteen, she lived with her large extended family on a small island. "From the sky, my island looks like an egg floating on a turquoise sea. On all sides are beaches as white as snow, and coral reefs with fish of every color and shape. Mangos, bananas, and papayas grow wild, and the coconuts have the sweetest milk." She giggles and says, "I know, too perfect. Right?"

"Please don't mess it up," I say. "Don't tell me people kill each other there. We've got to believe in something."

She flashes a smile and then continues on her journey into the heart of her island, where postcards of pristine blue waters and cloudless skies on occasion have frayed edges.

"The cycle of the year goes from bliss to rain to tropical storms to destruction, to being homeless. The only uncertainty is the strength of the typhoon and the level of damage. According to Filipino tradition, we've been living like this since our Adam and Eve emerged from the hollow branch of a bamboo tree."

"I envy you," Deborah says. "You grew up so differently than us. So close to nature. Our life cycle went from heat to air conditioning. We watched storms from the window and typhoons on television. Now it's different. We feel the heat and the rain, and the cold. Sometimes I love it and sometimes not, but it feels pure."

"*Pure* is what I miss," Louisa says with a trace of sadness in her voice. "*Simple* as well: my thatched hut, with my four grandparents, my parents, two sisters, my brother, and our dog. No electricity. No plumbing. We know nothing else, so we don't know we're missing anything. We were happy with what we had . . ."

Louisa closes her eyes for a moment. I drift into a thousand fantasies; her voice—like a warm, tropical breeze—glides us home to her island:

Filipino island life is very traditional. The men fish, the women raise the children, and everyone prays to Jesus—every day, many times a day, and much more during typhoon season. There's an island tradition that we roast a young pig as a sacrifice to Lord Jesus after the storms subside. If you don't hear the pig squeal before roasting it, it's considered a bad omen.

It's a beautiful, simple life, just not for the "girl with the dancing feet." That's what my mother called me. A girl on the move, a restless spirit in search of the big gods living in faraway places. My god was the goddess of movement and dance. I discovered her in Amsterdam, when I was an innocent island girl living alone in the big city. How I got there is a story unto itself. Let's just say (and she giggles) I was the smartest girl on our island and all the islands in our chain of islands. I won a scholarship to the Netherlands. By accident, I discovered dance or dance discovered me.

I was at a party, and someone asked me to demonstrate a typical Filipino folk dance. I asked the host to put two broomsticks on the floor—parallel and maybe forty centimeters apart. We call the dance the tinikling because you imitate the movement of the tinikling bird walking through the high grass. For a few seconds, I closed my eyes and I imagined I was in my village. The people in the room were my family and friends. The broomsticks became the two colorful bamboo poles we use for the tinikling dance.

In my head and body, I felt the drumbeat of the gambal and the guitar-like sound of the buktat. My feet started to dance to the clapping rhythm I know so well. I jumped back and forth between the broomsticks, going faster and faster, in tune with the tempo in my head. I moved so fast that someone said my feet disappeared.

I don't know how long I danced because I lost all sense of time and place. The Amsterdam living room was the town square. That night, I danced on the unpaved path between the church and the island's only grocery store—the one place where you could buy M&M's all the way from America. The light-skinned Westerners became all the people I knew from childhood, jumping and swaying to the rhythm of the instruments. When I stopped, everyone in the room stood up and cheered wildly. Overwhelming for the innocent island girl with the dancing feet.

That was my big break—my life-changing moment. A woman approached me and asked me if I'd like to join her dance group. I told her the only dances I knew were the ones I had learned from childhood. All she said was, "It doesn't matter. I'll train you."

Okay, enough about me.

Not quite yet. Turns out she had to learn how to use a flush toilet, to cross a busy Amsterdam intersection, and not to jump in fright when images moved on a screen. Louisa turned her world upside down and inside out. Hard to imagine what kind of strength that takes.

We play a back-and-forth game of transactional tennis. Louisa and Julian insist on hearing about us. We know who we are; we're curious about them. But they press us about our lives in the U.S., our careers as psychologists, our reasons for leaving. When we get around to sharing our war stories—or should I say, our stories of war—it touches Julian in a place he'd rather forget. Louisa encourages him to speak. The nonjudgmental culture of the road removes the fear of revealing oneself—as if our most natural state is to speak the truth.

He tells us he's an only child born two years after the war and thirty months after the Soviets liberated his father from Auschwitz. "Even as a child, I realized my father was a tortured man. I remember him sitting in his oversized leather chair, chain-smoking cigarettes, filling his lungs to capacity, and then exhaling a chimney's worth of smoke. He'd stare at nothing as if his mind had traveled to some distant place far from our home in Amsterdam. Sometimes, I would see tears streaming down his cheeks. And if he caught me looking at him, he'd say in a voice so gentle and sad, 'Julian, my son, don't worry about Papa. I'll be okay.' He wasn't okay. Still isn't okay. He's haunted by demons he won't speak about."

I gaze at Deborah. I wonder if my questions are hers. Why war again? Why us?

"Mother would tell me, 'Your father is an exceptional man, a giant among his peers. He's suffered terribly because of who he is and because of his principles.'"

He tells us that, over the years, he picked up fragments of a story from his mother. She wanted him to understand that the war years for his father were worse than the fires of hell. That he witnessed unspeakable cruelties and experienced unimaginable brutality. She never described those cruelties and brutalities. She didn't want to implant horrific pictures in his young brain.

"I so much wanted my father to smile. Yet, that chair where he sat, smoked, and stared was like a hypnotic magnet pulling him back to a horrific past he couldn't share. Not with me, not with my mother. No one had the power to erase his memories. Father never wanted me to feel responsible for his pain. He was unrealistic. I had to be good. His sadness weighed heavily on me throughout my childhood.

"I don't know if you have heard about the Second Generation—the children of Holocaust survivors."

We have not.

"I'm a classic second-generation child, except for one notable fact—I'm not Jewish. I share all the same feelings that any Jewish child of a survivor would feel—the guilt, the feeling of responsibility, the nagging sense that I don't have a right to be happy. It's probably why I love Louisa; she's naturally happy and positive. It was a relief to discover she knew nothing about the Holocaust. I remember Louisa saying to me, 'Don't let the Nazis steal your joy.'" Julian takes her hand and kisses it.

He pauses to ask us, "Are you sure you want to hear all this? It must be so depressing."

Deborah says, "Whether we want to hear it is not the right question for us. We need to hear your story and your father's. And you need to tell it. Julian, you're part of his story and you carry a heavy portion of his burden. So yes, please continue."

"Thank you. You're right, I need to tell his story—my story. Most people just don't want to hear about such things."

He tells us that his father's time in Auschwitz remains a mystery. "He has two responses: 'You should not hear of such things' and 'the world should never again know of such evil.' At times, he seems like he's wrestling with God, trying to find some answer to explain the madness. He once told me, 'God abandoned us. He let the monsters out of their cages. What loving God would do this? Not the God I believed in—not the one who told us to depart from evil and do good. My God went up in flames with the burning bodies of Auschwitz.'"

He tells us that his father organized workers' strikes against the persecution of the Jews. When the Dutch Nazi party torched an Amsterdam synagogue, his father—at grave risk to his safety—helped lead a march against the Nazis.

"Father was an idealist, a man who believed we can't be passive in the face of evil, that we must be ready to lay down our lives for a just cause. For him, the right cause was fighting fascism and everything it represented. He even wore the yellow star to show solidarity with the Jewish community."

I tell Julian about our encounter with Jacob and what we learned about the Dutch Jewish community and the Dutch collaborators. "Your father must have been a marked man," I say.

"He was. But that didn't stop him." He tells us his father became part of an underground Christian organization that helped to save Jews. In late 1943, one of the bounty hunters informed on him. He was sent to Westerbork, and from there, the Nazis deported him to Auschwitz. The Nazis tortured him so he'd inform on the members of the underground.

"He has the scars on his back and legs to prove it. I don't know if they broke him or not, and I don't know if his worst nightmares are about torture, or Auschwitz, or both.

"He believes he survived because of his blond hair and blue eyes. Even though the Nazis hated the 'Dutch traitor,' he was still an 'Aryan' like them. In my father's mind, the Nazis spared him for the same reason that the Jews were murdered—the evil of Aryan superiority. His survival tortures him more cruelly than the suffering he endured in

Auschwitz. In his mind, God deprived him of penance and martyr-dom—the chance to sacrifice his life like Jesus as an atonement for the sins of the Antichrist. For him, to have died in the gas chambers along with the Jewish martyrs he tried to save would have been his ultimate salvation."

He tells us his story is moving toward a happier ending. "Father has started to smile since Louisa, our angel of mercy, has come into our lives. My beautiful wife maneuvers through his misery and lights up his joy. When he's with her, he can forget his past and let go of his obligation to be miserable."

"You should know," Louisa adds, "that my father-in-law is the kindest, most gentle man I've ever met. There is something holy about him, almost saintly. And, my dear husband, Julian, has many of those same qualities. Perhaps God has taken me from my loving family and my peaceful island to share some of our joy and simplicity with people less fortunate than us."

Before we part company, I thank Julian. "As a Jew, I thank you and your father for your sacrifice. You've awakened something deep in me about being Jewish that will take time for me to understand. You give me hope that our better angels might overcome the worst of who we are."

Late that evening, Deborah and I can't sleep, as if we've both awakened from the same nightmare and have this intense need to talk. We struggle to find the right words to describe what we feel. Shock, sadness, compassion, horror, rage—all true, and yet, there's something we're missing, a deeper insight and understanding buried within the painful stories we've heard from Le Clown, Simone, Jacob, Nicole, and now Julian.

We search deeper to find the thread, to move beyond the expected emotional reactions their stories would elicit in any compassionate listener. Who wouldn't feel empathy and horror when listening to Jacob's painful tale of destruction, or the tragic account of Simone's family, or the suffering of Julian and his father? But, again, we sense that there must be far more to these encounters than an emotional awakening to human suffering or an empathetic understanding that the events of history reveal themselves in the scars of their victims.

No, this is not an odyssey in search of war stories. As the conversation continues, a new lexicon emerges, a participatory language that shrinks the distance between the listener and the narrator. Words like gratitude, responsibility, identity, and witness offer deeper meaning and direction. We get there when I ask Deborah what she meant by her statement to Julian: *We need to hear your story and your father's.*

"When he spoke," she says, "I asked myself the question we've been asking ourselves: Why does the war and the Holocaust follow us at every turn? The obvious answers crossed my mind: We're psychologists. We know how to help people open up. And the road is a truth potion. All true, but there's more. As Julian spoke, I felt a sense of gratitude and humility. He shared a precious and painful part of who he is, and I felt privileged to be there with him, honored that he invited us to be part of his story—as a witness to history. I don't know what it means to be a witness, but I know we'll figure it out, and we'll know what to do when the time comes."

Over the next few days, as we approach St. Pierre de Chartreuse, thoughts of the Holocaust and war recede to the back of our minds. The weather is too perfect, the scenery too gorgeous, and the French hospitality too inviting for us to remain focused on tales from the dark side. Almost imperceptibly, the flat road morphs into a chain of gentle hills, and then the gentle hills transform into foothills. From time to time, the slopes are so steep that a sign warns truck drivers to shift to a lower gear on the descent.

At the edge of the horizon, white specks appear that at first glance seem to be distant clouds, and then, with further examination, reveal their true identity: triangular mountain peaks. We're headed southeast toward those mountains. To reach Italy, our next country, we must traverse a steep pass with an altitude in the neighborhood of 8,000 feet. At our current location by the small white church in Entre-deux-Guiers, a village of fifteen hundred people surrounded by white-capped mountains, we're at a modest height of fifteen hundred feet. The distance to the Col du Lautaret pass is a challenging ninety-three miles, a nonstop ascent of 6,000 feet.

Nothing can focus a mind more intently than a steep climb up a narrow, winding road on a warm midsummer day in Southeast France. This mind has a singular intention: to keep its legs moving, its breath steady, and the sweat from burning its eyes. When you're climbing up an eighteen-degree slope, you don't feel that delicious feeling of flow that comes from maintaining a steady pace on a flat surface. No, pedaling up a mountain is all about effort and will.

I reach the crest of the hill a minute before Deborah arrives. She is struggling. I cheer—she's out of the saddle and pushes her entire body weight and strength onto the pedals, and with five more rotations, joins me on the top of the hill, breathing heavily and beaming like she just won the Boston Marathon. We extend our arms upward in victory and catch our breath before the fun starts.

To fight your way through eighteen degrees of resistance, you got to stare down gravity and make it blink. Call it mind over mass. Let's say you make it to the top—never once dismounting, refusing to sacrifice your will to gravity. Now, you get your prize: Eighteen degrees up means eighteen degrees down. Before you lies a beautiful sight: a long, steep decline that winds and falls at that same eighteen-degree gradient. Your former enemy, now your new best friend, will propel you down toward the earth's center of mass. The circular motion of your wheels will join to accelerate your fall.

And off you go . . .

If you're a serious skier, you know that sacred space where wild freedom and absolute control become one as you fly like the wind down a forty-degree black diamond trail. Fear is the enemy of freedom and mastery. It's a self-fulfilling prophecy—if you worry about falling, you will. On the other hand, if ego overshadows skill and experience, the skier puts himself at risk. All true for a bicyclist.

On an eighteen-degree hard surface road, you can reach speeds of forty to fifty miles per hour. You're one poorly placed pebble from deep shit. If your mind goes there, then you downshift your body by leaning back in the saddle until your bike slows to a manageable speed. Fear is your red light, your reminder to step on the brake. But let's say you're standing on top, breathing heavily, feeling like you just pissed on gravity. The time has come to cash in your chips.

You're a moment away from the divine, from that unearthly sense that your bike is more than an extension of you. You lean into the hill, let gravity work, and then you fly . . . You let go, and you let the road, and your bike, and your skill propel you at a speed that, only years later, will make you think, "I must have been crazy." Yes, at that moment you are crazy.

Two miles from Entre-deux-Guiers, Deborah has a flat tire. Not the first time—you can't travel thousands of miles on rough roads riding on thin bike tires and not get a puncture. Deborah leans her bicycle against a waist-high stone wall that marks the boundary between the road and a well-groomed, suburban-style yard. A large red house that looks to me like an over-the-hill dairy barn with a face-lift, tummy tuck, and a nose job sits about forty feet from the wall. A grove's worth of apple trees separates the former cowshed from the road.

A small, wiry man in his midfifties approaches from behind a cluster of trees carrying a basket filled with apples. A magnificent white Samoyed walks on his right, moving at the same pace as the owner. The man asks Deborah if she needs assistance.

She declines and says in French, "If I can't fix a flat, I might as well give up on our around-the-world adventure."

"Around-the-world adventure? What's your itinerary?"

To remove the rear tire, Deborah shifts the drive chain into the highest gear. "We're going over the Alps to Italy . . . India . . . Southeast Asia—" She loosens the rim brake on the flat tire.

"You can't go around the world on land."

While they talk, I'm amazed at how the dog sits by the man's feet, patiently waiting for his owner's next command—a far cry from our free-spirited mutt, Ajax, who is now on loan to my sister. I've heard that if you want to know what kind of parent someone will be, watch how he is as a dog owner. A calm, obedient dog is a cheerful dog. His owner must be an amazing father.

Deborah positions herself opposite the chain and pulls the quick-release lever. "No, we're taking a boat from Yugoslavia to Greece, and then from Egypt, we'll ship our bikes." She removes the tire, deflates the remaining air, and pulls out the tube.

"How do you make time for such an adventure?" he asks.

Deborah removes the inner tube, searches for the hole, and finds it. She removes the file, the patch, and the glue. "We're both self-employed psychologists, so it was easy . . . We both love to travel . . . and before we have kids . . . No, Michael doesn't speak French well, but he understands." She patches the inner tube, puts it back in the tire, and fills it with air.

"Please let me invite you into our home for something to drink and eat. We make our own cider. I promise you it will be the best you've ever tasted." He extends his hand to Deborah. "I am Louis, and you are?"

*   *   *

I considered skipping my journal passage about Louis and his wife Chantal. We met many fine and helpful people throughout our journey— most of whom I chose not to write about. Their kindness is noted as a group. As individuals, however, we either lacked sufficient time to get past the social level or, due to our own limitations, we failed to connect more deeply. To be fair, most of us have a natural reticence to open up to strangers, so to expect nonstop, soul-to-soul connections would be unrealistic, time-consuming, and way too much to absorb.

For reasons, at first unclear, I kept returning to my journal entries about Chantal and Louis. A photo I have of them and their dog, Otto, standing with Deborah holds an inexplicable fascination for me. My journal is vague: "Deborah has a flat . . . A man offers to help. Wonderful people, ask lots of questions about us, talk little about themselves . . . No dramatic stories. Warm feeling . . . Love their dog, Otto."

I stare at the forty-year-old photo lying on my desk before me. Deborah's on the left of the picture, looking like she's on the front cover of **Vogue.** *Her left hip leans toward Louis, who stands shoulder to shoulder with Chantal. Otto has repositioned himself. His forward-looking white head casts a shadow on Deborah's summer dress.*

Yet, there's something more to this picture than this self-assured, eye-grabbing American girl. To the camera's right stand a kind, modest-looking couple, a quiet contrast to the bold woman posing on the left. Slightly shorter than Deborah, bald and bearded, his right hand in his pocket, Louis focuses slightly to the right—nonchalant, like we caught him by surprise examining the apples on one of his trees. On the right side of the picture, Chantal stands, close in height to her husband, relaxed, smiling, at ease with herself. From the perspective of color and geometry, her blue-and-white striped, ankle-length dress clashes terribly with Louis's orange-and-white checked shirt. French, for sure. Parisian, not a chance.

Why did they make the cut? Simple. Louis and Chantal are extraordinary ordinary people—clueless about style, unpretentious and kind, gracious and curious, living a simple life in tune with the cycle of the seasons. They speak briefly about their three children and five grandchildren scattered throughout France. Chantal tears when she talks about how hard it is to be so far from her family.

Deborah tells me later, "When we have children, I want to feel that kind of love and attachment Chantal and Louis feel."

During the sixteen hours we spend with Chantal and Louis, we hear no tales of destruction, no painful war stories, no heroic encounters with evil. Instead of dramatic self-disclosure, the focus is on us—about this "adventurous young couple" that stumbled into their lives. They share a few anecdotes from their "ordinary" French life—a life of hard work, family, and now the simple pleasures of working their apple orchard, their vegetable garden, and being with one another and Otto.

I said earlier that Louis and Chantal are extraordinary ordinary people. But I sense they're more than that. I am convinced in my flesh, in my gut, and in my heart that Chantal and Louis would have been that

rare couple that would have risked their lives to save a Jewish boy like me
from the Nazis.

I am that certain of it—which is why they appear here.

*   *   *

We're in a St.-Pierre-de-Chartreuse café with a 360-degree view of the Alps, delighting in an out-of-this-world ice cream sundae. This is one of those radiant moments that invite all your senses to participate: You inhale the aromatic perfume of white gardenias standing tall in their flowerpots scattered around the deck. You taste the astonishing blend of cognac, chocolate, fruit, and ice cream. You experience it visually in this Alpine splendor of jagged granite, crystal blue sky, and the proud, erect pines that rise from the mountain slope, straight and true. And I feel my body stir from the touch of our fingertips. I breathe in the beautiful, dark-haired woman with the white gardenia threaded in her hair. I marvel at her lithe body shaped by weeks of hard climbing, at her golden skin tanned from the strong rays of the sun, and at her well-earned confidence brimming from her victory over gravity. She looks as lovely and as perfect as I've seen her—like it's the first time.

We take long hikes to the peaks close to St.-Pierre-de-Chartreuse, meditate in the utter silence of the Carthusian monastery, and indulge in every variety of pastry from a modest tart to a cream-filled chocolate cake. If you were to ask us, after three days and nights of earthly delights interspersed with hours of expanded silence and sacred communion, where would we say truth resides, we'd answer, very Zen-like, "Wherever you commit wholeheartedly." However, there is a caveat. A purely physical act divorced from its connection to the sacred is only a short-lived pleasure on the road to addiction. And a "dopey-eyed," disembodied spirituality that denies death and longs for blissful, sexless highs is a close cousin to psychosis.

To reach the 8,000-foot Col du Lautaret pass, we battle nonstop for four hot and humid days, zigzagging up narrow roads crowded with vacation traffic. The air is leaden with the black smoke of exhaust fumes and thick with noxious waste spewed from the open-pit mines—ugly, gaping holes like violent wounds oozing puss and blood. The polluted air burns hot and rancid in our throats, in our lungs, and in our eyes.

Yet, it seems as if a force far more powerful than the strength of our bodies and the determination of our minds propels our bikes higher, one rotation at a time, until we reach the summit where the air is crisp and clean, where an ancient glacier flows down the steep granite slabs like frozen lava, and where the pristine mountains remain as they've always been—untouched by the rapacious claws of progress.

We dismount. Deborah exchanges her bike shoes for sandals and yells at me to get the camera. She runs six hundred feet toward the snow and falls backward on the white crusty surface, and like a child after a snowstorm, she moves her arms and legs to form a snow angel. To my weary mind, her angelic body appears as a sacrifice lying on an altar of snow—an offer of gratitude to the force that carried us here. And then, Deborah gestures wildly upward toward the heavens, where a glorious eagle circles the cloudless sky. A sign that our sacrifice has been received in grace.

That night, we stay over in a noisy, crowded campground over-run with families in camper vans. The deafening volume comes to a halt at nine in the evening. I assume it's the vacation bedtime for the hundred or so children now sleeping peacefully in their motor homes. For us, the quiet is a delicious relief from the constant clamor of cars and kids. It's also the time to experience the afterglow of victory. We did it—we pedaled our way to the summit. We've earned the right to call ourselves champions.

As we sit by the quiet table close to our tent, we reflect on the last seven weeks in the country I love. Above us, generous clusters of con-stellations sparkle like fireflies in the moonless sky—a gift of departure for our last night in France. Tomorrow, we have miles and miles of downhill—around eighty-five to be more precise—until we reach the outskirts of Torino, where we'll spend our first night in Italy.

In the country I love. Perhaps we can blame it on the blazing trail of light traveling through the night sky. Or, maybe we can attribute it to Polaris's bright beacon guiding us toward true north. And let's not for-get the unique configuration of constellations coupled with a waning crescent moon. Whatever the astrological influence this August 9th night sky may have had on my answer when Deborah asks me why I love France so much, my response remains as much of a surprise for me as it is for Deborah.

"Because France makes me think of you."

"You're comparing your love of France to your feelings toward me?"

"No, actually the other way around. Like you, France is always a surprise waiting to happen. Just when you think you've got Paris neatly wrapped and packaged, she throws the Eiffel Tower and Pompidou at you. Kind of like Sweden, don't you think?"

"So now Sweden's a plus? Another reason you love me?"

"Let's call it the tension between love and hate or fear and excitement. You're a challenge, like the French weather and the mountain roads. Sometimes gorgeous and flowing, and other times, you're all hard rain and gravity."

"Go on . . ."

"You have enough existential angst to keep any French philosopher happy, and you're as calm and meditative as a Renoir painting."

"Impressive."

"You've got the classic bones of a French beauty even without the makeup, the perfume, and the clothes from Dior."

"Continue."

"You're sweet as a French tart, as simple as a perfect omelet, and as complex as the finest Bordeaux."

"And you're as insane as Toulouse-Lautrec."

Italy:
August 11 to September 7

At eight thirty a.m., we mount our bikes, ready to fly down the mountain to the French border town of Briançon, and then from there, to Italy. And fly we do . . . down slopes that would take hours of exertion to climb, beyond newly built resort hotels where a blur of tourists tan themselves in the Alpine sun. And soar we do. At speeds exceeding forty miles per hour, we overtake day trekkers carrying poles and packs; we plummet past climbers with heavy rucksacks on their backs and mountain gear dangling from their waists. We sail so fast that I barely catch the tail end of a brief bikini.

And descend we do . . . on cobblestone roads through picturesque Italian villages with red-tiled roofs and spires reaching to the sky . . . on sharp curves and switchbacks—leaning right, then left like we're downhill racers—and past sweet-smelling pine trees and meadows dotted with the blues, purples, and yellows of summer wildflowers, the wind alternately in our faces, then on our backs—at one moment forcing us to slow down and the next accelerating us forward at the same speed as the hyper-testosterone Italian drivers who strain their necks to gawk at the tasty-looking dark-haired bicyclist clad in shorts and a tight-fitting top. Beyond row after row of terraced vineyards, we descend . . . and, as we fall, the mountains fade behind dark clouds and the air becomes heavy and hot; our clothes drip sweat; our faces are gritty from dust and grime.

And, down and down we go, deep into the bowels where the

fresh aroma of pine and the grand Alpine vistas vanish like a one-night stand. What remains is nothing more than a lingering memory of fleeting pleasure. And in its stead, a separate reality: the putrid smell of industrial waste. The ugly blemish of deserted, broken-down factories—their windows smashed, their walls defaced with graffiti. The disturbing sight of plastic bags of rotting garbage abandoned by the side of the road. And the horror of rats feasting by the dozens on the discarded remains of human negligence. We have fallen into Dante's Inferno.

We find the least repulsive campsite near Torino to pitch our tent—an act of enormous skill and dexterity. Try to smack and swat mosquitoes the size of hummingbirds with one hand while hammering tent pegs into dry, dusty dirt with the other. As soon as we erect the tent, I unload our bikes and throw everything inside it while Deborah stands guard in front of the door, fighting off these nasty, blood-sucking devils.

It turns out that hell has decent showers, as long as you stay far from the light fixtures. It's where the mosquitoes congregate after a hard day sucking blood and mourning their loved ones. It takes some hard rubbing to get rid of the road grunge and the stench from eight hours of tough riding.

Thirty minutes later, we're sitting in a booth made from the finest Naugahyde—that fake leather that sticks to your bare skin and pops when you get up.

We're famished. I'd estimate we burned close to 2,000 calories today—a serious deficit that we tried to overcome with bananas, raisins, and chocolate. Problem is, they're all quick energy boosters. You get an immediate rush of glucose, which tricks your exhausted muscles into thinking they just got an injection of rocket fuel, and then—bingo—the tank is empty, you're running on fumes, and you sputter to a halt.

Now, sitting in this plastic palace, I'm suffering from a serious low-blood-sugar attack, and Deborah isn't doing much better. We need food now, but Signorina Deborah, my Italian rose, doesn't know what to order from this bright red laminated menu with photos of Italian flowers to demarcate one course from the next. She speaks passable conversational Italian, but what she knows about Italian cuisine begins and ends with pizza, spaghetti, and Chef Boyardee sauces.

Unlike me. When I was a student at New York University, I practically lived at Vincent Scungilli's House in Little Italy where you ate the best octopus, squid, and clams on a bed of linguini, swimming in Vincent's famous tomato sauce. I can close my eyes and taste the sautéed garlic, the sweet fresh tomatoes, and the oregano from Vincent's Mama's garden. Back then, you could test me on my pastas. Blindfolded, I could distinguish linguine from spaghetti, and rigatoni from ziti. And let's not forget those cannoli—those mouthwatering Italian beauties made from fried dough with a sweet filling of ricotta cheese.

But looking at this menu, I'm stuck. What's ossobuco? Risotto alla Milanese? Pizzoccheri? Cremona Mostarda? Cottoleta? Cappon Magra?

A triple-chinned, big-bellied man dressed in an oversized chef's hat and dirty whites emerges from the kitchen. I call him over and he approaches our table.

Deborah explains we're having difficulty understanding the menu. *"Buonasera abbiamo difficoltà a capire il menu. Potete per favore aiutarci?"*

"Americans? Don't worry, I speak excellent Engelees. I love America. My brodder in America. He in Boston. You know Boston, no?"

"Yes, quite well," I answer.

"Ah, maybe you know my brodder? His name is Alessandro Azzaro and he own car fix-it place. Me, Domenico Azzaro. My place, she called Ristorante Azzaro."

"Sure, I know Alessandro. We bring our car to him all the time. Call your brother and ask him if he knows Michael and Deborah."

He thinks for a moment and then laughs, "You think you can joke Domenico Azzaro? Me smart like fox. You want order. I tell you what to like.

"You Debrah, you start with nice salad. Da best in all of Torino. Fresh from garden of my wife, Maria da saint. You want ossobuco? We make best in all Eetalee."

"What's ossobuco?" Deborah asks.

"Veal and—"

"Sorry, no. I don't eat meat."

"Why no eat *carne*?"

"I don't like killing animals for food."

"Not good for pig and cow if he don't end up in you. He very sad. God tell animal, 'You serve man. Your job to make him strong.' Animal say to God, 'Bless you, God. Man and me one flesh.'"

"So, what's ossobuco?" I ask.

"Mama Mia!" In a uniquely Italian gesture of love, he curls the fingers of his right hand and kisses his fingertips and then throws his curled fingers in a heavenly direction. "Ossobuco. God Himself eat ossobuco."

After a few more grandiose gestures about ossobuco and passionate proclamations that his ossobuco is the best in all of Italy and the universe, he tells me it's made from braised veal shanks, white wine, and vegetables resting on a bed of risotto (creamy rice cooked in meat broth and onions).

To Deborah, he says, "I make you something special. No meat, no fishes, no chickens. No? You stay here in Torino and Domenico Azzaro make you like real Eetalee womens." He turns to me and winks like we're two guys from the same boys' club sharing a secret handshake.

"Ciao, my American friends. Now, Domenico Azzaro make great meal."

"Okay, what was that?" Deborah asks.

"That, I believe, was our introduction to Eetalee."

Ten minutes later, Chef Domenico returns carrying a wooden salad bowl filled to the top with crispy romaine lettuce; bright red, oval-shaped, cherry tomatoes; blood-red peppers; curled carrots; and dark purple olives. "Vegetables and spice all from garden of my Maria. All virgin. You both taste. Tell me, not good?"

According to the Quran, seventy-two virgins accompany a true believer to Paradise. I'm no true believer, but I can tell you this: Something akin to Immaculate Conception is going on in Saint Maria's garden. By my count, I just tasted the equivalent celestial pleasures of five fresh and spicy virgins—round and curvy, blood-red and coal-black, tall and thin, yielding and challenging.

"Good, no?" I'd completely forgotten that this bear of a man has been hovering over us like an anxious Olympic skater waiting for her score.

"Good? Yes!" Deborah says.

"Ah, if you happy, then Domenico Azzaro happy." I believe him. In Domenico's world, he's like the young calf that ends up on the dinner plate as ossobuco—he's here to serve.

To comprehend what Domenico Azzaro, the portly chef and owner of this plastic palace, did with a piece of veal and a few spices, you need to think Rocky Balboa, or simply Rocky, or the Italian Stallion—that everyman working-class hero with a deadly punch. Here, in Azzaro's Plastic Palace, Chef Domenico is my Rocky Balboa—my Italian Stallion with the tomato-stained apron, an oversized chef's hat, and a big belly. What my Rocky from Torino, Italy, does with a piece of veal is the culinary equivalent to Rocky's flawless left hook to the jaw. A total knockout.

I'd share all that with Deborah, except she's too busy sighing over her pizzoccheri, a flat, mostly buckwheat pasta layered with Swiss Chard, cubed potatoes, pieces of Valtellina Casera cheese, and ground fresh Parmesan. Doesn't sound so great, but it is. You take both cheeses, combine them with the vegetables, mix those ingredients with the earthy flavor of buckwheat, and then toss in butter-fried garlic, and trust me, your taste buds will shoot fireworks.

I don't know how much time passes before Chef Domenico comes back out with our desserts, Mostarda di Cremona, a local favorite made with candied fruit and a mustard-flavored syrup. Sounds weird—fruit and mustard together. Like the long and loving, if unlikely, relationship between that glamorous Italian diva Sophia Loren and her lover—the older, shorter, and rounder Carlo Ponti, the famous Italian director.

"Good, no?"

"*Mama Mia! Fortissimo! Fantastico! Incredibile! Straordinario!*" Over dessert, Deborah taught me these Italian superlatives and I practiced them together with the kiss of delight—curled fingers to the lips, a kiss to the fingertips followed by an outstretched hand to the heavens.

Pleased by our enthusiastic response, he rests his *enorme posteri-ore* next to Deborah and starts to inquire why we're in Torino. We tell him about our trip so far, and our around-the-world plans.

"Domenico Azzaro advice you. Don't go to fancy, touristic *ris-torante*. Go where the peoples go—like Ristorante Azzaro where real people eat real food. Not like French *ristorante*." He points to the left side of his head and says, "French food from here like French peoples. Too much fancy sauces. Too much in brain and not enough in heart. Chef need to feel God's blessing in the food, and he need to share bless-ing with the peoples."

As we leave, he gives us both a bear hug. I feel enclosed within his sweaty, earthy body like a bear cub nestling close to mama for warmth and protection. His garlic, raw onion, and olive oil breath burns my eyes and scratches the back of my throat. I taste the pungent flavors of garlic and onion on my tongue. The spicy aroma of olive oil stings my lips and smooths the sharp edges of the garlic and onion. Physically, we are standing outside the entrance to the plastic paradise of Ristorante Azzaro. In my imagination, we wander through the rolling hills and fertile fields of Lombardy, past the groves of olive trees, and around the Roseto rice fields where the sheep graze at the foothills of the Alps.

The following morning, we set out from Torino in dense wet heat. The air reeks from thick, unfiltered clouds of toxic waste that smell and taste like the sulfuric vapors vomited from the oil and chemical refineries that line the New Jersey Turnpike. As we head southeast toward Alessandria, a fifty-mile ride over flat, congested roads that pass by more filth, factories, and rats devouring garbage tossed by people that don't give a shit, my mood mirrors the environment— ugly and foul.

A black spirit of rage propels me forward. I move my legs fero-ciously to escape from this pervasive ugliness, from this consuming emptiness I feel overwhelming my soul. I'm not prepared for this. I haven't steeled myself against this assault on my senses.

I should have been able to say to myself, *Understand, Michael, the*

putrid air that burns your lungs, the terrifying rats only ten feet from
you gorging on garbage, the ugliness that penetrates you to the core have
nothing to do with you. They don't carry your address. Let go. It's life. It
is what it is. Accept it as the yin-yang of existence, the dance of dualities.

That's how Deborah thinks. She approaches the passing horror
with the attitude of a meditator, free of attachment as if it's an errant
thought she lets pass. To her reflective mind, the reality before us reminds us of the darker forces that lie within us. She says to me, "They
didn't do this to us. This is us. You know—don't give a shit and you
can't be bothered."

She reminds me of a scene we experienced together once on the
way to our office in Rutland, Vermont. A respectful-looking woman
driving a decent car stopped close to a dumpster. She stepped from her
car carrying a large plastic garbage bag. The distance to the dumpster
was no more than a third of a football field. The ground was muddy but
passable. She looked at the dumpster, turned her head to the ground,
looked again at the dumpster, then dropped her bag of garbage where
she stood, and returned to her car. She's us; we're her. When you can't
be bothered, when your brain convinces you it doesn't matter, then we
become the problem, the polluter, the cause we don't own.

We arrive at the Alessandria campground around six, shower, and
search for a pizzeria. We both want to dine on real Italian pizza, not
the phony Italian American substitute made with canned, overly
sweetened tomato sauce; processed pizza cheese; thick, doughy crust;
and raw vegetables tossed onto the ersatz tomato sauce after the pizza
comes out of the stainless steel, state-of-the-art electric oven.

Nope, we want the real deal: thin crust pizza with vegetables
baked in a wood-fired oven with mozzarella cheese, homemade tomato sauce, fresh oregano, garlic, black truffles, and mushrooms. We
find the place—an out-of-the-way mom-and-pop sit-down restaurant,
simple and clean. Pizza's their life, not a get-rich-quick franchise with
a soulless formula for tasteless pizza.

Oh my God! That's it. Nothing more to add.

We're out in the dark street in an hour—feeling good and happily Italian.

We walk through the poorly lit park. Deborah points out used syringes hanging from trees—hundreds of them dangling from nearly every branch. Some needles have dry blood on them, one drips fresh blood. We're confused. We see four young men huddled together in a circle. One fellow, around twenty, in jeans and a black T-shirt, with longish hair holds a spoon over a candle. He's cooking smack. Now we understand. Maybe two hundred feet from them, another group of four goes through the same ritual. To our left, four more young men and a girl are shooting up.

This isn't the back alleys of Harlem. This isn't Saigon in 1970, when scag (heroin) was as accessible as ammo. This is a public park in Alessandria, Italy, in August 1980. What the hell is going on? Where are the cops, the narcs, the social workers? The druggies own the park and they're all kids—strung out on smack, scag, brown sugar—whatever you call it, it's all the same. They're mainlining a deadly drug with unsanitary needles. Unbelievable.

This is the rats-on-the-side-of-the-road culture. Don't care; nothing matters. Life's a bitch, and then you die. No jobs. No meaning. No future. Just kill yourself slowly—and sometimes not so slowly, when your drugged-out brain didn't get the dosage right. Anesthetize yourself from a life you don't own, to a society that doesn't care, and from a dead-end future you can't control. If that's your life or if that's how your head sees it, then the needle's your friend.

Something's profoundly wrong in Italy.

Two days later, we're in a crowded, chaotic family campground in Cremona overflowing with scores of boisterous Italian children running to and fro. Their chaos has a mysterious rhythm to it like a flock of birds that at one instant soars high toward the heavens, and then, for some reason known only to the birds, makes a quick one-eighty and nosedives toward the earth.

As we stand by our tent, seven "birds" fly in our direction and stop before us. The oldest among them, their brave leader, I assume—an adorable ten-year-old boy with large, curious eyes and wearing the shortest of shorts—says to us in broken English, "You Americani? No horsa? Why bika?"

Deborah starts to answer in Italian, and he stops her, "No Italiano. Inglees. Learn school Inglees. You teach."

"No problem," I tell him. Pointing to each child I say, "I'll teach you, and you, and you, and you English." They all giggle. "We begin now. 'Bike.'"

"Bika," they say in unison.

"Listen, 'biKe,' not bika. Hard stop at the K."

"BiKa," my little flock of chirping birds sings out.

"Yesa!" I shout and they all laugh. Now we have some solid chemistry—just what you need to teach kids. "My name is Michael. Tell me your names."

First the leader. "My nome Antonio."

"Nice to meet you, Antonio." I extend my hand for a high five, and he responds immediately with a good slap to my right hand. The flock chirps and giggles.

"Antonio, try this: My name is Antonio."

Being the smart kid that he is, he corrects me and says, "You name not Antonio. Me Antonio. You name Mikeel."

"Yes, thank you for that."

He smiles proudly and introduces me to Mario, Giovanni, Alfredo, Sergio, and the two girls, Mia and Daniella. I have each of them introduce themselves.

"Me Mario."

"Sergio nama me."

"Mia mea," and everyone laughs, except for little dark-haired Mia, who's confused. I squat directly in front of her, eyeball to eyeball, and say to her, "After me. My name is Mia."

"After mea, my nama Mia."

"Excellent, Mia." I kiss her on her curly head, and she giggles.

Every fabulous public speaker knows that moment when they've got the audience hanging on every word. This is one of those moments. My birds are ready to follow me wherever I fly. So, in a spirit of joyful madness, I say to them, "I will teach you a song in English."

Antonio immediately translates, *"Ci insegnerà una canzone in inglese."*

I line them up with the four smallest in the front and three oldest behind them like a little chorus. "After me: *When the moon hits your eye like a big pizza pie, that's amore.*"

Antonio corrects me. *"Amore no Inglees."*

"Yes, true. You're a very smart boy. It's an Italian and English song together." He looks very pleased with himself. "Okay, again: *When the moon hits your eye like a big pizza pie, that's amore.*"

"When da moon hits your eyea lika biga pizza piea, dats amore."

I clap enthusiastically. They all laugh and clap their hands. "Again."

"When da moon hits your eyea lika biga pizza piea, dats amore."

"Fantastico!" They all shout.

Antonio then asks me. "Song just dat? No more song."

"It's all I remember. Sorry."

"No problem. I make 'em singa."

Maestro Antonio stands before his choir and together they repeat, *"When da moon hits your eyea lika biga pizza piea, dats amore."* And then with Antonio in the lead, they march around the campground singing the one verse I remember from this 1953 song sung by the Italian American singer and actor Dean Martin, the likable drunk with the bedroom eyes.

As I watch Antonio lead his six little singers around the campground, I say to Deborah, "As long as there are beautiful children like these kids, there's hope for the future."

"And, as long as there are crazy, beautiful souls like you to teach them to sing—even off-key—we'll be okay."

*   *   *

The next morning, we wander through Cremona without direction or purpose. You surrender to your fancy down blind alleys, twisted staircases, narrow pathways that seem to lead nowhere—whatever lures you, leads you. Maybe your fancy is the cobblestone Piazza del Comune, enclosed on three sides by white and pink stone, arched buildings possibly dating from the Renaissance or earlier.

If so, you find a café and you let your eyes experience the totality of what's before you—the domed church, the elaborately sculpted fountain, the flurry of pedestrians crisscrossing the plaza, the riot of colors. The soft pink stone, the tri-colored red, white, and green Italian flag, the blazing red dress, and the shapely legs of the sexy Italian women sitting by the fountain, before the pasta, pizza, and pastries transform their voluptuous topography of unimaginable curves into unsightly hills and mountains of flesh.

You let yourself feel the friendly vibe of this town square where the village jester once juggled, joked, and performed magic tricks. To our right, a lovely female violinist in form-fitting jeans and a tight sleeveless shirt plays a haunting version of the Beatles' "Norwegian Wood." Deborah notices my rapt attention and says, "You're leering like an Italian!"

"Really, I hadn't noticed. You know I only have eyes for you."

We don't carry guidebooks so we don't know, nor do we care to know, what most guidebooks say you should know—no must-see buildings from the sixteenth century, no have-to-know history of Cremona from ancient Roman times when Virgil wrote his poems here, or about the post-Renaissance period of violin making. No you-got-to-visit fountains where if you don't toss in a coin, you miss out on an authentic Italian experience.

We're aimless travelers, letting the spirit take us wherever it takes us. And right now, we're wandering down an alley through a courtyard that opens up to the smells of paint, sawdust, and glue. On all sides, violin makers in small workshops ply their craft. We stand by the door of a luthier named Zoltán Varga. He bends over his workbench, coating the neck of a nearly completed violin with dark varnish as if he's caressing a beloved cat gently and rhythmically down the length of her body.

It's a meditation of movement—one complete stroke followed by another. I would guess there is zero deviation in time between one complete pass of his brush from the top of the neck to the bottom and the next pass and the next after that . . . Only a master luthier blessed with flawless pitch would sense the faint resonance of imperfection—perhaps the result of one mindless moment, one slight variation from this rhythmic movement of the brush. Such are the demands of quality.

Zoltán Varga pauses and notices us standing by the entrance to his workshop and beckons us in. He asks us in crisp, formal English if we're violinists. We say no; we're merely curious about what he does and why he does it. Fine, he says, let me make you some tea and introduce you to the world of violin making—a generous gesture delivered rather solemnly as if he is about to initiate us into a secret world that few are invited to experience.

He asks a few questions about us and seems most intrigued to discover we're psychologists. "To be a master luthier, you must control your mind as surely as you must excel at the mechanics of the craft. A luthier must focus many hours each day with intense concentration, never for a moment allowing his mind to wander. Those of us who have remained in the profession move beyond the forced attention of a journeyman to become at ease with one's passion."

He explains: Far from the burning desire of the senses, hungry for instant gratification, the passion of a luthier is a slow-burning fire, offering constant warmth and heat—sustainable like an eternal flame. He associates it with being fully present, with being at one with your destiny, with being in touch with your deepest sense of who you are and what you're meant to do in this world—your every moment infused with meaning and purpose. "Is this not the life we seek to discover?" he asks.

"Quality is what I seek in my work. Perhaps one would call it excellence. Yet it is so much more than excellence. Excellence is merely the prerequisite of the luthier—the finely honed skills and superb technique of the craftsman. It is the perfection of sound that we long to express."

He makes a brief detour in response to Deborah's question about what brought him to the profession of violin making. Zoltán, thirty-four, was born in post-war Hungary. His father was a violin maker, as was his father before him. "From a young age, I was quite skilled with my hands. I sculpted from age six, and by my early teens, I learned to fix anything from cars to locks. When I was eighteen, I constructed my first violin. I knew then that to be anything else other than a luthier would be a negation of my true self."

For nearly two hours, we explore together the paradox of destiny and freedom and the challenge facing every creative soul—how to release the spirit trapped within the limited form of objects. Or, within ourselves—finite, but free.

"Yes, I was chosen to be a luthier, but that's not sufficient. I must resurrect my calling from moment to moment, with every stroke of my brush and with every movement of my saw. We all face the same challenge. We either run from our fate or we embrace it."

I'd like Dr. Claude to join us in this conversation.

For Zoltán, the pursuit of quality seems closely related to the medieval concept of alchemy in which the alchemist attempts to transmute finite base metals into gold. "A luthier," according to Zoltán, "like Stradivarius before him, must be obsessed with releasing the purest tone from an instrument made of created, bound materials. He must liberate the infinite from the finite."

I'm not sure whether Zoltán, a serious man who sees himself as part of a 350-year-old noble tradition of violin making, will appreciate my brief vignette about quality. But I decide to ignore my doubts and share this story about Frank, the short-order cook—the master of the perfect hamburger and the ultimate fried egg.

In the early 1970s, my friends and I practically took up residence at the Shaboo Inn in Willimantic, Connecticut, where we'd shake, rattle, and roll to some of the greatest singers and rock groups of the era, like Bonnie Raitt, B.B. King, and Aerosmith:

When the music stops at three a.m., we stop. Along with a procession of other Shabooers, we make the short pilgrimage to Frank's, a 150-square-foot, hole-in-the-wall, fast-food joint. A Formica counter separates Frank

from the mob of happy, stoned hippies crowded into his tiny establish-
ment. Like the proverbial quarterback for whom time slows, or perhaps
more like one gifted with the ability to distinguish discrete sounds among
the cacophony of chaos, Frank repeats the orders shouted from the crowd
of hungry and high Shabooers. Hamburger with fries; hamburger with
fries. Fried eggs, easy over, on toast; fried eggs, easy over, on toast. BLT on
dark bread; BLT on dark bread.

All the while, Frank's hands are moving faster than Ginger Baker's
drum riff on the Cream song "Sunshine of Your Love." And like a man
possessed, those high-flying hands of Frank's create fast-food Picassos—
juicy, fat hamburgers, pink on the inside and beautifully browned on the
outside; sunny-side eggs for which the sun itself would die of envy; fries so
crisp and light that you faint in pleasure on immediate contact with your
tongue. Meanwhile, as he's flipping burgers, cracking eggs, frying bacon,
and taking orders, he's collecting money and giving change. It's all one
seamless motion. Call it the Poetics of Perfection, the Zen of Fast Food,
Holiness in a Hamburger.

Zoltán smiles at my brief vignette and says, "I like this Frank. He's
a maestro in his own right. A man at ease with his passion. If I were a
religious man, I'd say about Frank that every flip of a burger and every
crack of an egg is a prayer and a sacrament."

CHAPTER 11

Italy: Part 2

Today is my birthday. I'm thirty-four years old and I'm on an around-the-world odyssey with the woman I love. I'm blessed.

The next leg of our journey takes us from Cremona to Sirmione, a fifty-mile ride over pleasant, relatively quiet country roads. The sky is a hazy shade of blue, the temperatures by noon are in the midnineties, and the humid August air envelops us like a thick, wet blanket. Vaporous heat rises from the black road surface like an endless bed of burning coals.

There's a short-term fix to help reduce the suffering from the scorching heat: To cool yourself, you ride fast and furious to create a fan-like effect on your damp, sweltering body. Meanwhile, the homeostatic mechanism housed in the hypothalamus sends a message to your sweat glands, "Release steam now!" On command, hot, sticky perspiration cascades from your pores as your thermostat fights desperately to cool off your overheated body. At that point, it's probably a smart idea to dismount, drink a liter of water, and find someone peddling ice-cold watermelon by the side of the dusty road.

When you live on the precipice like we do, the new normal is the extreme, the intense, and the unexpected—like going from being a moment away from heat exhaustion to the exquisite cooling sensation of sweet, cold watermelon as it slides down your throat.

An eighteenth-century philosopher once answered, when asked whether we should strive to walk the middle path, the golden mean between two extremes, "That's where the horses shit." His message: From the safe middle, your eyes won't witness the powerful waterfall surging over the boulders; your ears won't hear the explosion of sound as this terrifying cascade of power crashes against the rocks, nor will you experience the dread and awe of nature's ferocity.

Sirmione sits at the southernmost thigh of Lago di Garda, a body of water molded like the strong and shapely leg of a ballerina—round and full where Sirmione lies and then tapering toward its slender northern ankle. On all sides—standing tall like an army of soldiers—steep, pine-covered cliffs define and protect the pretty lakeside town, faded pale pink from the Northern Italian sun.

A cool, welcome breeze blows inland from the lake to the town. Our moderately crowded, surprisingly quiet, and mosquito-free camp-site faces the lake. We find a spot five feet from the shore to pitch our tent and leave the netted door open to receive the calm, refreshing winds.

Life is good on Monday, August 18, 1980, as we sit on the narrow strip of sand between the tent and the lake. The early evening water cools our feet, the gentle waves massage our calves. Deborah's left foot plays a very pleasant game of footsie with my right, and later that evening, while nestled in our lightweight sleeping bags, we celebrate my birthday in the most enchanting way.

We're now in a campground on the outskirts of Verona, the setting for two of Shakespeare's plays, *Romeo and Juliet* and *The Two Gentlemen of Verona*. Verona is also the birthplace of Catullus, the Roman poet known for his sexually explicit poems based on his many love affairs with both men and women. In one poem, he's in passionate pursuit of Lesbia, who plays with his soft head and his willing body, alternately stroking him and then pushing him away. Turns out Lesbia, whom Catullus modeled after a real-life seductress named Clodia, plied her feminine charms on our hapless poet and drove our poor lover mad.

So, in the spirit of love, suicide, and madness, we go to the opera to experience the tragic love story of Tristan and Isolde. The performance takes place in an open-air Roman amphitheater built in 30 C.E. from pink and white limestone. This well-preserved colosseum was once renowned throughout the Roman Empire for its gory extravaganzas in which gladiators replicated great military victories, replete with all the death and destruction one might expect from low-tech warfare. Fast forward to 1980, a more humane period in history, when lavish operas replace spectacles of blood and guts and when the stars of the arena are no longer gladiators fighting to be the last man standing, but tenors, sopranos, and baritones vocalizing the highs and lows of lust, longing, and the pains of a broken heart.

The best way for us non–opera buffs to understand an Italian's passion for these musical extravaganzas would be to imagine you're a Martian at a sports event. Now, what you'll notice about sports fans is that they seem to suffer from a severe mood disorder. In a nanosecond, they can fall from the height of euphoria to the pit of agony, and, in the next instant, soar to ecstatic peaks, then descend again into the depths of despair. All because of a near miss, a close call, or a leaping catch by the Yankees' centerfielder, Bobby Brown, to rob Boston's Carl Yastrzemski of a home run. You, dear Martian, may not understand why a ball one inch too low can transform wildly joyous humans on the verge of victory into a stadium full of shell-shocked fans moaning over that "one fucking inch."

But that's the way it is for fans. You live and die for your team. When the team's up, you're up. And so it is for the Italians and their opera. Holding lit candles, the Italian opera enthusiasts swoon and sob to the cantatas and arias of jealousy and longing, love and death sung by the tragic protagonists Tristan and Isolde. When the forbidden lovers partake of the poisonous aphrodisiac, the adoring crowd's hearts beat as one with our passionate couple.

With every tragic note of desire sung by Tristan, and with each aching octave of love that pours forth from Isolde's haunting voice, the brokenhearted mass of Italians grieve as one. A woman to my right sobs uncontrollably. An elderly man directly in front of me clutches his breast and weeps. A couple to our left embrace as if they're two mourners at a funeral, holding one another for comfort. For Italians, opera is far more than an elaborately costumed and richly staged form of musical entertainment. It's a stylized rendition of life itself.

But, like baseball, you've got to grow up with it.

Venice, Italy, August 24, 1980

We're in a rundown, mosquito-infested campground close to the taxi boat to Venezia. (Venice sounds so much better in Italian.) For the last four days, we've been commuting from this crude campground to the city *The New York Times* called "the most beautiful and the most romantic in the world."

I disagree. Paris has it all over Venice when it comes to love, aesthetics, and spectacular architecture. No doubt with its 118 miniature islands connected by over four hundred bridges spanning 150 canals, Venice makes for some outstanding photo ops, especially if you know how to manipulate light, water, and the shadows that the historic buildings cast on the Venetian waterways. The problem, however, is this: Try to find one unobstructed view free of the 60,000 daily tourists and the 22 million annual visitors jockeying for position to shoot their perfect Venetian picture—one among the many hundreds they will take on their two-week, fourteen-city European vacation of a lifetime.

Once upon a time, Venice was the center of European culture and commerce. Now it only has a past to peddle. Paris breathes; Venice recalls and preserves. I don't see or feel or sense the hidden Venice—the Venice without the beautiful mask, the Venice of Venetians. We don't happen upon neighborhood cafés where locals hang out to gossip and discuss politics. Sit in a touristy café and you won't find stylish Venetian women sauntering by, dressed in high heels and the latest fashion from the House of Dior. The only passersby are groups armed with camera bags draped over shoulders, dressed in shorts and walking shoes like obedient soldiers in an army of tourists.

So, that is our Venetian experience—visually pleasing, historically interesting, culturally engaging. I ask Deborah if she'd want to return. Her answer, like mine, is no.

Over the next five days, we ride 250 miles south along the Adriatic coast, past one spoiled beach after another, until we reach the port city of Ancona. Tomorrow, we travel by boat to Dubrovnik, Yugoslavia, the first and only Communist country we'll visit on our around-the-world journey.

The garbage-strewn beaches of the Adriatic communicate the same sad story about contemporary Italian culture that the discarded bloody needles tell. The bottles that bob up and down by the shoreline, the paper cups and plates strewn carelessly on the sandy beach, the plastic bags that fly here and there carried by a sudden sea breeze all stand as silent witnesses to a dying culture of rage and despair.

I once heard it said that rage is the last act of the incompetent. When you believe that making a difference is a myth, when you're convinced the system is rigged and you're a puppet that the powerful exploit, then why care when the government doesn't?

Anger and frustration can lead to change. Pain is a prerequisite to growth. But helpless wrath plays out in acts of bitter self-destruction like trashing the seashore, like defecating where you eat. Even a dog knows better.

Yet, amid all that ugliness and neglect, small, red-roofed cottages display window boxes overflowing with purple, red, and blue flowers. Like fortresses against despair, they make a stand for beauty and hope.

Dubrovnik:
September 8 to September 14

A tornado must have ripped through Ancona and transported us somewhere on the other side of the rainbow, gently depositing us in the make-believe world of Dubrovnik where we glide on marble as smooth and slippery as wet glass and where the three-fingered leaves of fig trees hold ripe purple fruit bursting with nectar.

Welcome to Oz.

To describe this orange-roofed, walled city on the Adriatic, I've got to dig deep into my lexicon of superlatives. Dubrovnik is a visual feast of vibrant colors, an imaginary universe of magical islands that drift on the horizon, a twisted labyrinth of beige stone streets that lead you up, down, and all around this phantasmagorical fortress by the sea.

From the fortified apertures built into the massive limestone walls that surround the Old City of Dubrovnik, we look down on the sailboats, yachts, and schooners floating on the sparkling blue waters below. From our vantage point, a rocky, forested island shaped like a dark green saucer hovers above the calm Aegean waters. At the edge of the horizon, the cloudless azure sky merges with the turquoise sea, creating an endless blanket of blue. The brilliant rays of the midday sun illuminate the bright orange roofs, pink stone buildings, and the occasional palm trees that dot the Old City.

Here within the walls of the Bokar Fortress, I imagine that the purveyors of power whispered sordid secrets, forged alliances of convenience, and schemed to overthrow the throne. No doubt these solid parapets hold secrets of past plots and plans—treacherous tales of mystery and murder and sinister stories of treason and betrayal. What better place to stage all this intrigue than the well-fortified fortress perched high above Dubrovnik, standing tall like a mighty God.

Our boat to Dubrovnik sailed under the Turkish flag. When we purchased our tickets twenty-four hours earlier, a very officious official in a starched brown uniform and a crisp mustache warned us in broken English, "Six o'clock morning, here at ship. You go seven o'clock. No you sleep late. No wait for nobody."

We arrive at the dock at 6:10, and the same severe, starched official from the ticket office now struts about like he's Napoleon. In leather boots, he stands no taller than five feet four inches. With the index finger of his right hand, he directs the passengers to one of two parallel lines that begin in front of a metal folding table—a very serious table indeed. Laid out on its stained surface are important stamps and authoritative documents with multiple sheets of carbon paper between each form. Ten of us arrive together: one family of four, two hippie couples in matching tie-dyed yoga pants and backpacks, and Deborah, me, and our bikes. In a scene eerily reminiscent of Auschwitz, our Napoleon wannabe commands the hippies to the right and the family to the left.

It's our turn. He stares at us, then at our bikes, and then back at us. I feel bad for our little general. From the confused look on his face, I'm guessing he can't find a place in his small mind for freaks on bikes. We're somewhere in that ambiguous gray area between the tie-dyed, probably stoned hippies to our right, and the respectable middle-class family of four to our left. I have relatively long hair and an earring in my left ear—a clear sign that I should be with the hippies. Yet, I'm older, cleaner, my hair's shorter, and we're on bikes.

He gives Deborah the once over from the top of her permed dark hair down to her chest, where he pauses for a brief rest, and then on to her bare legs until he returns eyeball to eyeball. She smiles at him, and then like a master hypnotist, she pulls a subtle trick on our hapless little commander. As she smiles, she moves her eyes ever so slowly to the left and turns the wheel of her bike toward the family. Napoleon points left.

It's three now—eight hours past our seven a.m. embarkation time. Napoleon's men and women strip search the hippies in the men's and women's porta toilets, empty their packs on the ground, and shake and search for drugs. No luck. *Idiots*, I want to tell them, *do you honestly think any self-respecting drug dealer would disguise himself as a hippie? You should check our line. The two kids probably have a kilo of cocaine stashed in their underwear.*

By four, the commandant and his men call names from passports. Of course, they mispronounce each name so badly that all you can hear are passengers screaming, "Did you say Rohinsky? Abalafia? Fortunato? Wolbromsky?" Good thing it's hard to mess up a one-syllable name like Risk and a simple two-syllable name like Tobin, which Napoleon calls *Tubin*.

At four thirty, we finally board this ugly tub for a seventeen-hour cruise to Dubrovnik. A word or two about the ship's cuisine: They feed us one slice of baloney between two pieces of stale white bread for breakfast, lunch, and dinner. Deborah, the vegetarian, eats six slices of stale white bread over a seventeen-hour span of time.

At ten a.m., we arrive at the Dubrovnik harbor and disembark. By ten thirty, we're mobbed by a gaggle of screaming witches, each one shoving and pushing the one next to her. A fierce competition rages to convince us to stay by them in their "most-bootifulest," "most-no-money," "most bestest," "most-no-dirt," and "most-freest-toilet-paper" apartment. For me, it's a no-brainer—toilet paper wins out in a heartbeat. "Only if," Deborah adds, "the place is clean."

The old woman, a dead ringer for the cackling witch from *The Wizard of Oz*, leads us through narrow cobblestone streets until we arrive at her small, well-tended house. She shows us our apartment, a clean and compact room with a tiny kitchenette, a bedroom salon, and a bathroom—as promised, piled high with toilet paper.

"Gud?" she asks.

"Good," we answer.

It turns out the witch has a tall, rugged, retired sea captain for a husband. He speaks pidgin English, and he likes to talk, especially about Tito, the recently deceased dictator of Yugoslavia.

"Tito was strong man like ox—a man with hot blood. Womens loved him. For Tito, many girlfriends and many wives. Strong men like that—love much women." I have a sense he's including himself here. "He was our Papa. He showed us how to be man. Not care what peoples think. He say, 'I'm Tito. I do what I want.'

"Tito not scared from no one, not even Stalin. And everybody shake like little girl by him. When Tito rule, Croatia no fight with Serbia, and Serbia no fight with Slovenia. Catholics no kill Muslims, and no ones kills Jews. Not peace, no war. Sure, we hate Serbs and Muslims. Why not? No good people. But Tito, he said, 'We all Yugoslavs, we be one people.' He made sure no fights. Someone no agree with him, then bye-bye.

"When Tito die, country cry much tears. Our Papa's no more. Who take care of us? Who show us what to do? No Papa, no peace. Childrens will fight. Much blood will fall in my country. You Americans think, 'Good. Tito dead. Now freedom in Yugoslavia.' Your government is stupid. Think you know best about my people. What goin' to happen here worse than civil war in your country.

"We want to stay safe, not vote. Vote make worse. Many parties for each religion and for each place in Yugoslavia. Only care about himself. Tito was smart man. He knows soul of people. He understood fear and power keeps peoples together. Now, nation be like pizza pie. Many pieces. Each one eat his brother.

"You want eat? Most-best fish in world from Dubrovnik water. You must eat bass from sea. Octopus from Dubrovnik, most-long arm and most-best. Brim most-best but not most-best from bass. No go where tourist go. Go where boat is." He makes a circle with his hand and says, "Dis is big clock. Clock never change. You go two o'clock to big plaza. So many tourists. No good eat der. Now go five o'clock to water. Den go three o'clock and der, you find much good restaurant at four o'clock."

He takes me by the shoulders, turns my body toward his two o'clock, points to a cobblestone pathway, and like it's straight out of *The Wizard of Oz*, he says, "Follow da cobblestone road."

The cobblestone road slopes up. From the top of the hill, we have an unobstructed view of the calm, blue waters of the Aegean. At the horizon, where the sky and the sea merge, you can see fishing boats casting nets and pots. The sky is crystal clear, and the afternoon sun hangs like a big yellow balloon in the western sky. When you focus your eyes on the sea, you automatically blink from the bright rays that scatter in all directions like golden pixie dust sprinkled on water.

The cobblestone road transports us to our two-o'clock destination—the touristy town plaza where restaurant barkers compete for customers for their "most-best-food," "most-cheapest-most-best food," and "most-freshest-fresh-fish." Tourists in shorts and T-shirts snap photos of Roman arches and columns. They vie for a spot to pose in front of the domed obelisk bell tower with a sundial midway down its facade.

According to the captain's instructions, to get to the harbor we need to turn from two o'clock to five o'clock, which we calculate to be southeast, assuming you know where two o'clock is in an open plaza—which we don't. So Deborah asks for directions to the water, which is toward three o'clock if the obelisk is twelve o'clock.

In five minutes, we arrive at the harbor and notice an outdoor restaurant filled with loud locals wearing bibs imprinted with an image of a wide-open clamshell that looks like a toothless smile. Beer suds fly in all directions from fast-moving mugs used as props for dramatic emphasis—reminiscent of a great conductor, baton in hand, wildly gesturing to the strings, then to the horns, and then back to the strings. No one seems to notice or care about flying beer or the clam juice that drips down people's chins onto their bibs, where it gathers to form clam-juice reservoirs.

We find a more or less quiet spot in the right rear corner of the terrace. From here, we can watch the fishing vessels return to shore with the catch of the day. After we've spent a few minutes rehashing the humorous tale of the captain and his clock, the waiter approaches to take our order. For me, black sea bass on a bed of risotto, accompanied by a cherry tomato, black olive, and endive salad dressed with truffle-flavored olive oil, balsamic vinegar, and herbs. Deborah orders a goat cheese, lettuce, tomato, and fresh fig salad topped with roasted almonds and cashews. She chooses the special house dressing, a vinaigrette of walnut oil, lemon, honey, white balsamic vinegar, and fresh herbs and spices.

Ten minutes later, the waiter returns with our orders. What the eye sees and what the nose smells trigger the salivary glands to salivate and the taste buds to taste. If I were a still-life painter, I would resurrect on canvas the delicately charred black sea bass lying in repose next to the mixed salad of blood-red cherry tomatoes, on a bed of spear-shaped, light green endive lettuce crowned with the blackest of black olives.

Deborah's still life radiates a full spectrum of color—sun bright and purple figs with bright red interiors, snow-white flakes of goat cheese, slices of juicy, fire-engine red tomatoes lying on a divan of emerald green lettuce, capped with dark brown almonds and light-yellow cashews. This canvas of luscious colors begs the question, "Why would God invest so much beauty in a simple fig and a modest tomato? Why such visual delights if the purpose of these fruits and vegetables is merely to nourish the body?"

If I were a perfumer, I would capture the deep, musky aroma of truffles along with the pungent, fruity smell of olive oil. I would add a few drops of concentrated cilantro and parsley to create an earthy perfume that would liberate the wild gypsy in every woman.

From Deborah's dish, I would extract the sweet aroma of fig nectar, the tangy essence of tomato, and the grassy flavor of goat cheese. To that fragrant tincture, I'd add a few droplets of walnut oil to create a potpourri of scents that, when unleashed, would re-create the experience of Mother Nature herself bursting forth. These perfumes compel the same questions the still lifes posed: "Why was God so kind to grant us such alluring aromas?"

So, how did our respective meals taste? What tantalizes the nose, tempts the palate. What entices the eyes, sets the taste buds dancing. There's nothing more to add. And that was just the main course. Here's the pièce de résistance—homemade peanut butter ice cream, along with its partner in pleasure: a generous dollop of fig marmalade.

The waiter explains that, for maximum enjoyment, we should add a teaspoon of the marmalade, thick with generous pieces of red and yellow figs, to a spoonful of sweet, creamy peanut butter ice cream, flavored with a hint of vanilla. What you have is an over-the-moon combination of sweet and nutty-flavored ice cream enhanced by the simple pleasure of concentrated fig nectar and the honeyed taste of fresh figs. To this genius of food combining, I raise my cup in praise and gratitude.

Over the next four days, we challenge ourselves with exceedingly decadent, intensely purposeless activity: indulging ourselves in every excessive way possible with fig-everything pastries and ice cream crowned with a peak of whip cream—yes, there's fig ice cream in Dubrovnik, and yes, these scoops of creamy nectar achieve a point of pleasure beyond imagination—and fish, salads, and broiled and baked asparagus dishes with olive oil, and goat's cheese that might have brought tears of delight to my eyes if I were a more exuberant personality.

To recuperate from this physical strain on the digestive system, we find hidden beaches on the surrounding islands where you can lie au naturel on the warm sand and think about nothing other than what new iteration of indulgence one might partake of on this lonely beach. So, if Eros loosens the limbs and weakens the mind—which this god of all things delightful might very well do when one is in the grip of a pleasure-seeking state of mind—then all that's necessary is a roll to the right, greeted by a shift to the left, and what you get are delights more delicious than a snow-capped peak of whip cream atop a mountain of fig ice cream.

CHAPTER 13

Corfu:
September 15 to September 27

Joseph Campbell, author of *The Power of Myth*, wrote, "The goal of life is to make your heartbeat match the beat of the universe, to match your nature with nature." If we were to take the greatest spiritual leaders on an around-the-world exploration to find the one setting on earth they thought best suited to achieve a sense of oneness with nature, Corfu would be that place.

Corfu asks nothing less than a total surrender to its charms—to align your heart to this mountainous island of four million olive trees, six thousand rare wildflowers, and fifty-five species of orchids, all bathed in a light so pure, it's as if God Himself were directing multiple spotlights on every one of His creative works.

The boat docks in Corfu City next to a row of cruise ships that, by ten in the morning, have probably dumped a few thousand tourists on to the besieged Old Town of Corfu. There's Mildred from Milwaukee showing her friend Ethel a recently produced relic from the Golden Age of Greece when Socrates was querying his students. Throngs of tourists line up to purchase T-shirts emblazoned with a picture of an unshaven Anthony Quinn as Zorba the Greek from the 1964 movie of the same name. A miniature replica of Venus de Milo, topless, armless, and nearly bottomless, has the boys from Milwaukee jiving around and talking trash.

Unlike my nasty but subvocal judgments, Deborah's reaction to the tourists is overtly negative. They remind her of the good folks from West Virginia. She tells me, "I can't stand this. I want to denounce my citizenship. Let's go someplace where the only English we hear is the sound of our own voices." I don't know if it's the West Virginia flashbacks, or some insidious female demon that's oozing from her past, or what I fear most—she's in a Swedish frame of mind—but since we've left Dubrovnik, she's been distant, and distant for me is a trigger. Is Niels lurking in the shadows?

We head out of town to the first quiet village where we can observe—anthropologically—Corfu as it's been for hundreds of years. More authentic than Venus de Milo's plastic titties, but let's not kid ourselves, we'll never get to experience the Corfu behind the curtain, especially when we don't speak the language, don't know anyone who lives here, and, as a cynical traveler noted, to the impoverished local residents, we're nothing more than a traveler's cheque.

That quiet village is Krini, an eighteen-mile ride to the western side of Corfu. To get there, we have a brutal climb from sea level to an elevation of around 1,000 feet. The treacherous mountain road twists and turns up a steep incline. On the right side of the road, dense clusters of emerald moss sprout from the moist crags of the sheer cliffs. An ancient olive tree hangs precariously from the cliff face, held in place by a wild maze of roots buried deep within the damp crevices. When the road curves left, the sky-blue waters of the Ionian Sea dazzle the eye and distract the mind from the discarded rubbish strewn among the olive groves that hug the side of the road.

Salty sweat burns my eyes and drips down the sides of my cheeks; beads of moisture cover my arms and legs, and my heart echoes like a beating drum as I push myself up this torturous incline. Deborah is a hundred feet behind me, struggling with every rotation, barely able to keep her bike steady.

Trucks spewing exhaust fumes pass us on blind turns. I count five drivers who toss plastic bags, bottles, and an ashtray worth of cigarettes from their windows onto the side of the road. I feel the heat inside my body rise close to the boiling point—proof that this metaphor for rage is grounded in physical reality. I want to cry out to every mindless polluter, to every indifferent spoiler of God's creation, "Stop! This is the earth God gave us. Cherish it!"

Only sweat and struggle can discharge this inner fury. So, I do now what I did when I was a kid: I convert my anger into rocket fuel. Then, it was *Fuck you, Dad,* and I'd drive myself to achieve the goal he said I'd never reach. It worked then, and it will work now: I stand on the pedals, let out a powerful scream, and churn like a madman up the mountain. The effort releases the toxic feeling of hate and anger. I stop to wait for Deborah, who is about 150 feet behind me, struggling to catch her breath.

I feel tears welling up from some faraway place within myself.

As I watch her, grim-faced and determined, pushing against resistance, I know in my heart that she's my life partner, my fellow traveler in search of a deeper truth. Yet, at the dim periphery of consciousness, I sense a deep disquiet that I can't identify—a feeling of disconnect. With myself? With Deborah?

Deborah is now twenty feet from where I've stopped. I love her deeply. Yet I feel something separates us. Sweden? Niels? I fear she harbors some secret yearning she'll reveal only during her most intimate encounters with herself. With me, she can push up a mountain. But when the sun sets and the fading colors dazzle the senses, does she long to share that experience with Niels? Maybe this is the trade I have to make to be with a woman like Deborah: One moment I inhale joy and the next I exhale unease and insecurity.

Perhaps one among these wizened and gnarled olive trees standing by the side of this winding, narrow road has answers to these nagging questions of the heart. They all appear wise enough—like twisted wizards bent in prayer. I have a sense that if I were to join them in prayer and meditation, I might reach a place of understanding and depth. Just gazing at these venerate elders—who for five hundred years have stood as silent witnesses to wars won and lost, to the rise and fall of governments, and to progress and the destruction it's brought—is a reminder that all things pass.

As we ascend, women balancing jugs of water on their heads walk by the side of the road. Unlike most Westerners, who lead with their heads because that's where their energy lies, these women walk erect. Like a yoga master, their neck, spine, and head are in perfect alignment. The earthen jugs sit upright on a round, cloth base that encircles the top of their heads. As these women in black move, their hands rest at their sides, their jugs remain perfectly still, and there's not a whisper of water against the sides of their earthen vessels.

To most of us Westerners, these women are charming relics from the past—a Kodak moment worth capturing. What most of us victims of progress fail to see is that in their graceful, confident movements, these women are living examples of what it means to be in your body, to be in touch with the natural rhythm of movement. I'd like to train my body to walk like these women walk—in alignment with gravity, moving from my core, not from my head, with simplicity and an economy of motion.

From a cliff close to the road, we look down on the still, turquoise waters of the Ionian Sea. When I studied natural sciences in high school, we learned that the combined factors of the sun's position in the sky, the degree of sediment in the water, and the vantage point from which we view the sea all impact how the rods and cones in our eyes see color. What natural science doesn't explain is what part the imagination and the associative process contribute to this highly subjective visual experience.

Like falling madly in love, a scene this captivating grabs your soul, spins you around, and tosses any vestige of sense and reason into the vast blue sea below. Is this what Joseph Campbell meant when he challenged each of us to match our heartbeat with the heartbeat of the universe?

The citizens of Krini must love their tiny village. Here, in this stone-everything piece of heaven, you don't see abandoned trash or discarded bottles mindlessly dumped here and there. Nowhere on the geometrically patterned pathways that radiate from the town square like spokes on a bicycle wheel can you find errant pieces of paper scattered about. Thank God for Krini, and thank God for this testament to our better selves. We may have stumbled onto an oasis, a quiet refuge to quench our thirst for nature as God meant it to be—before He kicked Adam and Eve out of Eden for mucking up His pristine world.

Life goes well in Krini. Takes us only five minutes to find a family-owned tavern where we can eat, sleep, and hang out on their outdoor patio all day long and read, write, reflect, meditate, converse, stretch, eat, and say goodnight to the sun.

For now, though, we'll take a leisurely walk around this miniature mountain retreat, ringed by groves of olive trees. Krini overlooks the greenish-blue Ionian waters that the sultry Greek goddess, Io, swam across to escape from the lustful clutches of Zeus. Hence, the sea's name.

Three hundred people live in Krini. Twenty-five percent of the male population—all of whom have droopy mustaches and caps like Zorba wore—sit crowded together or linger about in front of the two local cafés. Four pairs of men compete in four games of backgammon. From their aggressive and stern demeanor, it would appear that this game of backgammon has the element of a take-no-prisoner gladiatorial contest.

To my associative mind, this town where the jarring groans of donkeys pierce the silence, where olive trees grow wildly, where sheep and goats graze on the fields next to the village has me sitting under the shade of an olive tree listening to Aristotle pontificate on math, physics, biology, metaphysics, and astronomy.

From several angles, Deborah takes photos of the town square's stone surface. She wants to replicate its multiple geometric patterns on the floor of our next house—wherever that might be. I'd like to miniaturize this intricate mix of ancient rocks, stones, pebbles, and flat limestone tiles. What you'd see would be subtle shades of beige stones of various sizes and shapes, interspersed with an occasional dab of reddish-brown for contrast. The asymmetric interplay of curves, circles, and straight lines at first glance appears to be a cacophony of stone. Yet, as your eyes rest on this rock formation, you sense the underlying harmony in this ageless family of limestone and shale.

It's now six thirty p.m. and we're hungry and tired. We return to our new home and settle into our cozy room with a large double bed, wood-paneled walls, and a flat, stone tile floor laid out in the same geometric pattern as the town square. To the right of our bed, there's a striking photo displaying splashes of the light spectrum as the sun slowly relinquishes its authority to the night.

By the time we arrive on the terrace, it's thirty minutes before sunset. We both order large Greek salads and two glasses of retsina, a Greek rosé that originates from the Golden Age of the Philosophers.

Retsina must be an acquired flavor because it's remarkably similar to what I imagine gum turpentine tastes like. It smells sweet and piney like turpentine and tastes like pine tree bark, not that I've ever dined on pine bark. Deborah suggests we follow the standard protocol of a wine connoisseur and spin it, inhale it, swirl it around our mouths, and then swallow it slowly. This way, we'll train our taste buds to acculturate to the foreign flavors of retsina. It works. Our palates begin to have a more pleasant relationship with this unfamiliar, rose-colored wine. So much so that we order a second and third glass.

The American poet Emily Dickinson wrote, "I'll tell you how the sun rose—a ribbon at a time." Michael Tobin, twentieth-century psychologist and traveler, writes, "I'll tell you how the sun sets on a clear night over the sea—like an enormous light bulb at the center of the horizon, this fiery orb projects golden rays in all directions as it descends into the sea."

From the vantage point of this outdoor patio, a direct ray of light skips along the water's inky surface until it arrives at the shore's edge. When your mind is at ease, you perceive the orange and yellow hues, the golden arch that floats above the setting sun, and the white light that emanates from the center of the fiery yellow globe.

In our normal frenetic lives, cut off from the cycle and rhythm of nature, the transition from light to darkness appears to change as rapidly as the flick of a switch. We all know in our minds that the sun sets "a ribbon at a time," but do we sense in our bones how the sun relinquishes its power moment by glorious moment as if it's the last hurrah of a fading flame?

Night is the time to surrender, to release our creative powers to our receptive and reflective natures. Like the moon that lacks the power to generate its own light and can only reflect light from the sun, nighttime—and, in particular, this first night in Krini—is perfectly suited for us to dig deep and reflect on the activities and experiences we accumulated during the light of day.

You don't just dive headfirst into a conversation as intense as this one turns out to be. You first sip wine; you point out a meteor—or is it a comet?—that traverses the sky in a blaze of light. You notice how the moonlight outlines the silhouettes of olive trees leaning into the mountainside. You make small talk about rock art, and how the local olive oil tastes. And then a question such as "Did you notice the garbage by the side of the road?" puts an end to the light conversation and pushes it toward the darker side.

"How could you miss it? It was everywhere," Deborah responds, and then follows with her standard refrain. "It is what it is."

"No shit. Like what can you expect from us humans? We're just unconscious bozos?"

"Is that what you hear me saying—like I don't give a damn? The only way is to rage against the injustices to prove that you care?"

"Not to prove you care. To show you care. You'd make an excellent Hindu. It's all karma. Right? Why didn't you tell Simone, 'It is what it is,' when she told us the story about her brothers? Or Jacob? I'm sure he would have appreciated hearing, 'It is what it is' from you. That would have tied a nice ribbon around his story. 'It is what it is, Jacob. Just accept your losses.'"

"What's this really about, Michael? Something's bothering you and it's got to be more than 'It is what it is.'"

"You want to know what's bothering me? I'm tired of having a

parallel meditative experience. I'm tired of being two observers holding hands. Since we've left Dubrovnik, you're not here. You're in a box
labeled *Detached*. Something's missing. I don't know if it's with us,
with me, or both. With you, everything's fine on the surface, and then
you drop a bombshell. I'm still shell-shocked. So, when I sense distance between us, I wonder if you're in Krini with me or in Sweden
with Niels. No doubt you and Guru Niels could play it-is-what-it-is
all day long."

I can see the "fuck you" forming on her lips, and she stops herself.

"No, Deborah. Say it. Tell me to go fuck myself. That way you'll be
real. No fooling me with sweetness and love, and then blindsiding me."

"Fine, if it will make you happy. Go fuck yourself. And go fuck all
of your paranoid assumptions. What the hell's wrong with you? Don't
you see I'm here and I'm not going anywhere? You say I live in a parallel universe you can't reach. Well, I can say the same about you. Your
restless brain never stops working. I never know what new idea or new
discomfort you're about to dump on me. Say what you want, but you're
no more predictable than I am."

The waiter approaches and we order another round of retsina. If
we're going to shellac each other, why not drink turpentine? Deborah
reaches for my hand. I don't resist. Deborah's occasional forays into her
hidden spaces may be part of the problem. It unravels me when I can't
find her. But there's also something in *me* that I can't reach, a piece of
me that nags from some unidentifiable region of my psyche.

The restlessness Deborah spoke of is no less intense now than when
we left Vermont. Actually, it's more intense. There have been so many
exquisite moments when I felt so connected to myself, to Deborah,
to the world around me. Yet, deep inside of me, something's missing.
Whatever it is that we're presumably searching for is as elusive now as
it's ever been. I'm scared we'll continue to accumulate amazing experiences and then realize we've been looking in all the wrong places, that
the pursuit of experiences is like the hunger for money—the more you
have, the more you crave.

Restlessness for what? To discover God, to merge with the Infinite?

What's the formula? Is there a precise number of deep meditations one must experience before the last vestiges of ego and self vanish? How many glorious sunsets must you be at one with to say that your heart beats with the heartbeat of the universe?

The questions sound absurd, as if we could mechanize and quantify the one and only path to the truth. To achieve enlightenment, Siddhartha followed the standard blueprint of his time: obliterate the self through fasting, meditation, and renunciation. He failed. Wherever he turned, he found himself. So he left the path of no-self to discover his true self.

He asked why have an individual self that is as unique as the lines on our hands and fingers if the spiritual goal is presumably to shed individuality and merge with the greater whole? Why is it that no matter how far we soar we always return to ourselves? Maybe that explains why at one moment I can feel so expanded and connected, and the next so alienated and confused. Some parts of me won't let me run away from myself. I think this is what Siddhartha's teaching us: We need to dig into our alienation and confusion as surely as losing ourselves in a dazzling sunset.

Calmer, the storm passing, I share the above thoughts with Deborah.

"You need to think less and trust more," she says. "Trust this journey will take us wherever we need to go. You're letting your mind take over. You're trying to squeeze answers before you're ready to hear them. We're not even halfway through the story and you want to write the ending."

With our third glass of retsina, we order sykomaida, a dessert made from phyllo dough, dried figs, almonds, orange, pepper, cinnamon, retsina, and ouzo—eight distinct personalities that surrender center stage for the greater good, like five NBA superstars whose motto is "Team first."

So it is on Team Sykomaida. Orange doesn't compete with fig, cinnamon doesn't knock out pepper, and ouzo doesn't overwhelm retsina. Yet, each flavor maintains its discrete personality. An interesting model on how to be yourself and be part of everything—like Deborah and I are now, on this quiet deck on the western edge of Krini, fully present, the tips of our fingers touching one another.

Everything is as it should be on this nearly moonless night of September 15. The stars are bright and visible against the clear black sky. I can feel the heat of Deborah's body next to mine and the Sykomaida Octet plays tasty music on my tongue. Nothing needs to change in this small slice of God's Universe.

Yet it will. Because everything always does. You know—it is what it is.

*   *   *

Over the next two days, we wander among the groves to find a soft spot to eat our cheese, olives, and hard-crusted local bread that looks remarkably like a Viking warship. The light beneath the trees is misty and subdued, the air is cool and refreshing. Here and there, penetrating rays of sunlight pierce the leaves like swords. All around us stands a quorum of ancient olive trees bent in submission before their maker. Or, then again, perhaps they bow to us in a gesture of hospitality. "Come, my dear friends, enter our sacred space and break bread with us. One request, though: Please leave no trace behind."

We accept their kind invitation and find a soft, grassy spot at the foot of the most venerable of these kind hosts. With our backs against the Old One's gnarled and twisted trunk, we begin our picnic lunch. Perfect. Grab the moment; squeeze the juice out of it. Partake of it all: the wine, the cheese, the olives, the bread, the trees, the light . . . the unexpected.

The first book I ever read was Alice's Adventures in Wonderland. *To a six-year-old child—especially one who liked to hang out in his imaginary theater where heroes defeated villains and the underdog always prevailed—the Mad Hatter, the March Hare, the Queen of Hearts, and, of course, the Cheshire Cat were all new, wonderful additions to my make-believe cast of characters. Especially the Cheshire Cat—that mischievous, grinning devil that talks philosophy and then disappears from trees and reappears as rapidly as a name stuck on the tip of your tongue.*

"Hello."

"Did you hear someone say hello?" Deborah asks.

"I thought I did."

"Hello." We hear a slight giggle this time. Again, we look and can't find anyone.

"Hello, hello." The voice seems to be above us. We look among the branches of the trees, but no one's hanging on a limb like the Cheshire Cat.

"Ha, ha. You no see me. I see you."

"Come out. Come out wherever you are and let us see you," Deborah responds, like Dorothy to the giggling Munchkins.

"Me here, me there, me everywhere."

"Are you God?" I ask.

"No. Got what? You got? See me up in tree. Head up."

We look directly above us and there, standing on a thick branch, is our Cheshire Cat—a skinny little man in suspenders, a flannel shirt like a logger would wear, and pants fit for a short, chubby man. He wears a beat-up Panama hat that leans toward his right eye like Humphrey Bogart in *Casablanca*. He has the lithe body of a nine-year-old and a face as sundried as a raisin.

When in Wonderland, do like the *Wonderlands*, so I say, "Why are you in a tree when you can be with me and she?"

And then, just like that, he jumps and lands feet first with a smile and a bow. "Me Leonidas. You?"

"Michael, Deborah. Leonidas, how do you know English?"

"Know Engliss 'cause worked on beach selling drink to tourist with no clothes. Wife said no good for Leonidas to look at girls all day. I tell her, 'No look, just sell.' She no believe. Make me work now in Krini town. Bring grapes and olives to store. Up before sun and work hard. Now day done, and I tink in tree."

"Was your wife right?"

"No understand."

"Did you look at girls?"

"What you tink? Leonidas not man? Wife right, but she fat and boss like goat."

"Why do you need to think in the trees?"

"Olive tree smart. Tree be on Corfu for long time and see much tings. Tree tell me, 'Leonidas, listen to fat wife. She know.' Leonidas want to run from her bossy face, but tree say, 'No go, Leonidas.' So, I no go. In tree, Leonidas feel good. Tree tell Leonidas, 'Talk to people on floor.' Most tourists hear hello from tree and run. Not you. You no 'fraid. You Leonidas's friends." We invite Leonidas to eat with us. He graciously accepts.

For the next hour, he tells us every Corfu family has a male member named Spiro, after the island's patron saint and miracle worker, Saint Spiridon. "Much day," he informs us, "Leonidas go church, light candle, make incense. Me talk to Saint Spiridon. Leonidas know Saint listen. He friend and he watch me, fat wife, and three childrens. When Leonidas not work or be in tree, me be in church. You go church?"

"It's not our thing," Deborah answers.

"What mean not our ting?"

"Oh, sorry. We don't go to church."

"Why you no go church?"

"This is our church—the beautiful island of Corfu. God is here."

"God on Corfu, but son Jesus and son Spiridon live in church. God tell them speak to people, so people have mens to speak to, not just air."

"Then why do you speak to the trees?"

"Because my papa speak and his papa speak, so Leonidas speak. My papa teached me to listen to tree. All on Corfu know Leonidas talk to tree. Peoples come wit problem and want Leonidas to ask tree to help. Leonidas do, and people better. Leonidas speak to tree for you?"

I think for a moment if I should have Leonidas ask the tree one of my burning questions. I dismiss it as too complicated. Deborah turns to me and says, "Let's ask the tree if we'll have children."

Leonidas leans his ear against the tree and presumably whispers our question into the tree trunk. In a moment, he resurfaces with a big toothless grin on his face and proudly proclaims that we will have "much childrens, and childrens have much childrens."

Like so many places around Krini, the area close to the path abounds with a richness of flora nestled within and around the ubiquitous olive tree. Because these august elders create such vivid and direct associations to ancient Greek and biblical times, I've overlooked that enduring symbol of mourning, the tall, dark green cypress that towers above the groves like a needle-shaped spire.

The source for how the cypress became a symbol of mourning can be found in Greek mythology: Cyparissus, a handsome lad and the darling of the god Apollo, accidentally kills an innocent deer. This sensitive boy is so grief-stricken that he asks the gods to let him weep and mourn forever. In response to his soulful pleas, the gods turn him into a cypress tree whose running sap symbolizes Cyparissus's tears. I make a note to myself to hug this tragic symbol of loss whenever I pass a cypress tree.

Unlike their ravaged urban cousins dying from Dutch elm tree disease, the flourishing, green-leaved elms of Cyprus—their forked trunks joined at the waist like Siamese twins—shoot toward the sky in tandem like two parallel pillars. On a hill to the right of the mighty elms, the widespread limbs of the smaller Judas trees—known as the tree on which that turncoat Judas Iscariot hanged himself—twist around each other in a spaghetti-like maze of green and brown branches. The last of their bright pink and white blossoms blanket the ground beneath them, reminding us of those glorious days of late spring, when Judas proclaims his shame in a riot of colors.

Along the path, the scents of wild parsley, sage, rosemary, and thyme compete for the attention of our olfactory bulbs, those intelligent little centers in the brain that sort and delineate the multitude of aromas, like the piquant, woody odor of rosemary or the warm and lemony flavor of thyme. Scattered among the wild herbs, the lemon, fig, orange, and tangerine trees offer an abundance of multicolored fruit waiting for us to pluck them from branches bent from the weight of their heavy produce. The figs seem the ripest among this varied group of blossoming fruit trees, so we pick a few for our immediate pleasure. We're not disappointed—ripe to the moment, honeycomb sweet, and as mouthwatering as you would hope a fresh-picked fruit would taste.

The variegated autumn showstopper that sprouts from the cracks and fissures in the rocks, and from the dirt and dried manure on this well-trodden path, is the cyclamen, a spade-shaped flower colored in pink, lavender, and white, and connected to its emerald green leaves by long, olive green stems. Competing with the cyclamen for attention are the wild crocuses that mirror its brilliant tri-colored scheme with a similar, yet somewhat muted version of those same three colors.

Tossed between the cyclamens and crocuses, left in the spaces separating the fig and orange trees, and abandoned beneath the olive trees, lie the overwhelming evidence of how man communes with nature—those ever-present products of modernity: plastic wrappers, wine and beer bottles, and paper plates.

As we ramble down this footpath, a woman of indeterminable age, dressed in the traditional black garb of a mourner, approaches us. From the spryness of her body to her lined and leathered complexion, this woman could be anywhere between forty and sixty. Given her drab, painful appearance, she may be mourning for her husband, her parents, or any of her deceased relatives from this century or a previous one. I guess the shelf life for grief in this part of the world spans multiple generations.

On her head, she balances a water jug with the same precision and ease that we've observed in the other women in black—eyes focused forward, neck and head straight, shoulders squared. This young-old woman is an ancient mourner who moves with the grace of a gazelle.

Behind her march an unruly flock of speckled goats and unshorn sheep. Here and there, a boisterous goat and an unmanageable lamb dart in and out of the row. An ugly mutt nips at their heels to force his undisciplined flock in line. As chaotic as it appears, there seems to be a primordial instinct to follow the leader, namely our water-carrying woman in black.

At the rear of the procession walks a teenage girl of around sixteen, in jeans and a T-shirt. In her left hand, she holds a long, straight stick that she uses to coax a stray sheep or goat back into the convoy. In her right hand, she carries a boom box blasting the Bee Gees' "Stayin' Alive," from the soundtrack of *Saturday Night Fever*. I half expect the flock to form a horizontal row, like in the disco scenes. And like dancers in a chorus line, the flock kicks up its heels and jumps up and down in tune to the pounding rhythm that could bring the dead to life. Picture a goat—say the brown billy with white splotches and large gray horns—making moves like John Travolta.

It's impossible to stand still to the pulsating beat of "Stayin' Alive." So, as the girl passes, Deborah grabs my hand and we do some serious disco dancing on this makeshift dance floor overflowing with fresh sheep and goat shit. I spin her around, pull her toward me, and we pass our arms across each other's shoulders. We separate momentarily, then slide and groove toward one another. The moment Deborah reaches me, I grab her by the waist, and she bends backward. We met on a disco floor in Keene, New Hampshire; we fell in love moving to the beat of the Rolling Stones' "You Can't Always Get What You Want." I'd like to die together, dancing to "Stayin' Alive."

The girl stares at us wide-eyed for a few seconds and then continues on her way, lighting up the trail with the Bee Gees.

The following day, we're having lunch outside. On the two tables to our right, men with drooping mustaches engage in a spirited game of backgammon. A bent old woman in black, with prominent chin whiskers and gaping holes where teeth once stood, sits on a wicker chair next to the door. She weaves an intricate bouquet of red and white flowers interlaced with fresh basil and rosemary.

A young boy dressed in tight red shorts and a Bob Marley T-shirt

approaches us to take our orders. We order two moussakas. Deborah
explains to him we don't want meat. He looks perplexed until she
makes the *bah-bah* sound of a sheep, shakes her head side to side, and
says the Greek word for no, ουχί, which sounds like *oshi*.

"Ah, no want *seep*. No problem."

From the corner of my eye, I see the old lady observing the interaction with the boy, who I assume is her grandson. She smiles sweetly
in our direction and then slowly gets up out of her chair and approaches Deborah. She pats her on her head, kisses her on the forehead, and
hands her the bouquet as a gift.

Do you accept it for what it appears to be—a loving gesture from a
generous woman? Or, do you interpret it as an understandable attempt
by a poor woman to sell a local handicraft? If it's merely a kindness on
her part and you offer money, you insult her. It's like you're exchanging
her loving pat on the head for your patronizing one.

Deborah extends her hand to the woman's and says the Greek
word for thank you, "Ευχαριστώ," pronounced *efharisto*. The woman
sees that Deborah's eyes are welling up with tears and she strokes the
side of her face, then smiles and goes back to her chair.

"Do you think I should have given her money?" Deborah asks.

"No, this was her way to express gratitude."

A few hours later, as we wander around the fields close to Krini, a cackling voice calls us from behind an olive tree. Another old woman, this
one with a basket of dark purple grapes resting on her lap, sits under
the tree eating her grapes and spitting out the seeds. She motions us to
join her. She smiles, laughs, hugs Deborah, and then takes her by the
hand and leads us down a path to her vineyard.

She hands both of us a bundle of grapes and gestures for us to sit
on the ground with her and partake of her gift. Her generosity touches
Deborah. The grapes are sweet, juicy, and highly addictive. We finish
them and she quickly brings us two more bunches for our enjoyment.
She smiles and says, "Goot, no?" Deborah answers, with the Greek
word for *yes*, "Ναί."

The woman flashes us another toothless grin and again asks, "Goot?" Without waiting for an answer, she extends her hand palms up toward Deborah in the universal gesture for money. As if that nonverbal message weren't clear enough, she rubs her thumb repeatedly across the fingers of her right hand, demanding her money now.

We're seated in a family-owned restaurant in Mirtiotissa called Spiro's. The restaurant, a favorite for both tourists and locals, stands at the edge of a beach that Lawrence Durrell called the most beautiful in the world. I haven't visited every beach on the globe, and I doubt Lawrence Durrell did, but I agree Mirtiotissa is majestic. This sandy cove, bounded on three sides by sheer, tree-lined cliffs, looks out on water that seems to change from lavender to turquoise with every back-and-forth motion of the waves.

The restaurant is a hodgepodge of Greek and Western culture thrown together by a local with an identity crisis or a Westerner who's still finding his place in the world. On the walls hang a mélange of touristy photos that includes a red double-decker bus passing Trafalgar Square and a photo of the Acropolis at sunset. But what really throws class out the window and invites kitsch in its place is an outrageously tacky, absolutely dreadful, paint-by-numbers representation of Mirtiotissa Beach that would cause Lawrence Durrell to scream in horror.

Here, in this chaotic restaurant, a constant battle rages between the rock and roll favored by the Western tourists and the traditional Greek folk music preferred by the locals. At Spiro's, the winner isn't the guy who hits first, but the one who's first to the jukebox. From the back-and-forth discord of hard rock and haunting folk songs, I'd say it's pretty much a draw.

Amid all this noisy chaos, little kids run around taking and delivering orders while Papa, Mama, and Grandma are in the kitchen preparing moussaka, grilling meat, frying fish, tossing salads, and boiling octopus. The place is hopping. The kids are running, the music is blasting, the cultures are clashing, and at the table next to us, a woman is whining about her undercooked fish.

To whom, you might ask. Well, first to her diplomat husband, the only male in the restaurant with a tie and a jacket. Second, to anyone in earshot. I mean, she is looking from side to side to elicit sympathy. And third, to the twelve-year-old, thoroughly bewildered boy who brought her order of fried fish and salad.

"Young man," she says to the boy with the curly black hair, olive skin, and big brown eyes, "I'm quite disappointed with this fish. One can see that it has not been properly cooked."

"Huh?"

"Obviously," she says, "you haven't learned to speak or understand English. Bring this back to the chef and tell him it's undercooked."

"No understand."

To her husband, and to anyone else who is in earshot, she says, "How do these people expect to get ahead if they speak such poor English?"

Deborah leans in and asks, "May I help?"

"Do you speak Greek?"

"No. Excuse me for saying this, but you need to speak English in a way that a non-English speaker will understand. Would you like me to show you?"

"Be my guest. Why should I care if you dumb down your English for these people?"

Deborah smiles at the boy, points to the fish, and says, "Fish need more cook. Please bring to kitchen. Thank you."

The boy picks up the woman's plate and says, "Understand now. No cook 'nough. Right?"

"Yes," Deborah replies.

"I see you know how to talk to the natives," the woman remarks. "How did you learn that?"

"When I was a student at Wellesley, I spent my junior year at the Sorbonne. I traveled to places where people spoke very poor English."

"You went to Wellesley and the Sorbonne—very impressive.

I graduated from Smith. Wellesley was my first choice, but I didn't get accepted. I'm sure it's because I'm from Connecticut. You have a Southern accent. Where are you from?"

"I'm from West Virginia. That's why I got in, and you didn't. Not many West Virginians apply to Wellesley, and, of course, they lower their standards for those of us from impoverished backgrounds. That's probably another reason I can speak to the 'natives.' I was once a 'native' myself." She then switches to a West Virginia accent and says, "Sure 'nuf had trouble understandin' you Yankee girls. My people never talk fancy like yourn."

The diplomat's wife says, in her most Katharine Hepburn, perfectly refined voice, "It's quite impressive how you've raised yourself above your circumstances."

"Thank you. You're so right. I'm also from a poor Arab-American family. Same goes for Michael. He's from an immigrant Jewish family from Ukraine and he has a PhD in psychology. God bless America and the opportunities it's given people like us."

"Well, yes, I agree. Thank you for your help. The next time I converse with the locals, I'll do so in simple declarative sentences they'll understand."

"Good for you," Deborah says with a refined Southern drawl.

Man, do I love that girl's hot sauce.

Greece:
September 28 to October 4

The ancient Greeks—primarily Aristotle—taught us how to think:

Logically.

From a major premise, a hypothesis, to specific logical proofs. (Deductive Reasoning)

From specific observations to general conclusions. (Inductive Reasoning)

From a cause to an effect. (Linear Cognition)

Without Aristotle, there'd be no scientific progress—what we call left-brain analytical thinking—that method by which we observe, question, hypothesize, theorize, test, and categorize. To reason in an Aristotelian sense, i.e., to gain control over our environment, we must step back from our three-dimensional world of objects so we can observe, analyze, and ultimately progress based on new understandings.

Before diving into the who, what, and where of our four-day journey from Patras to Athens, let me first share our general conclusions based on specific observations (Inductive Reasoning). They are:

1. The food is inedible.
2. The modern architecture is forgettable.
3. The ancient ruins are regrettable.
4. The bicycling is more or less acceptable.
5. The one serendipitous encounter is incredible.

To remain true to the Aristotelian process of Inductive Reasoning, we need to ask, "Upon which proofs (data points) are these general conclusions based?"

To answer, let's use the Aristotelian hierarchical structure of the modern written outline to describe the first three of five categories:

I. Greek Cuisine
   a. Tasteless
   b. Repetitive
   c. Swimming in cheap olive oil—greasy, soggy, unhygienic
   d. Lacking a unique cultural identity like pizza and
      croissant

II. Modern Architecture
   a. At best, functional
   b. Gray boxes and rectangles
   c. No curves or other aesthetic touches
   d. Depressing—absent of any semblance of creativity,
      devoid of human spirit

III. The Ruins
   a. Ubiquitous—Wherever you turn, there's a pile of stones
      with an inscription stating that 2,000 years ago, a
      fortress once stood here.
   b. Unless you are a student of ancient Greek history, have a
      formidable imagination, or like to wear togas and quote
      Plato, a pile of rocks or the remaining one percent of a
      2,500-year-old wall is nothing more than a pile of rocks.
   c. What do the rocks tell us?
        i. Very little other than that empires rise and fall
        ii. Where we come from is merely a hair's breadth
            from this same ignominious fate
        iii. That after five minutes of rock gazing, my brain
             shuts down

d. What else do the rocks tell us?
  i. Look elsewhere: Broken buildings don't define a culture; transcendent ideas do.
  ii. Look elsewhere: Platonic philosophy, Socratic reasoning, and Aristotelian logic inform how we think, how we investigate our physical world, and how we point our moral compass.
  iii. Look elsewhere: Greek mythology maps the way to the archetypal regions of the psyche where we wage timeless inner battles.
  iv. Look elsewhere: Embedded within the structure of contemporary theater and architecture are the classical prototypes developed during the Golden Age.

We ride along the quiet, hilly coast road marred by potholes, bumps, and broken pavement. To ride safely over this obstacle course, we need to twist and turn from side to side to avoid the next hole in the road, and the one after that, and . . . A momentary lapse in concentration and the bike tumbles, a spoke breaks, the gear shift falls, a tire punctures, and you may be looking at any number of possible breaks and bruises.

Unlike the roads in France, the Greek roads don't ease you into the slope by zigzagging around a steep mountain. You power your way straight into the incline while negotiating the ever-present gaping hole that appears on average every three to five feet.

Deborah suffers behind me, cursing the pervasive holes and the murderous slopes. A particularly nasty road brings out the killer.

"Listen, you son of a bitch, you won't beat me," I hear her mutter.

You animate the road, see it as your mortal enemy, and then crush it. Deborah dismounts, glares down the twenty-degree slope she just conquered, and gives a two-handed, middle-finger salute to her defeated foe.

The Greek roads pass through the poorest, saddest, and drabbest towns imaginable. The only remaining residents are emaciated dogs, old women in black, and ancient men sitting in silence drinking coffee and smoking hand-rolled cigarettes. Perhaps the young folks are in the fields harvesting the grapes, or in some regional school far from their dying villages, or perhaps neither. More likely, in an act of self-preservation, they've moved to Australia—say, to Melbourne, where 400,000 Greek immigrants live.

On our way from Patras to Athens, we stop at the beach resort of Akrata, and in the ancient cities of Corinth and Mycenae. As we push our loaded bikes around a town's streets and alleys in search of a restaurant and a place to stay, we consistently bump into several curious and helpful individuals. Curious: locals with limited English, eager to know where we've been and where we're going. Helpful: always ready to recommend a place to eat and sleep—invariably owned by a family member.

"Want good eat?"

"Yes."

"Want good sleep?"

"Yes."

"Yiorgos take you to best place." Of course, Yiorgos's uncle owns "best" restaurant and his aunt runs "best" guesthouse. And, of course, the moussaka is cold, the omelet tastes rancid, the room has no toilet paper, the faucets fall off, the water leaks, the roaches follow you into the bedroom, and the bed sags in the middle where the springs once were.

Deborah insists we spend three nights in Corinth. She wants to take day trips to Argos, Mycenae, Nafplio, and Epidaurus to see more broken-down temples, unidentifiable bathhouses, and the one remaining stone of the home of a wealthy merchant—a most likely patron at Aphrodite's Palace of Pleasure, the finest whorehouse in all of ancient Greece.

We wander around Corinth until we stumble on a relatively decent guesthouse a block away from the water. No cockroaches, the faucet doesn't come off in your hand, and toilet paper is included in the price. Inflation's out of control during Jimmy Carter's presidency, and thanks to my friend Zandy, who suggested we invest in inflation-proof bonds, we actually have more money after four and a half months of traveling than when we left. That minor diversion is just to say that we'll splurge tonight at Corinth's finest restaurant—a semi-touristy tavern by the sea.

The interior of the restaurant has an intelligent feeling about it, with its rough stone floor, olive-wood tables, and somber black-and-white portraits of mustached, leathery fishermen laying nets, preparing lines, and cleaning fish. There's an empty round table toward the rear, next to where an attractive, intelligent-looking thirty-something with black hair sits alone reading one of my favorite books, Sheldon Kopp's *If You Meet the Buddha on the Road, Kill Him.*

This is a meant-to-be moment I can't let pass. So, as I sit, I say to him, "I love that book. I've read it many times."

He looks up, smiles, and replies with a slight Greek accent, "Isn't that a coincidence." He extends his hand and says, "I'm Solomon."

We introduce ourselves and Deborah says, "The gods must have arranged this meeting. Come sit with us." The coincidence doesn't end with Sheldon Kopp's book. My first name in Hebrew is Solomon (Shlomo in Hebrew; Solomon in English). He and I are thirty-four and we're both Jewish. All three of us practice psychotherapy—Solomon's a psychiatrist studying psychoanalysis in Athens, where he lives.

He tells us he often visits Epidaurus, an ancient Greek city close to Corinth, which was once known far and wide as a powerful healing center. He visits the Temple of Asclepius's ruins in Epidaurus for inspiration and courage. Asclepius was the son of Apollo and the god of healing. The healing symbol the medical profession adopted is Asclepius's staff carved in the shape of a twisted snake.

Solomon tells us he's researching an article for a Greek psychoanalytical journal on the dualism of Eros and Thanatos in Freudian Theory, which, he adds, is an exercise in futility since the journal will reject it. "Too controversial for the True Believers."

Much of my doctoral work was about proving the fallacy in Freud's dualistic thinking. So, to discover another crazy fluke, especially one as esoteric as this, is more than a bit freaky. It's been ten months since I convinced my doctoral committee that Freud got it wrong—that Eros and Thanatos, or life and death, are not the irreconcilable opposites that Freud claimed they were.

"So, are you a Freudian?" I ask.

"Do you know the Jewish prayer, the Shema?" he answers.

"Yes. Hear, O Israel, the Lord our God, the Lord is One. Why the question?"

"It's 'The Lord is One' part that troubles me. It doesn't fit with Freud's dualism. Freud needed to kill God to prove oneness was a myth. Not enough space in Freud's universe for God and a self-denying Jew like him. My problem: I'm more of a believing Jew than an orthodox Freudian. That doesn't sit well with my teachers, especially the Jewish ones."

I sense there's a subtext here, that we're not just dealing with an intellectual dilemma. Feels like we're about to touch on core issues of identity and religious commitment—a far more threatening discussion for me than proving that Freud fried his brains on cocaine and then theorized that life and death are core dualities.

"Solomon," Deborah says, "I'm curious how a committed Jew goes to a Greek temple for inspiration and courage."

"Because I'm Greek and Jewish. My soul and intellect are in both worlds."

His Jewish-Greek roots extend to the third century B.C.E. His ancestors were part of the Greek Jewish community called the Romaniotes, a proud and distinct sect. The Romaniotes never adopted the Greek gods, but they did embrace Hellenistic ideas about philosophy and the sciences.

"Maimonides, the greatest Jewish philosopher of all time and a doctor, was Socratic to his core. As a Greek doctor and a classically trained thinker, my place for inspiration and courage is the Temple of Asclepius."

"Why do you need courage?" she asks.

"To take on Freud and his anti-Jewish ideas, which is why the Institute will reject me."

He asks me about my Jewish background. I tell him I've been in a synagogue once in twenty years, and that was last Yom Kippur when Deborah insisted I go. I tell him about my escape and Deborah-the-shiksa's profound experience.

"Some rabbis say that a 'shiksa' like Deborah might bear the soul of a Holocaust victim." He turns to Deborah and says, "If Yom Kippur was that meaningful for you, then you may be a reincarnated Jew. So many of our people were murdered during the war that the only reason a Greek would want to convert has got to be because his reincarnated soul demands it."

He tenses his forehead; his eyes blink rapidly, and he exhales deeply. "Do either of you know what happened to the Greek Jews during the War?"

"No," we both reply.

He tells us that the Nazis wiped out the once-vibrant Jewish community of Salonika—96 percent of the 43,000 Jewish citizens were murdered. A final solution like none other. His father grew up there and left when he was eighteen to study in Athens. He married Solomon's mother, an Athenian Jew, and remained in Athens. During the war, they escaped to the Italian-occupied section of Greece until the Allies defeated Italy and the Nazis replaced the Italians. His parents spent the rest of the war fighting with the Greek partisans.

"After the war, my father discovered the fate of his parents and his entire extended family. The Nazis murdered every member of his family, either in the gas chambers of Auschwitz, Majdanek, or Sobibor, or on the crowded trains that brought them to the death camps. My grandfather, Solomon, my namesake, was the one exception. He died in the Sobibor uprising.

"I grew up in a house of mourning. My father says Kaddish for over forty relatives. My mother's full-time job is to console her tortured husband. I'm not like you. If I turned from Judaism, I'd feel the eyes of my murdered relatives burning a hole in my back. I wanted to run from the guilt, from the burden of being a Jew, from the eternal suffering, but I couldn't, or I wouldn't, and now, I no longer want to. I'm proud to be a Jew."

I didn't grow up surrounded by apparitions from the past. There were no photos of family ghosts reminding me who I am and where I come from. He could hardly say what I could say—that for me, Judaism was irrelevant, a meaningless impediment, and, occasionally, a hateful and shameful association. I think of the incident with the Holocaust survivor, Mr. Farago, when my mother punished me for making fun of his Polish accent. I was ashamed that this foreigner, this weak victim, this man who didn't know who Willie Mays was, was a Jew just like me.

"Michael, the difference between you and me is that you escaped from the synagogue on Yom Kippur and didn't feel guilt. Despite what most American psychologists claim, guilt can remind you of who you are and what you're running from. For some, it's the spark that ignites a search for depth and meaning."

I burn at Solomon's description of Freud as a self-hating and self-rejecting Jew. Not because it's not true about Freud—but because I know it is true about me. Since I've been a child, I've been running from my Jewish identity. The question is why. Why reject a part of oneself? Why be so ashamed of being a Jew, especially the weak Jew I projected onto Mr. Farago? Why do I despise Woody Allen and his portrayals of the neurotic New York City Jew? I cringe the moment I hear his whiny, depressing voice. Why did I feel such discomfort when a guy walked into the café below my Rutland, Vermont, office wearing a yarmulke? I felt like screaming, "He and I are not the same!"

But now, four months into this journey, I don't want to run anymore.

Mykonos:
October 5 to October 15

To fall in love with Mykonos is to fall in love with being lost. Enter any one of its many twisted cobblestone streets and you're trapped in a dazzling labyrinth of whiteness from which there appears to be no exit. Lawrence Durrell called Mykonos a nightmare.

Perhaps it is, if being lost in a conglomeration of ghost-like sameness paralyzes your brain and unnerves your sense of Aristotelian order, then yes, this could be "a flaring nightmare of whiteness." Like a nightmarish acid trip when you don't know where you are, how you got there, and where you're going, and your thoughts race like a stampede of wild stallions. Then yes, that experience of being trapped—for you—would most definitely be a nightmare.

Unless...

You let go. Of control. Of needing answers now. Of expectations. And...

You embrace what is. You let your mind soar. You let the unexpected happen.

You trust.

Then the flaring nightmare of whiteness transforms into a magical maze of joy. And you fall madly in love with not knowing where you are.

Welcome to the mystical madness of Mykonos.

*   *   *

The ferry, as expected, leaves Athens four hours late for the five-hour trip to Mykonos. We arrive at the port at five p.m. and head for the least touristy restaurant we can find. We find a tavern by the water. At the entrance, sunning himself, sits a great white pelican with the coolest tuft of white hair above his narrow eyes and his long pink bill. He looks like a swan in desperate need of a nose job.

I kneel to talk to him. Why not? He's blocking the way like he owns it. Plus, he seems quite comfortable with the human species. I'd like him to step aside so we can pass without ruffling his feathers.

I bend down, focus my eyes on his, and say, "Hey, Mr. Buster, hope you're having a nice day. I sure am. Sun's out, no clouds, temperature's just right. I'd call it a perfect day for doing nothing. You agree?" (I call him Mr. because he seems very male to me and I want to treat him with respect, and buster like, "Hey, buster, you're blocking the way.")

Maintaining strong eye contact with him, I ask, "Hey, Mr. Buster, do you mind moving so me and my woman can pass by?"

Mr. Buster turns his beak in my direction and looks at me with his squinty eyes and—*sort of*—says, "Whatever."

A good-looking couple, probably Americans from their clothes and accent, sit at a nearby table watching me talk to Mr. Buster. They're both laughing. The guy throws me a piece of bread and says, "See if this will get him to move."

"Brilliant idea. You obviously have more experience with pelicans than I do."

I take the bread, put it close to Mr. Buster's beak, and then back off a bit. Mr. Buster gets up, follows me to where I place the bread, plops down, and swallows it whole. Cathy and Matt from Monterey, California, invite Deborah and me to join them.

Maybe because Mr. Buster is our matchmaker, or maybe because Matt and Cathy are the first intelligent Americans we've met on this journey, or maybe because they're both serious practitioners of TM, or because they're both artists and they see things differently than two psychologists and that makes for interesting perspectives—whatever the reason or reasons may be, there's instant chemistry between us.

Together, we look for rooms. On the outskirts of the village, at water's edge, we find a freshly painted white stucco house with blue shutters and doors. Continental breakfast included.

The owner, Amari, an ex-Ethiopian diplomat under the deposed former Emperor Haile Selassie, is a tall, regal man in his midfifties. With a few well-placed questions from Deborah and me, we learn that a violent political party, the Derg, murdered a significant portion of his family during the Qey Shibir, the Ethiopian Red Terror campaign during the 1970s. He tells us the Dergs assassinated over 750,000 innocent civilians. Amari's a formal man, not used to showing emotions, yet a trained eye can sense the suffering and loss barely beneath the surface.

After we unpack, all four of us go outside to sit by the water. Cathy asks, "How did you do that? In a heartbeat, he was ready to tell you his entire life story."

"Did you notice his expression when he told us he was from Ethiopia?" Deborah asks. They both reply no. "His gaze shifted downward. You could see his chin quiver, and his voice became softer. All signs of sadness. I had a sense he wanted us to probe further."

"If he didn't want us to ask," I add, "he would have changed the subject. It's happened a lot on this trip. We seem to bump into people traumatized by war. They need to talk about their pain, and we need to listen. Their horror is personal, but it touches each of us."

We tell Cathy and Matt about Le Clown, Simone, Jacob, and Julian. Through tears, Deborah describes Simone's story in detail. Cathy continuously wipes moisture from her cheeks. Matt looks stunned.

"How do you listen to these stories and not break down?" Cathy asks.

"My answer may sound strange to you," Deborah says, "but I felt a sense of reverence when I heard Simone's and the others' stories. Like I was participating in something far more than a catharsis. More like a holy ritual that we were invited to participate in." But then, Deborah stops, cups her eyes with her hand, and sobs.

Cathy and Matt listen like meditators. Total focus. Their eyes are riveted on Deborah; their parallel expressions say, "I'm with you. Your words touch me." Both seem to understand that the comfort Deborah needs now is space and respect. Moments pass.

Deborah lifts her head and says, "Thank you. I didn't realize how much I've been holding on to. I feel their stories so deeply like I went through each of their traumas myself. I feel such love for each of them."

"I'm speechless," Cathy says, her eyes welling up with tears.

Matt laughs. Cathy shifts her gaze to Matt and then back to both of us. "Even when I'm speechless, I speak. I once heard about a Jewish myth that says you're allotted X amount of words at your birth, and when you exhaust your supply, you leave this world. It's a good thing I'm a meditator."

I glance at Cathy and Matt. They look like a California dream couple—blond, athletic, with striking blue eyes. They have this open-to-the-world vibe about them. Straight out of Ram Dass's book *Be Here Now*—when you learn to listen, everyone's the guru.

"Enough about us," Deborah says. "It's your turn to bare your souls."

"You're a tough act to follow," Cathy says. "Our lives are so mundane compared to yours. We're just two struggling artists trying to bring a bit of creativity to the world. Matt stares at a rock and sees its soul. I trip out over color."

"What does that mean?" I ask Matt. "To see the soul of a stone?"

"This may sound strange," Matt says, "but sometimes, I'll experience this powerful connection with a slab of marble, like it's telling me, 'Matt, you know who I am. Chisel away what's not me and you'll find me.'"

My sense about Matt is that he's awkward talking about himself. He deliberates, chooses his words carefully, almost like he's carving each word one by one from a solid mass of thought. What's natural for us is an effort for him. What's natural for him is dust and shards for me.

Cathy is the extrovert. We've known her for five hours and we're lifelong buddies. She sparkles with energy, touches when she talks. Her neurons pop with every new insight as if she just discovered the Truth. Her face radiates joy and creativity like every moment is about to be life changing.

"Oh, my God. I just got it. You have no idea how into colors I am. I feel so alive when I paint. I want every creation to burst with joy and hope. You help people express their pain; I want to remind them of beauty."

I notice Deborah beaming. Cathy's infectious energy lights up your mitochondria, sparks your creative energies, and makes you want to stay up all night and pack your seconds with dynamite.

We spend our days playing lost and found in the labyrinth's intertwining network of cryptic pathways. To enter the maze, the price of admission is your mind, your ordered sense of self, your fear of the unpredictable. On most days, Cathy and Matt join us on this magical excursion into Wonderland. They have the meditative, be-here-now heads to enjoy whatever bizarre phenomena this jungle of interlacing alleyways might throw at you.

We go right. An old woman covered in black sits on a stoop grasping a cane for support; she flashes a toothless grin and beckons us to step inside her modest room for tea and cookies. We accept and follow her into her tiny kitchen with a two-burner hot plate and a wobbly table. There are no cabinets. We sit two on a chair as she prepares our tea. She talks in nonstop Greek, laughing as if she just told herself a great joke. We smile and ask stupid things like what's her name and does she live alone. (Of course she does. There's a small bed in the one adjacent room. I don't see a bathroom.) She just chatters on and on, oblivious to our efforts at small talk. The four of us look at each other with an expression that says, "Do you have any idea what's happening?" We finish our tea and cookies; she kisses Cathy and Deborah on their cheeks and pats Matt and me on our heads, and we leave. She returns to her place in front of her house until the next visitor passes.

Then left: A lonely travel writer for Fodor's wants—no, needs—to share his adventures with us. We listen attentively, not because we're fascinated, but because it's the compassionate thing to do. The writer for Fodor's doesn't realize how he leads with his loneliness and that stories by themselves don't create soul-to-soul connections. He wants us to stay because he knows without knowing that we've found the person within the story. We remain for a while to hear about governmental brutality in Burma and the poor mountain people of Nepal who sell their daughters to the whorehouses of Delhi and Calcutta. Only when Deborah asks, "How do you feel when you hear these stories?" do we see a glimpse of the person within the storyteller. A chin that trembles and a voice that chokes tell a story that moves us.

We step into one of the 360 churches on the island. You bend your head to enter its cave-like interior lit by a row of candles. From the out-side, the church looks like an igloo—oval-shaped, small, snow-white exterior with a turquoise door. Inside, there are rough benches, icons, and a small statue of a cartoon-looking Christ nailed to the cross. The smell of burning incense makes me sneeze. Cathy says it's frankin-cense. All four of us find a spot and meditate for thirty minutes. I'm not sure why, but not one of us offers the usual post-meditation evaluation: no "deep, amazing, incredible." For me, a positive sign. Cathy and Matt don't quite fit into the California, everything-is-beautiful box.

In some blind alley, we bump into Bo Adams, a photographer, walking arm-in-arm with his latest boyfriend, a skinny Scandinavian with flowing blond hair. Bo is probably fifteen years his senior. Bo in-vites the four of us to join him and his boyfriend in his studio down the narrow alley to the left. He brings out a bottle of ouzo and we get slightly inebriated. While Bo strokes the blond boy's bottom, he leads us on a lecture tour of the spiritual heights of same-sex love. He waxes biblical about the great love and passion between King David and "his lover" Jonathan. "The sexual is the only route God gave man to achieve union. David and Jonathan's love united the male energies of David with the female energies of Jonathan."

"Bo," Cathy says, "I don't get it. Why would sex between two men create a union of female and male energies?"

"It's obvious," he answers, as if her question is beneath his dignity. "The female energy represented by a woman is inferior to the anima of a male. I see you've not studied Jungian psychology. If so, you would know that when Jung described the female side of the male—what he

called the anima—he was referring to the purest form of female energy." He points to his Scandinavian possession, who's been moaning in
tune to Bo's caresses, and says, "This beautiful boy represents the ideal
of female energy one can only find in a male. When he and I come together in holy union, we are rectifying the split between the male and
female aspect."

"What a fucking asshole," Cathy screams as soon as we are out of
earshot from his studio. "Does he actually believe his bullshit?"

I rarely remain in bed beyond six a.m. So, while Deborah sleeps, I stroll
along the water, letting my mind drift. I find myself landing on questions—more like incongruities. My strange reaction to the Christmas
tree. The discomfort I felt seeing the guy with the colored yarmulke ordering ice cream from his cousin's restaurant—*how dare you enter my
world acting like a proud Jew.* Simone's right: Not the reactions you'd
expect from someone who claims being Jewish is irrelevant.

Yet a different question seems to emerge, which is: "How Jewish
do you feel now?" An answer follows: more than ever—though not
a growing religious awareness. More like a feeling of identification
with the Jewish victims and heroes—a sense that it didn't happen to
them alone, but to me as well. I experiment with saying to myself, *I'm
Jewish.*

I don't squirm or want to run. I savor the words; they feel warm
and intimate—like I've discovered a disowned part of myself that's
ready to come home.

I think about Cathy and Matt: Americans like us, fellow travelers
like us, meditators like us. So much in common; so much ease and
flow between us; so many shared cultural associations and meanings,
like the Cold War, assassinations, Vietnam, the search for meaning and
purpose in the affluent world that is our common bond.

Cathy and Matt are bona fide WASPs, straight from the *Mayflower*
to the covered wagons that brought their ancestors through the Native
American lands into California. Deborah and I are second-generation Americans, mostly melted, but with enough unabsorbed pieces

remaining to remind us that our roots are not pure red, white, and blue. And, in my case, I've heard enough stories of assimilated Jews who ended up in the gas chambers along with their ultrareligious co-religionists to cause me to question where my true identity lies.

The days flow by like the rhythm of the tides—without a ripple or an errant wave crashing to the shore. Everything's as it should be: Mr. Buster languishes in his favorite spot in a repose of arrogant nonchalance; mustached Greek men with their fisherman's hats, mischievous eyes, and deeply grooved cheeks sit silently in front of the cracked white walls of their cafés and homes. Spiro spins, jumps, and twists in his restaurant to the recorded sound of an oud, a tambourine, and a Greek drum. Like a guardian angel, a radiant shield of pure ethereal light protects Mykonos from sunrise to sunset. The old, wrinkled women crouch in the doorways and hobble down the alleys as twisted as their overburdened spines. Bo Adams pontificates to the converted and the almost converted about the purity of homosexual love from the Golden Age to its glorious rebirth in the late twentieth century. And Cathy, Matt, Deborah, and I sit together on a stone terrace facing west as Cathy describes the subtle changes in color as the sun disappears into the dark blue water.

This is our final evening with Cathy and Matt and our second-to-last day in Mykonos. We'll spend the next nine days island hopping and then we'll head for Cyprus, our point of embarkation for Lebanon.

Halfway through our dinner of Greek salads and vegetarian moussakas, Matt raises a challenging question. "Cathy and I wonder why you want to go to a place as dangerous as Lebanon. We love you both, and we're worried about you—not only for your physical safety but for your psychological and spiritual well-being as well."

Cathy echoes Matt's sentiments and says, "You have such positive attitudes about life; you bring so much light to others. I'm scared the horror might be too much. Everyone has their limits, even people as strong and as caring as you both. I'm especially worried about you, Deborah. You have such a sensitive soul; you feel suffering so deeply."

Both Deborah and I are silent for a few seconds before Deborah responds. Several thoughts run through my mind, ranging from appreciation for their concern to criticism for what I consider to be their California-keep-your-head-buried-in-the-sand-everything-is-beautiful attitude.

"Thank you for your care and your love," Deborah says. "Believe me, I don't dismiss the impact Lebanon might have on us. What you don't understand is that I want the exposure. It's the stories of the survivors—whether from parental abuse or ethnic abuse—that give me hope and optimism."

"I want to piggyback on something Deborah said. I remember a quote that I read: *The road to depth passes through darkness—not around it*. I don't want to learn about war from gruesome images on television. I want to hear the stories directly from the survivors of horror, and I want to experience their pain as deeply as an outsider can feel it. To be honest, there may be a part of me that's a war tourist, that's seeking the adrenaline rush of battle. I hope not, but I'm not certain. What I do know is this: Both of us do want to feel life fully without cynicism and illusions.

"Maybe the difference is that we're psychologists and you're artists. You focus on beauty and try to replicate it in your work. We go into the sewer to find the humanity in the filth. To transform despair into hope. And you're overlooking something—Deborah's roots are there."

When we say goodbye, we exchange hugs, kisses, and tears. We promise to stay in touch.

CHAPTER 16

Cyprus to Beirut:
October 26 to October 29

I t's an axiom that you can only be where you are, and where you are is not necessarily the place where you stand. Cyprus exists only as our transit point to and from Beirut. All journal entries dating from October 26 until October 29, the day we depart for Beirut, focus on contacting Deborah's Beirut cousins on her mother's side, Yvonne and Samya. Both Yvonne and Samya are in contact with Deborah's aunt Ruth from Florida, who plays a central role in finding family members living in Lebanon.

Deborah's more distant cousin, Georgette, on her father's side, lives in Kab Elias in the Beqaa Valley near the Syrian border. Kab Elias is the birthplace of Deborah's paternal grandmother, Affifie to her Beirut-born husband, Dieb, but Sito (the Lebanese Arabic word for grandma) to her grandchildren. She left Kab Elias in 1911 when she was twelve years old.

Neither Sito, nor any of her American Haddad family, nor any of Deborah's grandfather's American Risk family have had any contact with their respective Lebanese families in nearly seventy years. The last time Sito saw her parents was when they hugged and kissed good-bye in 1911. According to Aunt Ruth, the only way to find Georgette is through Yvonne, who lived in Kab Elias twenty years ago when Muslims and Christians lived side by side in peace.

Aunt Ruth, who's not a bona fide aunt but the cousin of Deborah's maternal grandmother, Rose, spoke with Rose about our planned trip

187

to Lebanon. Rose, who immigrated to the United States from Beirut when she was two years old and can hardly cook tabbouleh or baba ghanoush and prefers that her grandchildren call her Mamie rather than the Arabic *sito*, told Aunt Ruth that Debbie and "her Jewish boyfriend" want—for some "unfathomable reason"—to visit the Lebanese family "that's so different from her."

Aunt Ruth, the most orthodox Syrian Orthodox Christian in the family, also emigrated from Beirut when she was a child. Since "it's the Orthodox Christian thing to do," she alone in the family maintains contact with the folks from the Old Country. So, when Rose, the widow of Mitchell Thabit from Damascus, a failed poet in the tradition of the oft-quoted Christian Lebanese poet/philosopher Khalil Gibran, expressed her concern to Aunt Ruth that her first grandchild Debbie wanted to make this "foolish trip" to Lebanon with her Jewish boyfriend, Aunt Ruth said, "You should know, Rose, it's because of that TV show *Roots*, about the colored man who goes back to Africa to find out where he came from. I'm sure that's what Debbie's doing— you know, finding her roots."

So here we are, at the telephone company, attempting to call Yvonne with the number Aunt Ruth gave Deborah. Aunt Ruth promised to give Yvonne a heads-up about our visit to Lebanon, so this call shouldn't be coming out of nowhere.

No luck. The Lebanese maid speaks only Arabic.

At eight o'clock in the evening, we return to the phone company to make another attempt to call Yvonne. Two guys in line are speaking Arabic. One of them has blond hair, blue eyes, and looks Scandinavian. The other has olive skin, dark wavy hair, and a Lebanese nose like Deborah and her mother. Deborah approaches them and asks, "Are you speaking Arabic?"

The blond answers in excellent English, "No. We were speaking Phoenician—the language of Lebanese Christians."

"That's strange. Sounded like the Arabic my grandparents speak."

"It is. In these times, we don't use the word Arabic or Arab when we talk about ourselves. Are you both Lebanese Christians from America?"

"I am. Michael's not."

"Oh, so you're a regular American?" he asks me. "Not Italian or Jewish before American?"

"Nope. Regular American," I answer. I lied on the visa application when I wrote "Protestant" under the religion category. So best to continue the charade. "You're both from Lebanon?" I ask.

"Yes," the dark-haired one answers. "I'm Mario from Beirut, and my crazy friend, Yousef, is from Tripoli, in the north of Lebanon." We introduce ourselves.

"So," Yousef says to Deborah, "you're about to fly to your ancestral home, the place of peace and love?"

"Yes, that place—with your help. We need someone to speak 'Phoenician' to my cousin in Beirut."

"No problem. You're my Phoenician sister. It's my pleasure to help."

Yousef calls the number and the same maid answers. He asks for Yvonne. A moment passes and Yvonne comes on the line. They exchange a few words and Yousef hands the phone to Deborah. Yvonne says to Deborah in English, with a slight French accent, "Oh, you're Betty's daughter. Yes, Ruth spoke to me about you . . . and yes, when you're settled in your West Beirut hotel, call me and we'll get together."

"What West Beirut hotel? What's she talking about? Why didn't she invite us to stay with her?" Deborah asks Yousef.

"Because it's too dangerous to stay in East Beirut. And, because you don't know what her story is, and she may not want you to know. And you chose the wrong country at the wrong time to have an emotional reunion with your long-lost family." He turns to Mario and says, "Let's take these fine people to dinner and enlighten them about our peaceful little country."

Yousef is a force field, a rapid-fire machine gun, a go-for-the-jugular charmer who moves in for the kill and then backs off a second before thrusting the knife. Mario is his straight man, his good cop, the guy assigned to resuscitate Yousef's casualties.

"So, Deborah, you're looking to discover your Lebanese soul in the tortured homeland of your grandparents?"

The straight man steps in and says to Deborah, "So why Lebanon and why now?"

"Yes," Yousef says, "why this roots experience? Don't tell me your grandparents have been pining away for the old country. When the Lebanese leave, they leave for good and never look back. Not like the Jews. They carry their history wherever they go. You're breaking the mold. Was it the zaatar on Sito's pita or the incense at the Syrian Orthodox Church?"

It's hard to know what Yousef's endgame is. He controls the narrative, and only he knows where and why he wants to drive this conversation. I sense that Deborah's thinking is along the same lines.

"Are you asking me to justify why I want to visit Lebanon?" Deborah asks. "Or should I feel guilty that my grandparents left Lebanon for America?"

Yousef looks down for a moment, shakes his head, and stares at Deborah. "Watching your people die and your country collapse isn't good for your soul. Turns you into a cynic. See, Deborah, you come and go. We stay and fight."

"So, why don't you move?" she asks.

"I can't, or I don't want to. Lebanon is where I belong; I need to do my pathetic part to save my hopeless country."

"What's your part?" Deborah asks.

"Not for discussion," he answers.

Yousef owns a boat—presumably, a fishing vessel. Hard to imagine him casting nets, setting bait, and waiting patiently for his catch. More like he's smuggling Kalashnikovs, Uzis, and M-16s to his Christian friends, the Phalangists.

He looks directly at me and continues, "Unlike us, the Jews to the south are smart and tough. No one plays the power and influence game better than them. I admire them. Jews know how to survive. They help their own. Not like the Lebanese Christians. If your own people don't give a shit about you, who will?" He stares at Deborah and says, "Tell me, Deborah, has your community done anything for their brothers and sisters in Lebanon?"

"No. No one speaks about the Civil War or the suffering of the Christian community in Lebanon."

Yousef looks at me and says, "If we were Jews, the world would know about our suffering."

I don't know if what I'm hearing from Yousef is reverse anti-Semitism—the Jews are cleverer, more caring of one another, and more ruthless at playing the power game. But strangely, this most vile and threatening of Jew haters makes me feel proud to be a Jew.

He proceeds to give us a rather lengthy obituary about the death of the Lebanese Christian community that begins with Israel's War of Independence in 1948, in which hundreds of thousands of Palestinians sought refuge in Lebanon and continues through to Black September in 1970 when the Palestinians in Jordan tried to overthrow King Hussein. Hussein killed twenty thousand Palestinians and expelled hundreds of thousands to Lebanon. According to Yousef, Arafat played the Palestinian victim card with the Lebanese Muslim politicians. He convinced them to let Lebanon be his base against Israel so the Palestinians could redeem "their homeland" from the Jews. Israel's response was to bomb the refugee camps of southern Lebanon with an occasional sortie to Beirut to remind them "who's got the biggest equipment," explains Yousef.

He tells us the Palestinians hate the Christians almost as much as they despise the Jews. "We don't bow down five times a day and we don't identify with their dream of returning to Palestine." During the early seventies, there were frequent skirmishes between Palestinian and Christian militias. In 1975, Yousef witnessed Palestinians massacre a Maronite priest at a PLO checkpoint on Avenue Sami El Solh in Beirut.

"The Palestinian filth rounded up a bunch of us Christians and held us at gunpoint. They placed a priest on a raised platform and tied sticks of dynamite around his neck. The filth ran a wire with a fuse attached to it from his neck to a place around fifty meters from him. I thought, 'They're just trying to scare us. No way they can be this sick.' They set the fuse. Seconds, like hours, passed before his head and brains splattered everywhere. One eye rolled out of its socket and lay on the ground next to part of his brain. That was my introduction to the reality of my beautiful country by the sea.

"Our Christian ship is sinking." He stares at Deborah and says, "Your people are doomed." He glances at me and then looks back at her. "It's not smart to side with the underdog. Go where the power is."

"What's that supposed to mean?" Deborah asks.

"Michael understands," Yousef says. "He'll explain it to you."

It's rather hard to transition to small talk after sloshing through the entrails of hell. Yet, with the help of Yousef's straight man, Mario, we talk about the upcoming election between "Cowboy" Reagan and the "Little Mouse" Carter. By the end of the evening, Yousef decides Mario will fly with us to Beirut and will help us find a hotel. He's granted protection to "the 'Jew' and his Phoenician girlfriend."

When we return to the hotel, Deborah asks me what Yosef meant when he told her to "go where the power is."

"He's telling you to stick with the Jew boy. Your people don't look after their own. There's something else he's telling us as well. 'Open your eyes to what you're about to walk into.' For us it's an adventure and an experience. To Yvonne and her family, it's a fucking nightmare."

"To you it's an adventure and experience, Michael. Don't you know it's much more than that for me? Yes, I was insensitive and naïve to think that Yvonne should host us. More like an entitled baby expecting the family to jump through hoops for their brave cousin from America. But let's be clear: If Yvonne didn't want to share her painful life with us, she could have told Aunt Ruth that we shouldn't come. She extended the invitation, so she obviously wants us to experience her life. I don't expect you to have the emotional connection I do, but I do expect you to respect it and to understand my need to connect with my Lebanese family. It's my DNA, not yours."

*　　*　　*

From an aerial shot, Beirut by the sea sparkles like a floating diamond caressed by the clear aqua blue Mediterranean, with forested mountains to its north and east. As we descend, the first thing we notice is the steel and glass skyscrapers you'd expect to find in any cosmopolitan city. At 3,000 feet and falling, Beirut definitely deserves its reputation as the "Paris of the East." From this perspective, you'd think all this talk about war and destruction is much ado about nothing.

Without questioning Deborah or me about why two Americans are vacationing in Lebanon, the comatose official stamps our passports and visas, and says in a most matter-of-fact voice, "Lebanese food is the best in the world."

"Thanks for the tip," I answer. We collect our two small backpacks and meet Mario by the exit.

So much for the "Diamond by the Sea" moniker. In this Beirut, the only sparkles I see are from the sunlight bouncing off the metal barrels of the Kalashnikovs (AK-47s) and M-16s set on automatic. Directly in front of us are three machine-gun nests protected by cement barricades. The M-60 machine guns are mounted on tripods. Helmeted Syrian soldiers in beige camouflage uniforms grip the barrels. I stare at the soldiers as they rotate the guns from side to side, scanning the plaza for any person who doesn't fit. Their weapons are an extension of themselves, cold steel and deadly.

I know the M-60 well from my military training. It's a killer. We called it the "Pig" because of its weight. Firing hundreds of rounds per minute, it shreds flesh into chopped meat—like a Vietcong platoon of forty soldiers wasted in seconds. One burst from these M-60s would turn this entire plaza into rivers of blood and piles of body parts.

I notice Deborah. Her mouth is taut, her shoulders are tight, her eyes dart from the Lebanese and Syrian soldiers in front of the airport to the machine guns momentarily aimed in our direction. Beads of sweat appear on her forehead. She grabs my left hand and motions with her head toward the Syrian soldier to our left who is interrogating a Westerner with a suitcase.

Mario whispers to us, "Don't stare at the soldiers. Make yourself invisible. Don't let anyone notice you—especially the Syrians. They're psychopaths. Follow me and look down." He hurries us through the plaza to a taxi stand.

Just as we're about to enter a taxi, a Lebanese soldier approaches us and asks for our names and addresses in Beirut. Mario tells the soldier we're family staying with him in East Beirut.

"Why does he want to know?" Deborah asks.

"Because if you disappear or you're killed, he has a record you left the airport on such and such date."

"That's reassuring," she says.

Shocking scars of conflict glare at us through the window of the taxi. Skeletons of bombed buildings, their interiors eviscerated by constant shelling, stand as monuments to the horror of the ongoing civil war. Wherever you focus, the remnants of war stare back at you: rubble, broken glass, fragments of buildings. Lives shattered.

I can't help but think about the people who once worked and lived here—the innocent Christians and Muslims gunned down in their living rooms and offices, while walking the streets, while praying in church, while jumping rope or kicking a soccer ball. Alive one moment, dead the next, their broken bodies crushed by a collapsed wall or a fallen beam. Two lovers embrace and then it's over, their lives ended by a stray bullet or a misplaced mortar quicker than you can say, "I love you."

Mario points to the remains of a four-story apartment building. "Five years ago, it was considered the crème de la crème for wealthy Christians. In 1976, Palestinian fedayeen armed with shoulder-fired mortars destroyed the building along with most of its residents. The Palestinians stormed the building. They lined the survivors against a wall and murdered each one of them. Didn't matter if they were women, children, and old people. Each one got a bullet to the head."

Mario points to what looks like the remnants of an enclosed window with ornate wood latticework. "It's called a *mashrabiya*. It's an example of traditional Arabic architecture you find—or, I should say, used to find—on many of the fine residential buildings in Beirut. You see that broken stained glass? The windows in the mashrabiya were all made from decorative glass. Before the Civil War, you'd walk down any one of these streets and you'd see amazing displays of these colorful protruding windows. Every building had its own personality. Now, nothing. Just a broken reminder."

Anarchy and chaos rule Beirut. There's no police, no fire department, no community services. "It's a jungle. You survive by wits and instinct. A stranger's an enemy. Especially another driver. It's a war—you against the other guy." Like our taxi driver, who is weaving in and out of traffic, blasting his horn, cursing the other drivers—a road warrior fighting for his piece of this broken boulevard of potholes, mini-craters, and blocks of stone lying haphazardly like lost puzzle pieces.

On the way to his apartment, Mario tells us that during the worst of the fighting in 1976, his parents, three younger siblings, and his grandmother huddled together in the basement of his building. "For one week, we ate stale bread and water. There was nonstop fighting in the street between the Phalangists and the PLO. It was too dangerous to go outside and too terrifying to be inside—trapped in a building that at any moment could collapse. The fighting stopped when the Syrian Army entered the neighborhood and the battle moved somewhere else."

"How come you don't fight with the Christians?" I ask.

"Because I promised my parents I wouldn't. I lost two close cousins to the fighting. Their deaths broke their parents. I couldn't do that to my mother and father. My mother was close to having a nervous breakdown, so my father decided to move the family to Rome, where he's from. Because of my jewelry business, I remained with my grandmother. She's a stubborn woman—tough as nails. She tells me, 'Don't worry, God will save us from the Filth.'"

After an hour of driving, we arrive at Mario's mutilated building. A cement balcony on the right side hangs from its metal base, waiting for the forces of gravity to pull it to its death twenty feet below. An adult stands watch outside the building. Mario tells us the parents don't allow the children to play in the piles of stones directly beneath the balcony. "Do the children listen?" I ask.

"Yes," he answers. "They're all battle-scarred little warriors, wise to the dangers."

The interior of his spacious apartment borders on the edge of elegance. A large cross with a crestfallen Jesus nailed to its olive-wood arms commands an entire wall. From this spot, this symbol of messianic deliverance protects the living and dining rooms. Oversized dark leather sofas line all four walls of the living room.

The dining room is set for four. Mario called his grandmother from the airport to tell her he was bringing a couple from America. Mario told us that his sito's thrilled that a Lebanese American girl and her husband will be guests in her home. ("Sorry," he said, "no way I can explain *living together* to my ultrareligious grandmother.")

When we enter, Sito rises from the couch to greet us. She's around seventy, young-looking, well-dressed, and well-coifed with stylishly cut, silver hair. I wonder if a pilgrimage to the beauty parlor's like a middle finger to hopelessness and despair?

In passable English, Sito greets us and invites us to join her in the dining room. She apologizes for not having sufficient time to prepare a proper Lebanese meal. The food is fabulous—stuffed grape leaves with rice and saffron, tabbouleh, baba ghanoush, kibbe, and pita. The vegetables are fresh from the nearby farmer's market.

After concluding she's not related to Deborah's family, Sito asks Deborah, "Do you go to church?"

"I did when I was younger. We went to the Syrian Orthodox Church."

"Now, no more? Not good. Only He," Sito says, pointing to Jesus, "can save us from the evil. I tell Mario he needs faith and hope. He thinks I'm foolish old woman. I think he's a blind boy. The Lord understands more than one sad moment. He knows that in end, it will be good, and pain will stop. It says in Bible, 'Don't believe in powerful horses and their riders, only believe in Me. Only I will save you.'"

* * *

The plan is for Mario to drive us to West Beirut, the Muslim section, to find a place for us to stay. The first stop will be the American University of Beirut (AUB) to find out if there's free housing for the next nine days.

To drive from East Beirut to the western side, Mario follows a convoluted route of detours, bypasses, and intuitive turns that takes an hour and a quarter—five times longer than before the civil war. He stops at a bridge and tells us the following story:

"My cousin was shot here." His voice expresses the bitter tones of anger and futility; his eyes reveal his grief.

"Philip was twenty-one years old, studying medicine when the Phalange recruited him. They targeted young Christians by convincing us justice demands revenge. Their slogan: *five Muslims for every Christian soul.* It worked. Everyone knew someone the fedayeen had killed. Phillip's best friend, Elias, was murdered in a drive-by shootout. He was playing soccer in the park. Phillip became something he wasn't—hateful and obsessed with revenge. After Elias's murder, he began to fall asleep in classes and stopped coming home. At night, he trained to be a Phalange fighter.

"He believed he had to kill five Muslims so Elias's soul would rise to heaven. One night, his commander tested his resolve. He ordered him to gun down a Muslim mother and father and their three young children who were crossing this same bridge together. He now had his five Muslims—all easy targets—but he couldn't do it. Killing a Muslim family of five is not the same as killing five Palestinian fedayeen. His comrades screamed, 'Kill them! Kill them! Kill them!' He put his rifle on automatic and murdered the entire family—the parents, two boys, and a girl. This ugly conflict turned a good, gentle boy into something he wasn't—a monster. He wanted to be a doctor. A few weeks later, a Palestinian gunman shot him in the head where we now stand."

As soon as we cross into West Beirut, we notice the obvious: Here, the evidence of war exists on a far smaller scale.

Quantitatively, I'd estimate the walls of the West Beirut buildings reveal a fraction of the scars, wounds, and gaping holes we witnessed in East Beirut. Here and there, pockmarked buildings testify to a local skirmish between any possible combinations of combatants. However, unlike East Beirut, you see far fewer skeletal remains of buildings destroyed from hours and days of constant shelling.

"From what I see," I say to Mario, "it looks like the Muslims attacked your neighborhoods, not the other way around."

He tells us there are no clear good guys and bad guys. "In Lebanon, everyone's a perpetrator, a victim, or both, like my cousin Phillip. He massacred a Muslim family to revenge the death of an innocent victim murdered by Palestinian terrorists." To Mario, it's an endless chain of madness, perpetuated by a distorted logic of revenge and retaliation.

He tells us a story similar yet different from the one Yousef told us: In 1975, Christian militia slaughtered twenty-five Muslim women and children on a bus. "Why? Because you don't differentiate a baby cockroach from an adult. You exterminate as many as you can and you terrorize the survivors. The Christians in 1975 were on a holy mission to drive the Moslems from Lebanon."

The Muslims retaliated by murdering innocent Christians. Christians attacked residential and commercial areas of West Beirut. In the Battle of the Hotels, close to here, Christians and Muslims fought for control of downtown Beirut. "The Holiday Inn will give you all the proof you need that West Beirut has seen its fair share of destruction."

The Christian forces lost the Battle of the Hotels. The Muslims drove the Christians from West Beirut. The Syrians changed sides, aligned with the Muslims, and shelled East Beirut for days on end. "If anyone tells you who's guilty and who's not, be skeptical. The biggest evil is our own nature."

There's life in West Beirut. Stylish pedestrians wearing the latest fashions from Dior and Yves St. Laurent share the street with Arabs in traditional dress. Some women wear scarves fastened by knots under their chins. Others wear the full-body burka that conceals everything other than their eyes. Arab men dressed in white ankle-length shirts and red-and-white checkered keffiyehs draped over their heads walk ahead of their modestly dressed wives.

Carts peddling everything from authentic Rolex watches to expensive Chanel perfume stand side by side with street vendors selling shawarma wrapped in flat Syrian bread, slathered with tahini, lemon, and garlic sauce, and stuffed with fried eggplants, tomatoes, and onions. The pungent smell of street food sets my taste buds on fire.

Ten minutes later, we're at the AUB campus on the edge of the Mediterranean. College students in jeans sit under palm trees reading from texts and writing in notebooks. Four guys play an animated game of Frisbee football on the campus lawn. A coed softball game takes place on the south side of the lawn. A hot girl in a red shirt hits a sharp single to right field. She tries to stretch it into a double; the right fielder throws a strike to the second baseman, who tags her out. Everyone cheers, including the girl.

"Where the hell are we?" I ask.

"In Beirut, the insane asylum by the sea," Mario responds. "Where reality and illusion are two sides of the same coin: baseball and bullets, frisbee and fanaticism."

A sign promoting a free lecture on Transcendental Meditation greets us at the main door to the administration building. It says to contact either Robert or Khalid for more information. A poster in English depicts a map of Israel draped in a Palestinian flag. Another announces a solidarity march to support the PLO. A third displays a swastika covering the blue and white Israeli flag. A flyer calls for volunteer stagehands for the upcoming musical *Oklahoma*. The chess club offers a workshop on opening moves.

No luck finding free housing on campus, so Mario suggests the Bedford Hotel, a five-minute walk from here. The Bedford's an Old World, classy place with chandeliers, Persian carpets, and domed Arabic windows. Our fourth-floor room has its own bathroom with porcelain sinks and polished brass faucets, a large double bed with two pieces of chocolate on each pillow, and a long balcony that looks down on the wide boulevard below where carts sell cheeses, pastries, shawarma, nuts, and candies.

CHAPTER 17

Beirut, Lebanon: October 30 to November 7

W e're not the only guests at the Bedford Hotel.

There's Peter, Gustav, and Mariana, young Germans from Frankfurt who drove three Mercedes to Beirut to sell at nearly double the sticker price. As soon as they complete their transaction, they're off to Goa "to blow smoke and do nothing."

Meanwhile, Mariana seriously needs a sedative. She talks nonstop about the guns and soldiers, doesn't listen to a word you say, gnaws on her nails, and picks at her skin, terrified a Palestinian gunman will rape and murder her.

There are two more older teens sharing a room on the second floor. I wouldn't exactly call them guests—more like unwanted residents the hotel can't expel. Riad, the bellhop, calls them criminals and drug addicts. They snort speed, smoke hashish, and, when they're totally stoned, they steal jewelry and sell it from their room. Dressed like bad-ass fedayeen, armed with AK-47s and bandoliers draped across their chests, they move in and out of the lobby multiple times per day. They don't look older than eighteen.

Sometime around nine p.m., Deborah and I relax on our fourth-floor balcony eating pistachios and drinking wine. The sky's clear; the moon's full. The street below bustles with activity. From this vantage point, we have a clear view of the Mediterranean. Intersecting beacons of light scan the coastline as far as the eye can see. It feels good to decompress and discuss the day's events. To protect our fragile brains from overexposure to the sights, sounds, and stories of war, we'll need to take time to process our daily sensory and emotional experiences.

So, as we sip our wine, savor the delicate nutty flavor of roasted pistachios, and share our experiences, Deborah points out a red flash of light streaking across the sky, followed by another, and then another. On the street directly below us, we notice people duck into buildings and run for cover. With each successive bolt, the red stream heads closer and closer to our hotel.

"Deborah, get off the balcony now and get into the bathroom!" I shout. "Those are tracer bullets coming toward us."

Huddled between the protected walls of the bathroom, we hear thud . . . thud . . . thud . . . as bullets penetrate the outside walls of the Bedford Hotel. From the second-floor room where the two thugs live, AK-47s on fully automatic return fire.

From my military experience, I know well the repetitive sound two machine guns make as they exchange fire. I received hours of live-fire training on the infiltration courses at Fort Knox, Fort Gordon, and Fort Sill. Our trainers taught us how to control our fear and to focus our minds as hundreds of rounds flashed over our heads. You slow your breath, tune out the incessant sound of machine-gun fire, and focus on the mission.

"Deborah, breathe slowly and let go. We're safe here. Nothing can happen to us."

She grabs my hand, squeezes, and continues to let out long, deep breaths.

After ten minutes, the firing stops. We wait awhile longer to be sure we're safe before exiting our bathroom bomb shelter. We return to the balcony, look below, and everything is as it was before this mini skirmish: The pushcarts peddle their French perfumes and Swiss watches. We can smell the aroma of shawarma roasting on a spit, and stylishly dressed Lebanese share the boulevard with Arabs in traditional garb. All appears to be just fine in downtown Beirut on Friday evening, October 31, 1980.

We go downstairs to the lobby for another glass of wine. Our new friend Riad, the bellhop, stands by the empty reception desk looking a bit off-color and stressed. "I hate this fucking place," he tells us as soon as we're in earshot. "Those fucking Palestinian gangsters make our lives miserable. Management is too scared to kick them out. They play this game once a week and no one wins. Their Fatah enemies try to kill them; they try to pick off the Fatah fighters."

"Riad," I say, "where did you learn to curse like that? You sound like an American."

He laughs and says, "I've watched the American film *Blue Collar* with Richard Pryor four times. It holds the record for the most *fucks* in any film." He then goes into a perfect Richard Pryor imitation: "When I take over your muthafucking job, know what I'm gonna do, baby?"

I put my arm around Riad's shoulders and say to him, "Riad, teach us about life in Beirut."

"What's there to know? It's a shit storm. A fucking nightmare. A place to leave."

"So why are you here?"

"Because I haven't gotten a visa to the U.S. My uncle in Chicago's working with a lawyer to get me political asylum. He's trying to use connections in the local Lebanese community, but so far no luck."

Riad's a twenty-one-year-old secular Muslim university student and part-time bellhop at the Bedford Hotel. He tells us he's from a "traditional Islamic" family. "Traditional," according to Riad, who speaks English like a fast-talking Afro-American with an Arabic accent, means his mother wears a scarf when she's outside; his father and two brothers fast during Ramadan; nobody prays five times a day, and everyone, except for mom, cheats with an occasional glass of wine. "Allah doesn't give a shit about Lebanon. If he did, he'd feed Arafat and his PLO criminals to the dogs," he says.

"Here's how to survive in hell," he teaches us. "First rule: Never walk down an empty street. A bored fedayeen might shoot you. Second rule: At the first sound of gunfire, hide behind a car or run inside a building. Third rule: Don't look at a Syrian."

For the next hour, we sit with Riad, attending his class entitled "How Not to Get Your Ass Shot Off in Fucking Beirut." He teaches us where to sit in a restaurant in case of a "fucking" suicide bomber; how to recognize, avoid, and speak to—"if the fucker approaches you"—a drugged-up "fucking Palestinian psychopath" like the ones living in the Bedford Hotel. "Don't make eye contact, look scared, and don't react to their insults."

At eleven thirty, we return to the room and sleep well until we wake up peacefully at seven. We're scheduled to meet Yvonne at two p.m. at the Café Hamra, an upscale restaurant and bar close to the hotel. Yvonne tells Deborah this will be the first time she's crossed the Green Line between East and West Beirut since the start of the Civil War in 1975.

"She sounds terrified," Deborah tells me. "Makes sense. Aunt Ruth told me that Samya's and Yvonne's husbands were murdered by Palestinian gunmen. Who knows who else she's lost and what traumas she's suffered? I believe we're about to meet a very tortured soul."

We return to the AUB campus to see if we can find the two TM initiators, Robert and Khalid, listed on the posters we saw. Deborah tells me that when she worked for the TM movement in Spain in 1973, she and Niels designed that poster, which is now on display in the AUB's administration building.

At the TM desk sits an attractive coed dressed in jeans and a red pullover sweater. When Deborah tells her about the posters and that she's an initiator, she jumps up and gives Deborah a hug. "You've got to meet Robert, our director. He'll be over the moon to find out an initiator from the U.S. has landed on the AUB campus."

Khalid's twenty-two, from a secular Muslim family. After a brief discussion about our trip and why we're in Beirut, she shares—like every Lebanese we've met—her perspective on the conflict.

"I'm a chemistry major, so I look at it like this: You add the unstable Palestinian element to the stable Lebanese ethnic compound and what you have is an explosive chemical combination that continuously reconfigures itself into new volatile permutations." Like a mutating virus that morphs into a more lethal version of itself.

We spend the next few hours with Robert and Khalid. Robert, thirty, is Christian Lebanese, speaks five languages, has a doctorate in mathematics, plays the violin at an elite level, and works full time for the TM movement. He shares his grand vision with the flair, dramatic gestures, and relentless energy of a man on a mission.

"You both know meditation strengthens the nervous system and releases stress. That's probably why Lebanon won't make you crazy. You've got meditators' brains."

In one grand gesture, he plans to initiate the entire wing of the most militant and violent Christian forces. The leader of this militia, Robert tells us, is a twenty-four-year-old "psychopath who loves Lebanon."

"I'll show him how meditation will make his men alert, energetic, and focused—better warriors." Robert laughs and says, "It's a trick. Have you ever met an angry, out-of-control meditator? Can a meditator be a psychopath?" He makes direct eye contact with Deborah and me and says, "Help us bring peace to Lebanon. Where else can you make such a difference?" But much to his disappointment, we decline his offer to change the world.

We wait for Yvonne in the glass-enclosed patio of the Café Hamra. The restaurant's a cross between Bogart's smoke-filled Casablanca pub and a dimly lit Upper West Side singles' bar. Prints by the French Impressionists Renoir, Matisse, and Monet create a surreal, almost meditative background. Every table boasts a French-Arabic menu on a bright red tablecloth, a vase of freshly cut yellow roses, and two Gauloises ashtrays. The pungent smell of French cigarettes mingles with the fragrance of L'Air du Temps, a popular perfume.

At my insistence, we grab a table approximately twenty feet from the entrance. I've been eyeing that spot from the moment we entered the café. The table is strategically protected by a Romanesque column, a rather obtrusive and peculiar structure for such a pseudo-hip watering hole.

It surprises me that no one else wants it. From what Mario and Riad tell us, drive-by shootings and an occasional hand grenade are de rigueur. The formula is simple: Take three terrorists high on speed; a beat-up Subaru; one AK-47 set on automatic; a few hand grenades and possibly an RPG, depending on the arms dealer's current inventory; and then, with one quick pass in front of Café Hamra, you can count at least five dead, ten wounded, and enough dismembered limbs and un-recognizable body parts to fill up the back of a small farm vehicle like the one I saw yesterday, piled high with crates of persimmons. It takes a week to scrape off the burnt flesh from the walls, floor, and ceiling, and another two weeks before the stench of death dissipates.

At two forty-five, a woman enters the café and looks around as if she's searching for someone. "Yvonne," Deborah calls. She acknowl-edges Deborah's greeting with a barely perceptible nod and a tense, almost angry look. Her black turtleneck and pants underscore her mood. As she walks toward us, she glances from side to side.

"I hate driving in this damn city."

The waiter starts toward her. She dismisses him with a slight movement of her wrist. "I had to fight my way through every in-tersection to get here, and then it took me another half hour to find parking." She sits.

She pulls a filtered Gitanes cigarette out of a leather case, taps it twice against the back of her hand, and lights it with a gold mono-grammed lighter. She inhales deeply and exhales two long, straight streams of smoke from her nose. From the lingering aroma of her Gitanes, I can taste the biting flavor of dark and bitter espresso.

"How's your vacation in hell going so far?" she asks Deborah.

"As expected—upsetting," she answers. "The residents in hell are helpful and hospitable, their stories painful to hear. The destruction's overwhelming to see."

Yvonne takes another deep drag on her cigarette, turns her head to the left, and blows out a cloud of smoke. She stares at Deborah for an uncomfortable few seconds and then begins her interrogation.

"Why are you here? You don't have to be. Don't you think it's fool-ish to expose yourself to so much danger?"

"I know you do, Yvonne. And maybe you're right. There's no way that I could begin to comprehend what you've been through and what you go through on a daily basis. Perhaps, if I did, I wouldn't be here. But I am, and if that makes me foolish, then I am. But to be honest, I don't feel foolish. Quite the opposite. I'm learning a great deal and we've met some amazing people. But why the questions? Does it bother you we're here?"

Yvonne crushes her cigarette in the ashtray, separating the paper from the lipstick-stained filter. She takes out another cigarette and places it on the table. She looks at Deborah for a moment and then responds.

"Yes, it does bother me. You've come when we're at our worst. You can't fake being hospitable when you're suffering. But we're Lebanese and you're family, which is why I agreed to host you when Ruth said you wanted to visit. You know we're required to show you a pleasant time. But we can't. The only thing we can share with you is our misery. If that's what you want, we've got plenty to offer you."

"Yvonne," Deborah says, "we didn't come to Lebanon expecting you to fake it. We understand what the situation is. We came to listen, to learn, and to meet our Lebanese family. If suffering is what you can or want to share, then that's okay."

"It's okay with you; it's not okay with me. Your presence makes our situation too real. I look at both of you—tanned, healthy, looking happy—and it's a reminder of how miserable we are. When it's just us, we're all in the same boat, suffering together. But you're the outsiders. You get to listen to our awful stories, and then you leave. Maybe we'll be material for a book you'll write about the death of the Lebanese Christian culture."

"We're not here to cause you more pain and inconvenience," Deborah says. "If it's too much for you, then we'll say our goodbyes now. I understand it's not fair to show up at your doorstep and expect you to take care of us."

Yvonne takes the cigarette lying on the table, lights it, and exhales a long stream of smoke. "Deborah, you're hearing and seeing an Yvonne

I don't like, but that won't stop me from spending time with you. I'll do my best to be a proper host. Just understand I can't pretend to be happy or calm."

"Yvonne," Deborah says, "we don't have those expectations."

"Fine. But I still want to understand why you're here."

"The simple answer is because all my ancestors were born in Lebanon. For some reason that neither they nor I can understand, they instilled this deep desire in me to explore my roots. Maybe that's not a good enough answer for a Lebanese living in hell, but it's the best I can come up with. Yvonne, I can't nor do I want to justify to you why I'm here. My reasons must sound incredibly naïve and even selfish to you. I'm almost ashamed to admit it, but let's just say I'm here because it feels like I'm supposed to, I want to, and I can. I don't know if that speaks to you or not. It's the way we live our lives. If I could, I'd share that blessing of freedom with you."

"I envy you. You're free to come and go. We're burdened by circumstances we can't ignore or leave. There's something else—Kab Elias. Don't go. There's more fighting between the Christians and the Palestinians." She exhales another long stream of smoke and continues, "The road is dangerous." She grinds her freshly lit cigarette into the ashtray. "You're taking a big chance. I tried calling the number I had for Georgette. The phones are down—probably cut. She doesn't know you're coming, and I don't know if she still lives there."

Yvonne pulls yet another cigarette from the case, taps it again, lights it, and continues. "Your grandmother's Kab Elias doesn't exist anymore. It's an ugly, poor village. Georgette means nothing to you. Who is she? A third cousin your grandmother never met. Even if she could speak English or French, you'd have nothing to talk about. Why take a risk like this? For what?"

She sighs deeply. For a moment, I make eye contact with Yvonne. She doesn't notice. She's gone, caught in a web of black memories. Deborah tries to reach the Yvonne beneath the pain, but she can't. Yvonne and her suffering are one. There's no place for connection.

"Do you even know what happened in Kab Elias?" This is not a question she expects or wants Deborah to answer. "No, of course you don't. Why should you? I doubt you, your sito, or any of the Lebanese American community thought about Kab Elias in January 1976. You had more important things on your mind."

Between puffs of smoke, she tells us that in January 1976, Palestinian militia murdered sixteen Christians in Kab Elias. Among other atrocities, Yvonne singles out a story about a bomb tied to the neck of a Maronite priest. Different from the story Yousef told us, but with the same outcome—the explosion splattered his brains in all directions. The Palestinians then rounded up a group of Christian children and cut off each of their three middle fingers so they'd never fire a rifle.

Grinding the half-smoked Gitanes into the ashtray and taking out her fourth cigarette from the leather case, she repeats the ritual—tapping, lighting with her expensive gold cigarette lighter, and exhaling a long stream of smoke through her nose. She looks at both of us and then spits out the inevitable words, "I hate Arafat and his Palestinian criminals, but it's the Jews I hate the most."

Tuning back in, I only catch the end of her story. "We're a poor country; we can't take care of 250,000 Palestinians. They rot in their filthy, overcrowded refugee camps with no chance of a better life. It's the Jews' fault. They gave us this tumor."

With no visible reaction from either of us to her performance, she grinds out the last cigarette, stares at Deborah, and goes back to basics, "Deborah, I still don't understand why you're going to Kab Elias."

I know I should feel empathy. I should understand her vile, Jew-hating curses as the desperate cries of a victim in pain. But something visceral in me won't let me see her humanity—some part of me that's beyond logic and understanding stops me from feeling her suffering.

I exhale deeply, attempting to let go of my disdain and contempt, trying to dig into the therapist in me to find enough compassion to temper my judgments. I remind myself she lives in the devil's playground; she's experienced the worst of who we are; and who knows how dark any of us would become in these circumstances.

I glance at Yvonne—she's all black: shoes, pants, turtleneck, hair, mascara, eyes, and the deep half-moons underneath them. However, it's the blackness of her anger and hatred that swirls around her like the smoke she exhales.

I try to imagine her as my client, encouraging her to express her resentments:

I resent you for waltzing in and out of our lives.

I resent you for having choices, for coming to Lebanon to have your sentimental "roots" experience while our country burns.

I resent your American naiveté, your meaningless support and compassion.

I resent your pseudo-Lebanese identity. Suffer with us. Then, you'll know who you are.

"Because I have to," Deborah answers. She momentarily looks away as if she's searching for the right words. "Yvonne," she continues, "I know you think I'm chasing some frivolous dream. I'm sure Kab Elias is a poor, ugly village, but to me, it's the place half my family called home. It's part of my childhood. I'm one hour from Kab Elias. I haven't come this far to turn back."

"Okay, Deborah," Yvonne says. "Go to Kab Elias. But not now. Wait until a safer time."

"A safer time?" Deborah asks. "The Lebanese Embassy in Athens told us that this is the safest period in five years. Do you really think there'll be a safer time than now?"

"I don't know," Yvonne answers. I notice her eyes tearing. She shuts them for a moment and pulls on her bottom lip to stop it from trembling. For the first time, I see a person under the blackness.

Over the next few days, Yvonne takes us on a whirlwind tour of Beirut and the mountainous areas surrounding it. She drives her BMW sedan on steep hairpin turns in tune with her rapid-fire commentary about "how lovely Lebanon was before the Palestinian filth destroyed the country." As she curses the Palestinians and their Jewish "persecutors," she tosses her cups, cigarette butts, and candy wrappers out of the window. When she tells us to dump our bottles and wrappers, we politely decline. "What difference does it make?" she says. "The entire country's just a Muslim landfill."

On the way to her sister Samya's, we stop at a reality-bending exhibition of ultramodern Lebanese furniture called The Lebanese Home of the Future. Using asymmetrical geometric shapes and multiple metallic colors, the Lebanese artisans bowed, curved, and twisted steel, plastic, and wood to create futuristic chairs, sofas, and tables. As Deborah and I maneuver about tomorrow's tables and chairs, we wonder whether we should consider this exhibit delusional, defiant, or hopeful. I want to ask this ultrachic crowd of avant-garde Lebanese how, while Lebanon dies, do you create a vision for tomorrow?

Deborah asks a similar question to Yvonne, who answers, "What choice do we have? We have to go on living."

We arrive at a building wasted with bullets in the Christian section to meet Samya. She tells us that in 1978, Samya's husband and her own husband, Maurice, were gunned down together during a crossfire between Phalangist and Syrian troops. "They were best friends from childhood. For Samya and myself, the last two years have been a nightmare."

When we enter the interior of Samya's spacious apartment, it feels like time has stopped. Artifacts dated from before Christ share space with Lebanese landscapes depicting a more peaceful period in the country's history. An angel-like, porcelain Madonna spreads her broad wings over a sizeable portion of a mahogany and glass breakfront.

Dressed in a contemporary dark pantsuit and Italian heels, Samya's a younger version of Yvonne, only more hidden within her suffering. There's no flesh on her frame; her black eyes stare ghost-like from deep sockets carved from skin and bone. She greets us graciously. She beckons us to the living room where plates of pistachios and dates await us.

"I hope your stay in Lebanon has been enjoyable."

"More like eye-opening than enjoyable," Deborah replies.

"Yes, of course, eye-opening. I prefer to keep my eyes shut. I don't like to think about what there is to think about. Do you know how to not think about what everyone around you thinks about all the time?"

Deborah reaches out to touch Samya's hand. Samya waits a few seconds before she pulls away and announces dinner is ready.

This multicourse Lebanese meal appears and disappears in less than thirty minutes. In retrospect, I imagine what Samya prepared was gourmet quality. There's no doubt the lentil and lemon soup, the grape leaves stuffed with zaatar-flavored rice and raisins, the five different salads made with tabbouleh, toasted pita, fresh vegetables, and an abundance of mint and olive oil, could rival any Michelin-starred restaurant. But I wouldn't know. It all passed amid a flurry of agitation and invective.

As much as Samya and Yvonne try to be polite and inquire about our trip and our American lives, the conversation quickly reverts to the situation. Samya asks us who we supported in the recent presidential election. She doesn't wait for our answers; she and Yvonne tell us they supported Carter because "he's not a Jewish puppet."

Samya informs us, "The Jews control the U.S. government, the press, and the banks. Hitler had the right idea. It's a shame he didn't have enough time to complete the job."

I listen without reacting.

CHAPTER 18

Kab Elias, Lebanon: Monday, November 8

The first driver we ask wants five hundred dollars for the thirty-five-mile trip to Kab Elias.

"The trip bad." He moves close to me, looks from side to side, and whispers, "Don't like Syrians. They bad."

We go from driver to driver. Most just shake their heads. One driver laughs; another walks away. Our emotional pleas fall on deaf ears.

"I have family too," a portly driver tells us as he nervously fingers his beige worry beads. "Much danger in Beirut, don't want more."

For a two-thousand-dollar deposit, an old, beat-up Ford could be ours for the day.

Finally, Khalid finds us a driver named Mahmoud who will take us to Kab Elias and back for thirty dollars.

"Why is he willing to do it so cheaply?" I ask.

"He's got to go to Damascus anyway, so he'll drop you off on his way there and pick you up on the way back. Besides, he owes me a favor . . . and Mahmoud's different."

An explosion jolts me out of bed.

I bolt to the window. Lightning flashes across the gray morning sky, followed by another explosion. Thank God it's a thundershower. I glance at my watch. It's five—three and a half hours until Mahmoud arrives. I go back to bed.

At six o'clock, Riad calls to wake us up. He tells us he'll bring us some sambousek b'jibn (cheese pies). The rain has stopped, and the clouds are breaking. At six thirty, Deborah wakes up. She puts on her close-fitting, blue and red floral print dress with short sleeves and a revealing neckline. By American standards, it's fairly conservative. I'm wondering if her relatives in Kab Elias will approve.

I'm also wondering if this wild goose chase is insane. Despite many attempts to reach Georgette, we haven't gotten through—either the phone lines are down, her number no longer exists, or Georgette has met the same fate as Yvonne's husband.

"While you've been sleeping, I've been worrying," I tell her. "Everyone thinks we're crazy for going to Kab Elias. Maybe we should call off this wild goose chase."

"No problem. Stay here in *safe Beirut* and I'll go on my wild goose chase."

"Thanks, I'll pass," I say. "But be real. No doubts. No worries. About this . . . wild goose chase?"

"No, not doubts. Something else. Remember Sito's reaction when I told her I planned to go to Kab Elias?"

"She didn't say much of anything."

"That's the point. At the time, I read her silence as critical—as if she didn't want me to go. Almost like I was messing with her dream. I heard lots of romantic stories about vineyards and olive groves and juicy pomegranates, but if it was so great, then why leave and why not come back to visit? I want to see *her* Kab Elias with my eyes. I want to know where I come from."

At eight forty-five, Mahmoud arrives. Twenty-five, I'd guess, with black bedroom eyes, a smooth, olive complexion, and a suggestive half smile. He wears a black and lavender shirt open to the fourth button, revealing a large gold medallion and a liberal amount of chest hair. His pants are green and tight. He combs his well-lubricated, longish hair straight back into a perfect 1950s rendition of Elvis Presley's "duck's ass." I half expect him to rotate his hips and break into a bar of "Love Me Tender."

He appraises Deborah's physical assets from ankles to eyes. He's pleased.

"*Je suis Mahmoud*," he murmurs.

I extend my hand. He looks at me for a brief moment, doesn't reciprocate, and walks toward the car. I'm a slight impediment to his obvious designs.

I tag along while Mahmoud escorts Deborah to his 1970 black Chevy with broad red side stripes. The interior is adorned with black velvet curtains, Playboy Bunny dolls, decals of semiclad women, and a padded steering wheel. He motions for Deborah to sit beside him. She ignores him and joins me in the back.

He presses the accelerator to the floor, leaving a significant part of his tire in front of the Bedford Hotel. We both breathe deeply as we head for Kab Elias.

Mahmoud makes a screeching left turn onto Boulevard Mahatma Gandhi. Breaking and accelerating, blasting and cursing, he skillfully weaves his way through the traffic. It's hard to imagine him functioning in a civilized society.

At the intersection of Bliss and Gandhi, the heavy traffic forces Mahmoud to slow down. AUB is on our right. Three stylishly dressed coeds carrying book bags meander along the dense tree-lined paths, while a group of four middle-aged joggers, probably visiting American professors, run across the lush lawns that extend throughout the campus. Farther ahead, on the baseball field, another softball game is in progress. Men are in scoring position on second and third and the infield is drawn in. There's a large gap in right center field, and—

Mahmoud turns right onto Avenue de Paris. On our left, the road overlooks the Bay of St. George, an inlet of the Mediterranean. Sun and clouds form blue-gray shadows on the still surface. On the shoulder of the road, overflowing bags of rotting garbage cover the remains of a flower garden. An occasional hardy perennial pushes its way through the rusty cans and broken glass. The repulsive stench brings an instant olfactory flashback of Ajax, our lovable mongrel, joyfully rolling his furry body on the rotting carcass of a twelve-point buck. My immediate reaction—to vomit.

Avenue de Paris becomes Boulevard Charles de Gaulle. On our right is an abandoned amusement park. Weeds and trash cover the ground. A once-majestic Ferris wheel, commanding a spectacular view of the bay, stands painfully abandoned. Below the amusement park, a water skier gracefully traces a figure-eight across the smooth surface of the inlet. You've got to admire this obsessive need for normalcy.

Mahmoud also sees him and says in French, "Two weeks ago, they shot a water skier. He died with his skis on."

"Why was he shot?" Deborah asks.

"He was a nobody," Mahmoud answers. "They used him for target practice."

"What are you saying?" Deborah asks. "They just killed him for no reason?"

"Yeah," he answers.

"Who did it?" she asks.

"Who knows? Phalangists. Palestinians. Amal. It makes no difference. In Lebanon, murder's the national pastime. You don't ask why. It's just the way it is."

We enter a section of Beirut where the destruction is total. This is what Mario meant when he called Beirut "The City of Death." Burned and gutted buildings riddled with bullet holes loom over craters filled with ash and crumbled stone. Here and there, a staircase stands alone, severed from the floors it once connected. The dust from bomb-scarred buildings chokes and violates the senses. The dense mass of rubble forces the question: Who's buried under this graveyard of destruction? A large red stain on a charred stone wall captures my attention.

"Death to America," scream the bold red letters. A large photo of Yasser Arafat—grim-faced, unshaven, and dressed for battle—stares out at the street. The slogan underneath reads: "To Jerusalem." A poster of a Jewish star in flames covers the entire side of another wall.

I assume we're in one of the Palestinian neighborhoods of Sabra, Shatila, or Burj al Brajneh, names that have been seared into the collective consciousness of the Palestinian people. It was in this ugly, angry place that the Palestinians sought refuge following the infamous month of September 1970—"Black September"—the month King Hussein of Jordan brutally crushed a Palestinian rebellion, killing thousands. This is the "tumor" Yvonne referred to in her history lesson.

Mahmoud turns the corner onto a narrow, shattered street littered with broken glass and plastic bags that rise and fall aimlessly on currents of hot, dusty air. On both sides of this devastated street stand the stark evidence of rage: Dark-eyed Palestinian teenagers wearing X-shaped bandoliers draped over thin chests. In their hands, they hold AK-47s and an occasional M-16. The oldest among them can't be over fifteen years old.

Out of nowhere, traffic materializes—not American-style, slow-moving, listen-to-a-tape, commuter-type traffic, but a bumper-to-bumper swarm of battered buses overflowing with sweaty, sullen passengers; cars and taxies sputtering sounds frighteningly similar to an M-16 on automatic; trucks emitting enough black clouds of toxic fumes to cause an immediate, violent rupture to the ozone layer; primitive pushcarts piled high with tomatoes, carrots, and squash; and even an occasional rusty and tattered bicycle carrying two or more riders balanced precipitously on the front and back wheel guards. Blasting horns create an ear-splitting cacophony.

I feel trapped. Something's about to happen. I can sense it. Deborah stares at the Palestinian boys. "They're only kids!" she says.

Mahmoud turns to me and says in broken English, "You like Rolling Stones?"

"Yes," I say, wondering what that has to do with anything.

"Good," he says and then slips a cassette into his four-track stereo and turns up the volume. The traffic inches forward. From all corners of Mahmoud's taxi, Mick Jagger screams, and the lyrics of "Sympathy for the Devil" reverberate through my head. Jesus Christ. What is the nature of this game?

"Christ Almighty!" I whisper to Deborah. "Who does he think he is? Francis Ford Coppola's sound man?" Deborah manages a weak smile and nods toward the right.

A helmeted PLO fighter cradles an M-60 machine gun behind a sandbag bunker. He stares at us. I turn to the other side. Fragments from the street scene flood my vision: Crowds move toward the shrill cries of street vendors selling Parisian fashions out of broken carts. Pairs of turbaned Shiite Muslims walk slowly with arms linked, followed by their black-veiled wives.

Swarms of children covered in filthy rags play on piles of rubble. Pieces of a crystal chandelier lay among the ruins of a battle-scarred building. A tattooed Kurdistan peddler squats in the mud with his merchandise spread before him. A long-sheathed knife rests against his thigh.

Mick rages on. Tanks. Blitzkrieg. Bodies. The stink.

Suddenly, there's an explosion. A gun? A car backfiring? Crowds freeze. Moments pass. Nothing. We breathe deeply.

A filthy, pockmarked beggar in a tattered, soiled caftan hobbles toward us. A cigarette hangs from the corner of his mouth. He extends his nicotine-stained fingers and then thrusts his hands through Deborah's open window. She gasps and jerks to the side. Mahmoud lets go of the wheel, reaches across the front seat, and shoves him away.

I heard a voice in my head shouting something about the Kennedys and who was to blame.

Deborah grasps my arm. Her hands sweat with tension. She shakes her head from side to side as if she's vacillating between terror and disbelief. Traffic screeches to a halt. Drivers are screaming. A man leaps from the back of a car, fires his automatic weapon in the air, slams the butt of his rifle onto the hoods of adjacent cars, and with the barrel, motions them to get out of his way. Frantically, they move. He jumps back into the car and speeds away.

Mahmoud turns and says, "Crazy place, huh?" Deborah and I exchange glances and we both laugh. For a moment, the absurdity of it all seems more real than the horror. The traffic now starts to move. In a few minutes, we're on the Beirut-Damascus road. The traffic is light and Mahmoud flies.

Glancing at us in the rearview mirror, Mahmoud says, "In Lebanon, you never know what the next moment will hold or whether there'll be a next moment. What is life? We all die. Me, I'm not afraid of dying. De-bo-rah," he says emphasizing each syllable of her name, "I only want to enjoy. You understand me?"

The twisted road to Kab Elias winds its way treacherously up a steep mountain. On either side of the road, Syrian soldiers lean against tanks and sandbag emplacements, their machine guns aimed directly at every passing car.

The view from Mahmoud's speeding taxi—when it's not being obstructed by massive Syrian armor—is stunning. Meticulously constructed stone walls define one row of terraced fields from another. The silvery leaves of olive trees reflect the sunlight, creating moving patterns of light and shadow. The air has that fresh smell that follows the rain. The foreboding rain clouds that envelop Beirut contrast with the luminous blue sky directly above us.

Mahmoud's determined to display every nuance of his driving skill. On blind curves, he passes lumbering Syrian tank-carriers, barely missing the oncoming traffic. I pray he can intuit what lies ahead. Deborah says, in a rather unconvincing voice, "I don't think we've come this far to die in an automobile accident." I don't share her confidence. With one hand on the wheel, Mahmoud turns around, looks at Deborah for a dangerously long time, and then continues to enlighten her on life in Lebanon.

"For us, there's no tomorrow," he says. "You in America say, 'This is the first day of the rest of your life.' I say, 'This could be the last day of your life.' Lebanon has no future. Who cares about us?"

Pointing to the Syrian soldiers standing by tanks and sandbag bunkers, he says, "They're pigs! I hate them. They want Lebanon for themselves." Spitting out the words, he asks, "You want to know what Lebanon is about?" He doesn't wait for a reply, he launches into Yvonne mode, what psychologists in the future will identify as the first mark of post-traumatic stress disorder: the endless stream of talking, repeating traumatic scenes again and again, as if for the first time.

A Syrian soldier motions for us to pull off the road. Mahmoud bangs the steering wheel and lets out a stream of Arabic curses. "Get your passports and visas ready," he says.

"What do they want with us?" Deborah asks.

"Probably nothing," he answers. "You're Americans."

That's no protection! a voice in my head screams. *What about the American hostages in Teheran? At a whim, they can throw us into a dungeon.*

Deborah's hands are shaking as she takes out our passports.

"Passports and visas!" the soldier demands in Arabic. He looks at our passports, glares at us, and then examines them page by page. "Where born?" he asks in English.

"Philadelphia, Pennsylvania," I answer, feigning control and acting like it's natural for us to be driving to Kab Elias. He takes our passports to his commanding officer, who's standing by a large mortar mounted on a flatbed truck.

"Is there a problem?" Deborah asks Mahmoud.

"Who knows?" he mumbles.

The officer looks at us, says a few more words to the soldier, and walks toward us. He's in his midthirties and has a kind face and smile. I'm suspicious.

"What brings you to Lebanon?" he asks in perfect English.

Trying to appear cool, I explain to him about Deborah and Kab Elias. He smiles and says, "I hope you find your family." He returns our passports and visas and waves us on. Each one of us lets out a lengthy sigh of relief.

As we reach the highest point of the road, a marvelous scene leaps out at us. Below us lies the Beqaa Valley—a fertile swath of land covered with shades of green, highlighted with occasional specks of red and yellow. Mahmoud points out Kab Elias, a distant spot on the right surrounded by mountains.

I'm trying to imagine we're climbing Mount Dunmore, close to our Vermont house, safe in the shadow of the giant nameless trees, far from this crazy country.

Deborah, on the other hand, is right here.

Tears flow down her face. Mahmoud notices and remarks, "This must be a special moment for you—to return to your grandmother's birthplace." He seems almost embarrassed by his spontaneous expression of tenderness. A few moments pass, he breathes deeply, and the harshness returns to his voice. "It's good she left."

At the sign for Kab Elias, Mahmoud turns right onto a narrow farm road that has more potholes than pavement. Fiercely displaying his disregard for death, he heads directly into an oncoming truck. Deborah covers her eyes. At the last possible moment, Mahmoud concedes, veers sharply to the right, barely avoiding an almond tree.

The road passes through cultivated fields of potatoes and other root vegetables, followed by groves of apple, olive, and pomegranate. On the side of the hills, neat rows of grapevines overlook plots of wheat and barley. Muslim women, wearing scarves and dressed in long multicolored skirts with pants underneath, load bunches of vegetables into baskets strapped to the backs of their donkeys. A frustrated boy, with a whip in one hand and the handle of a primitive plow in the other, attempts to convince a disagreeable mule to make a 180-degree turn. The mule refuses; the boy threatens; the mule whines. They remind me of an old married couple.

Close to the road, we notice a cluster of open Bedouin tents. Donkeys, goats, dogs, and Bedouins move freely within the space in a kind of symbiotic extension of one another. Cooking utensils, rugs, and bedding lie in a pool of urinated mud and manure. Two children and a dog chase a lamb in and out of a tent.

A tattooed Bedouin girl stands by the side of the road. An explosion of blue lines and dots transforms her hands and face into a work of ethnic art. A turban of red and black wool hides her hair. From her neck to the soles of her feet, layers of multicolored wool, cotton, and linen cover her thin body. Beads, silver, and copper dangle from her neck and wrists.

Farther down the same road, Mahmoud points to a squalid Palestinian refugee camp of tiny, box-like, cement structures with slits for windows. Except for an occasional child sloshing in the mud or a dog scavenging for food, the place appears abandoned. Mahmoud informs us that most of the men are in a Palestinian military unit somewhere in Lebanon or work in another Arab country. Rarely, he says, are entire families together.

The nauseating smell of rotting garbage welcomes us to Kab Elias. Despite the morning rain, the air is thick with dust. A fine sediment of caked, brown-red mud covers the car, our clothes, and the silver leaves of the olive trees. Swirling clouds of dirt and debris dim our vision.

Sand piles, building materials, and heavy equipment create an impression of activity and growth. The equipment is still, the scaffolds are empty, and the half-completed foundations appear forgotten.

Kab Elias slopes along the side of a steep hill with steps leading from one level to the next. This multilevel construction is similar to towns we visited in France—but without their beauty and mystique. Constructed from cinder blocks, the box-like buildings mirror the ambiance of the town. The old is dilapidated; the new lacks inspiration.

I break the silence and say, "This place—"

Deborah cuts me off with a terse, "Not now, Michael." Her tears and the tone of her voice tell me Deborah and I are not in the same Kab Elias. Mine is filth and fear; her Kab Elias is family history.

Mahmoud suggests we start our search for Georgette at the town hall. As we pass well-armed Syrians, my eyes meet those of a soldier. I look away. The remnants of evil stare from all sides. The walls of the building to my right are ripped and disfigured. Like a memorial to the horrors of war, piles of gray rubble—the work of a mortar, no doubt— lie neglected on the sides of the street. Kab Elias is dead, removed from any attempts at life support, abandoned to its tragic fate.

We arrive at the town hall where we enter a large rectangular room with bare, dirty beige walls, a beat-up desk, and two metal folding chairs. I'm intrigued by the absence of filing cabinets. Behind the desk sits a rather nondescript, bored-looking Muslim woman in her midtwenties wearing a bland dress and scarf. With her eyes glued to her desk, as if engrossed in a serious decision regarding the town's welfare, she fails to acknowledge our presence, which I find absolutely astonishing. It's not like two Westerners looking for information at the town hall are a daily phenomenon. If I didn't know better, I'd say we'd entered the Vermont State Psychiatric Hospital. Mahmoud asks if she knows Georgette Haddad. She shakes her head.

"How could she not know her?" Deborah asks. "Everybody must know everybody. Tell her we have her telephone number. They must have records somewhere. Ask her to check." The woman doesn't meet our eyes. We're invisible.

Mahmoud asks, "Could you please call this number for us?"

"The phones don't work," she mumbles. Who knows, I think, maybe she just discovered that her brother or husband has been murdered. To be fair, there's an endless number of ways to feel miserable in Lebanon. I remind myself to be less judgmental.

Deborah's search has touched Mahmoud. He says to her, "Don't worry, we'll walk around town and look for someone who knows Georgette. I'm sure we'll find her."

Deborah's relieved. I'm not. Looking at the empty, filthy town hall with its lifeless clerk, I think Kab Elias exists for one reason—to leave it. Why would any sane person want to live in an abandoned, hopelessly depressing place controlled by a foreign army? Who says Georgette still lives here? Yvonne hasn't spoken to her nor received news about her since the beginning of the civil war five years ago.

The three of us turn to leave, not sure what to do next. I think, *Let's stop everyone in Kab Elias and ask them if they know Georgette Haddad. Someone will know where she is or what happened to her.* I'm about to share my thoughts when—

Directly in front of us stands a tall, immaculately dressed, white-haired gentleman, perhaps in his late sixties—the ghost of Cosmo Topper, the dapper banker from the fifties TV series of the same name. His sharply creased three-piece suit with wide lapels is reminiscent of a style worn by a man of taste some thirty years ago. His shirt is white, severely starched, and adorned with gold cufflinks and a stickpin. Out of his stiff collar flows a broad red striped tie. A gold chain, undoubtedly connected to a timepiece, hangs between a buttonhole and a breast pocket in a perfect semicircle.

For a moment, I wonder if I'm not hallucinating. Who is this distinguished gentleman standing before us, so untouched by the filth and violence—as if he's dropped in from a more humane era?

The man takes a step forward, looks directly at us, and asks in flawless French, "May I be of assistance to you?"

"I hope so," Deborah replies. "We're looking for Georgette Haddad. Do you know her?"

"I do," he says.

"You do?" I blurt out in English. "Incredible!"

The old man looks at me with a bemused expression and says to Deborah, "If you like, I will take you to her."

"Yes, please," Deborah says, restraining tears of joy, astonishment, and gratitude, and probably a number of other emotions neither she nor I could identify.

Silently and slowly, with our guide in the lead, Mahmoud, Deborah, and I wind our way through a misshapen maze of blind alleys filled with the ever-present trash, rubble, and dried mud. Here and there, a grossly disfigured wall reveals its part in some skirmish.

There's no life in these dark, musty alleys. The only sound is our shoes making contact with the well-worn stone blocks.

Suddenly Deborah exclaims, "These are the alleys! The ones she spoke about! This is where Sito played hide and seek—the only cool place in Kab Elias."

The alley opens up to a gray, four-unit apartment building. Flower boxes filled with bright red geraniums hang from the balconies. Their health and beauty are evidence of loving hands.

Our guide points to an upper-level apartment close to us and says, "This is Georgette's home." We climb the stairs; he knocks on the door. No answer. He knocks again. I can't tell if it's my heart or Deborah's that's beating madly. Softly, I whisper, "Please be home."

Again, a knock; again, no answer.

"Georgette, Georgette!" he calls. More time passes. A woman responds from the lower balcony. They exchange some brief words in Arabic. She hurries up the stairs. We watch this short, plump, plain-looking woman in her early sixties come toward us. She has light, olive-colored skin, dark hair—perhaps dyed; she wears a light-green dress and heavy support hose; a large gold cross hangs from her neck.

Everything about her is unremarkable, except her kind smile and warm brown eyes.

The elderly man turns to Deborah and says, "This is Georgette. What would you like me to tell her?"

Displaying remarkable self-control, Deborah looks at Georgette and says, "Please tell her I am Deborah Risk from America, and I am Affifie Haddad's granddaughter. She and I are cousins."

He translates. Georgette's smile disappears. She looks shocked—or is it confusion I see on her face? She says nothing. She stares intently at Deborah. Does she see the family features in Deborah's face?

Silence.

Her lack of response elicits doubts in me. Who is Affifie Haddad to her? An older cousin from America she's never met. And now her American-born granddaughter just appears. Is she supposed to react like it's the second coming of Christ?

The silence continues. Deborah seems to be on guard, poised to go in any direction. Maybe she's preparing to react to Georgette's disinterest, or even resentment. We did just drop into her life unannounced. More time passes and still there's no answer—in words or gesture.

But then it comes.

First with her chin. There's a slight tremor, and then the color returns to her cheeks. The first sign of moisture appears in her eyes. Tentatively, she moves toward Deborah and extends her hand. Deborah responds and moves forward to meet Georgette. She takes Deborah's hands in hers and kisses them.

Georgette and Deborah burst into tears and embrace one another. It's too much for me. I cry—followed quickly by Mahmoud, who's coughing, rubbing his eyes, and looking very embarrassed. Only the elderly man remains dry-eyed. He kisses Georgette and Deborah on both cheeks and then politely takes his leave, disappearing like an angel who has come for this singular purpose and now must return.

With tears streaming down her face, Georgette invites us into her home. It's a small, immaculately clean apartment. We follow her into the salon. Like Mario's *sito* and Samya, Georgette has arranged her two sofas on opposite walls. The solidly built and well-cared-for cedar wall-unit reminds me of Sito's beloved china closet, an anniversary gift from her husband, Deborah's *ghido*—grandfather—who saved every penny he earned peddling watches door to door in the dreary coal mining towns of West Virginia.

I remember something Deborah once told me. "Every Sunday after church, and for every holiday, birth, and death, the whole family would go to Sito's home. The men would sit silently on one side of the room with Ghido in the center, and the women would be on the other side, babbling about food and kids. I'd be on the floor near Sito."

As I stand in Georgette's living room, I can see them all here.

Georgette tells Mahmoud she'll be back in a moment and dashes out of the apartment. Mahmoud, balanced on the edge between tears and laughter, tells Deborah he's sure Georgette ran to announce to her friends, neighbors, and family that the relatives from America have arrived. No doubt, he tells us, she's recruiting a significant portion of the Kab Elias female population, both Muslim and Christian, to help with the Feast of the Returning Cousin.

In ten minutes, Georgette, who's standing at the bottom of the stairs, yells to Mahmoud to help her. She refuses *our* offers to assist. You serve guests; you don't ask them to help. Mahmoud and Georgette return, carrying seven bags full of nuts, cheese, fruit, candies, and assorted other Lebanese delights.

Through sign language, she points to the small dining room table near the door separating the kitchen from the salon. Mahmoud, Deborah, and I take our seats as Georgette darts back and forth between the living room and the kitchen bringing an extravaganza of cookies, persimmons, olives, goat cheese, pita, pistachios, hummus, candy, and coffee. With each appearance, she asks Mahmoud to tell us she loves us.

"Deborah," I ask, "what would she have done if she knew we were coming?"

"I have a feeling this is just the beginning," she answers.

Mahmoud, who's gorging on cookies, pita, and candy, announces he has to leave, and he'll return at five o'clock to take us back to Beirut. Georgette begs him to stay overnight, but he tells her he can't.

As Mahmoud departs, two oversized Muslim women enter, wearing a collection of brightly covered scarves and long embroidered dresses. Georgette tells them who we are. They throw their arms up in joy and waddle across the room to smother us with hugs and kisses. As they jabber at us in a peculiar mixture of pidgin English and Arabic, they serve us more food.

"Is good? Is good?" they ask.

"It's good. It's good," we answer.

One of them disappears and then reappears a few minutes later, followed by two more women in long multicolored dresses carrying screaming infants, an elderly Muslim man with a beautifully waxed mustache and a white keffiyeh, three teenage girls in school uniforms, and assorted other adults and children. Each one embraces us, kisses us on the cheek, and tells us to eat. And then they all vanish—including Georgette.

"What's happening?" I ask, as if Deborah's the expert on Lebanese culture.

"Oh, my God! Oh, my God!"

"Oh, my God, what? What's the matter?" I ask.

"Oh, my God! Don't you know?"

"Know? Know what? Did I miss something?"

"Do you know where Georgette just went?" Deborah asks, her voice full of terrible knowledge.

"No, where?" I ask.

"To buy meat!" she cries.

"Meat?"

"Yes, meat! I'm sure of it. She's going to cook us a feast with meat. Lamb! For sure, lamb! What am I going to do? I haven't touched meat in eleven years."

"Calm down!" I say. "Just tell her you don't eat meat. What's the big deal?"

"In sign language?" she asks. "I can't. This isn't America. They don't know about vegetarians. She and her friends are probably spending their entire week's food budget right now on lamb. She'll think she failed as a hostess if I don't eat. I'll disgrace her and probably most of Kab Elias. What am I going to do?"

"So, eat it! Think of it as an act of love. If you chew quickly and take a lot of vegetables with it, you won't even taste it."

Deborah's wringing her hands as she paces back and forth across the room whimpering, "I'm sick, I'm sick. What am I going to do? I'll gag for sure. I'll vomit. Oh, my God, I can't possibly. No! I must. I can't ... You're right—an act of love . . ."

"This is great," I say. "We travel halfway around the world on bicycles, get terrorized by rats in Brussels, ride through freezing rain in France, fight off ravenous mosquitoes in Italy, shit our guts out in Greece, dodge bullets and bombs in Lebanon—and you have a nervous breakdown over a little piece of flesh! Consider it a small price to pay for discovering your family."

And then, as if God Himself sent her a sign, she glares at me and says, "I assure you, I will not eat meat and I won't embarrass Georgette."

"So, what's your plan?"

"You'll see," she answers.

After fifteen minutes, Georgette returns with two bags of groceries and, with a big grin, shows off what looks like the entire rear half of a lamb.

I can see from Deborah's repetitive attempts at swallowing that she's determined to control her gag reaction.

Holding up a leg of lamb and pointing to the clock, Georgette "tells" us to return in an hour. She encourages us to explore Kab Elias while she prepares the meal.

Deborah wants to photograph the Missionary School that Sito attended. As we retrace our steps toward the center of town, we pass groups of schoolgirls in gray uniforms and beige scarves standing near armed Syrian soldiers. The girls giggle when they see us; the soldiers stare. We are as inconspicuous in Kab Elias as a Hasidic Jew at a Baptist revival in Biloxi, Mississippi.

Near the town hall, we stop to photograph an old monument erected in the 1800s in memory of French troops. A tiny middle-aged man approaches us and says in French, "Hello, are you looking for someone?"

"No, we're looking for the Missionary School. Does it still exist?" Deborah asks.

"Yes. Why do you want to see it?" he asks.

At the mention of Sito's name, he leaps forward to hug and kiss Deborah on each cheek. "We're cousins! We're cousins!" he shouts. "I am Ibrahim Khouri. Come! You must meet my mother."

He leads us to an old, shabby house marked by bullet holes. It's dark inside. An old woman in black sits in a corner, illuminated by a ray of light. Ibrahim tells her who we are. She reaches out to kiss Deborah and says in Arabic, which her son translates to French, "I remember Affifie Haddad. Her mother and my mother were cousins. We went to school together. She's had a good life in America?"

"Yes, very good," Deborah answers. "She has eleven grandchildren."

"It's good she went to America and they raised you there," she says. "I told my children to leave. I have two sons in Australia and a daughter in Brazil. Only Ibrahim is here. I tell him to go, but he says, 'Momma, what would I do without you?'" She stops, looks down for a second, and says, "It's hard here. We have no future."

She tells Ibrahim to bring us food and coffee. She points to family photos, Sito's relatives, I guess. One photo—at least fifty years old—sends chills up my spine. A well-dressed elderly gentleman stands next to a woman in black. I swear he's the same man who introduced us to Georgette.

"Who is he?" Deborah asks Ibrahim, who carries a tray laden with yet more Turkish coffee, pita, hummus, olives, cookies, and candy.

"He was your great-grandfather's cousin," he answers.

Ibrahim offers to drive us back to Georgette's. He's Kab Elias's only cab driver and owns what may be the only car in town. He first takes us to the Missionary School, where Deborah photographs a group of uniformed schoolgirls standing near the entrance.

The school has not aged well. Letters are missing from its name. The stone exterior is badly cracked and broken. There are no trees, grass, or flowers to brighten its sad and neglected appearance. After a few minutes, Ibrahim drops us off at Georgette's.

An overpowering smell of roasting meat greets us at her door. Grease is in the air. Deborah's tottering like a top at the end of its rotation. Georgette announces the meal is ready.

Georgette has moved the small table into the center of the salon and has set it with her best Sunday linen and china: a slightly frayed and faded white tablecloth, two old, chipped dishes engraved with a pastoral scene, and once-proud silverware that's probably been around since before Sito left Kab Elias.

Suddenly, out of nowhere, four hefty women shaped like overstuffed pitas make their appearance. After enveloping us with hugs and kisses, they join Georgette in the kitchen.

Almost immediately, they return in single file, each one carrying a platter of food. One by one, they set our first course before us:

Baba ghanoush, pita, hummus, batangen makdood (eggplant with pine nuts and olive oil), and labane (yogurt).

The chorus of women are all singing, *"Zahtane, zahtane!"* (Eat! Enjoy!) "Is good? Is good? You like? You like?"

One of the women speaks barely recognizable French and relays Georgette's barrage of questions: "How is Fudwa? How is Nora Ghiz? How is Sito? Where are Michael's people from? When were you married? Where are your children?"

I'm impressed with how quickly Deborah invents such plausible answers to conceal that Fudwa is dead, Nora Ghiz has been divorced three times, I'm Jewish, and we're not married. They all bob their heads up and down and smile at her answers until Deborah tells them we've been married for six years and have no children.

"Why?" Georgette asks. Deborah explains about career choices, priorities, and other foreign concepts, and all the women can do is shake their heads and feel sad for us.

Silently, two of the women clear the table. Georgette enters carrying a tray with tabbouleh, green bean salad, fatayer (spinach pies), and zaatar talamee (flat bread). She places each dish before us and extends her arm, inviting us to partake.

"*Zahtane! Zahtane!*" the chorus cries. The women seem genuinely concerned about Deborah's lack of excess flesh and insist she eat more. She meekly obliges.

I reach under the table to loosen my belt to prepare for the next course. I turn to Deborah who's nervously picking her thumb and whisper, "Don't worry, Deborah, this is merely foreplay—the meat will soon arrive."

The largest of the four women clears the table while the other three seat themselves on the couches as if waiting for a performance to begin. Then, slowly and proudly, Georgette appears, carrying one of the largest trays of food I've ever seen. Reverently, as if ministering to royalty, she sets the next course before us and serves us.

In the top left corner of our plates, she places a mountain of reddish-brown, raw lamb. I'm struck by how similar the color is to the dry, caked mud that covers much of Kab Elias. To its immediate right, she spoons chunks of brown, fried lamb, swimming in its fat. Directly below it, she covers the entire bottom third of the plate with pieces of grayish lamb and green beans.

Deborah's ghost white. I imagine her fainting and falling face first into this large, brown, and bloody pile. Meanwhile, she takes her fork and moves the pieces of lamb from one side of the plate to the other.

Georgette returns to the kitchen. The four matrons follow her.

"Michael, you know what you have to do, don't you?" Deborah says.

"What?"

"You eat it!"

"That's your plan? Forget it; I can't eat anymore!"

"Oh, yes, you can!" And then she dumps her entire pile of meat and vegetables on mine. Afraid of being caught, I devour the entire mound of meat in seconds.

Georgette returns, overjoyed at her success. Again, she loads our plates and disappears, and again Deborah dumps her food on mine.

"Woman, you owe me big time," I say, resigned to the fact that there's nothing I can or will do to avoid eating another plate of Georgette's gift, lovingly prepared for her relatives from America.

"Look at it this way, Michael," Deborah says. "Consider it an act of love to your new wife and her new cousin. Just know you ate your way right into our hearts."

"Very cute," I mutter to myself as I pick up my fork. So what if I get a stomachache? It's the least I can do to express my appreciation. Georgette and her friends have opened their hearts and wallets to us. Our gratitude is our receiving. Also, it's a kind of spiritual scrubbing— a refuge from the encounters with Yvonne. With each gamy bite, I feel restored, released from the hate of the last eight days.

Mahmoud was right—the word has spread: The relatives from America have returned to Kab Elias!

It's a genealogist's dream.

Kab Elias cousins are leaping from the family tree. Georgette, acting like the Godmother of the clan, has invited every known relative, even if he or she is a distant tenth cousin, once removed. Family is family. Somewhere on top of the tree, they all connect. Maybe eight generations back, there was a young farmer named Yousef Rizid who married Rose Haddad, the oldest daughter of Diep and Mary Haddad, and that's the link. I remember hearing Sito mention those names on one of our visits to Charleston, but when Deborah asked her who they were, she couldn't recall which branch they belonged to.

It really doesn't matter because, as we are about to find out, Sito had no idea how many family members she left behind and what became of them.

But *we* do.

Hovering near the entrance of the living room, looking rather uncomfortable, stand three men, two women, a teenage girl, two boys probably ten years old, and three young girls ranging in age from six to nine.

They all wear their Sunday finest.

The men and boys sport dark, wide-lapelled jackets, baggy cuffed pants, white shirts, and wide ties. The women and girls wear gold crosses, and except for one of them, out-of-fashion skirts and blouses with clashing colors and lines forming multiple geometric patterns. Their black patent-leather purses match their Sunday shoes.

One of the men announces in poor French, "We are your cousins. Welcome to Kab Elias."

They form a line, from the oldest to the youngest, and each one stiffly hugs, kisses, and introduces himself in terrible French.

"I am Elias, Georgette's brother, and this is my wife Sulwa." They're both in their late fifties. Elias is a tall, erect man with the rough hands of a farmer. Sulwa's a plump, cheerful-looking woman with a dark olive complexion and a prominent nose.

"I am Chaffic, Georgette's brother, and this is my wife Nazha." I like his face. He has a beautiful, bushy mustache; dark, laughing eyes; and the permanently tanned skin of a man who lives outdoors. Nazha is a small, sad-looking woman. She takes Deborah's hands in hers and kisses them.

"I am Assad, Georgette's son." Assad, a man in his midtwenties, has his mother's round face and ready smile.

"I am Mona, Chaffic and Nazha's daughter." Mona doesn't fit. Her French is excellent. Her clothes are more appropriate for the Beirut scene. She's probably only sixteen, but there is a seriousness and determination in her face you rarely see in an American teenager. This town seems too small for her dreams.

Following them are the five children. "I am Yousef, Chaffic and Nazha's son." "I am George, Elias and Sulwa's son." The younger children giggle; the older ones rigidly embrace us.

"I'm overwhelmed," Deborah says as she looks at each member of her newfound family. Mona immediately translates Deborah's words for the family. "This is a wonderful surprise for me. I had no idea I had such a large family in Kab Elias. I am so happy to—" and the tears flow. The women cry, the men try to maintain control, and the children squirm.

A strange thought enters my head. In January 1976, when Deborah and I were attending a doctoral seminar on creativity and madness, her entire Kab Elias family may have been running from Palestinian terrorists. I can't help but glance at the children's fingers. Thank God, they're all there.

The adults and Mona join us at the table; the children sit on the couch and chairs. The questions start. "How is Sito? How is Fudwa? How long have you been married?"

The story is the same. "Michael and I have been married for six years—"

"What kind of work does Michael do?" Mona asks Deborah.

"We're both psychologists."

"Psychologists? What's that?" Mona asks for Elias.

"We help people with personal problems," answers Deborah.

"What types of problems do you have in America?" asks Mona, as if the last thing she could imagine is a struggling American.

I'm intrigued to discover how Deborah will answer that one. How do you talk about American psychological issues and discontent to folks whose problems are so concrete, so much about the daily challenge of staying alive, and so much about genuine loss, that anything we say would have to sound unbelievably trite and foolish?

I imagine telling Georgette, Chaffic, Nazha, Mona, and the whole clan about my client Ann. *She left her husband and two young children for her female lover. "I had to," Ann told me. "How else would I discover who I am?" She felt compelled to rebel against her puritanical Catholic upbringing. She loved her husband and children, but finding herself was more important. Was she courageous or selfish? I wasn't sure. Neither was she. She made a serious suicide attempt and her ex-husband saved her.* No doubt they'd resonate with Ann's existential angst and her wholehearted search for authenticity.

Or, what if Deborah were to tell them about our Gestalt group clients who beat pillows while raging at their projected parents seated in an empty chair? Sure, these people would understand the need to spill your guts before a group of strangers.

234 | *Riding the Edge*

"We need more of what you have in Kab Elias," Deborah answers. "Never come to Charleston unannounced. It would take two weeks to organize a family reunion. And then, half the family wouldn't show up. Just not interested or too busy. Family is not as important as it is in Kab Elias. Too many Americans don't feel connected."

Mona translates, and an animated discussion in Arabic follows between Sulwa, Chaffic, and Elias. "Aunt Sulwa wants to know how you can help someone who doesn't have a close family?"

I like the innocence of the question. It's like asking, "How do you help someone breathe when he doesn't have lungs?" I want to help Deborah out—we've got a serious cross-cultural divide here. There are no common icons. Our American hero is an orphan—a self-reliant individual. He needs nothing from no one. We find our truth by leaving the family. Not by staying glued to it. It's how we learn to breathe on our own.

Deborah's Kab Elias cousins find their sense of belonging within the family. It's their respirator.

"It's different in America," Deborah says. "Just like you, we need friends and family. But making money and having a career takes over. So, there's less time for family. And, we usually don't live close to each other."

Deborah turns to me and says, "Help me out. How do I answer the question?"

I laugh. "Try this: We help our clients figure out who they are and what they want. Then we support them to follow their dreams. Sometimes with the encouragement of family, sometimes without, and sometimes against what the family wants."

This triggers another lively discussion among the adults. After a few moments, Mona turns to Deborah looking somewhat nervous and says, "My mother wants to know why you and Michael don't have children?"

Deborah tries to explain the challenges of a professional lifestyle. What she won't say is that, like many of our peers, we chose career over family.

I'm watching Mona as she listens to Deborah. Her lively, light brown eyes focus on Deborah as she tries to understand what she's saying. This time, Mona doesn't translate but asks, "Oh, you mean you and Michael could have children, you just don't want any?"

"Mona," Deborah says, "it's not that simple. We want children. We're just not ready yet. We plan to start a family when we return from this trip."

"It's different for us," Mona says. "If I'm not married by twenty, my parents worry. But it's harder now. There are fewer young men. They run away to Australia or America, or they stay and fight." Her face tenses, and she turns toward her parents. "I have two older brothers in Sydney and a sister in California. And . . . my brother Moses, he died last year fighting Syrians. It's hard for my mother. She cries all the time. She won't eat. I sometimes think she wants to die." Her father interrupts and says something sharply in Arabic. A heated interaction follows between Mona and her father.

Mona translates. "My family doesn't want me to burden you with our problems. My father says with God's help, everything will be okay. We must believe everything is for the best and we shouldn't question God's ways. He says today, we celebrate the coming together of our family—a blessing and a miracle."

It's strange. I don't know who should give strength to whom. The family carries deep wounds. How do we respond? Do they need to share their pain with us? If so, should we ask questions? Or respect their need for privacy? The psychologist in me is stumped. The cultural divide is too deep.

Their religion brings them solace. Family gives them security and a sense of belonging. Definitely not very American, but do we Americans, who know nothing of the horror and pain of war on our own shores—and who, for years, have slowly dissolved the family unit—have any meaningful answers to give this family? Silence and respect seem to be the only appropriate response.

One of the women offers us more pie and coffee. This is our sixth cup of very strong, black, and bitter Turkish coffee. My stomach screams; my brain buzzes like a high-tension wire.

Over the next couple of hours, the family continues to question us about life in America, our professions, and the sights and scenes of our trip. In response to their questions about American family life, Deborah emphasizes the disconnect. What she's really telling them is: "Despite your suffering, you have each other."

The discussions are mostly about us. They gently deflect our attempts to elicit information about their lives. "It's difficult, but we manage. And we have each other." I can't tell whether it's stoicism or serenity, but there's a noticeable lack of complaints. They've opened their hearts to us, and we feel their love.

At five, Mahmoud returns. The family begs us to remain. Unfortunately, we tell them we can't. Mahmoud's our only link to Beirut. Amid tears, hugs, and promises to write, we separate. As we're about to enter the taxi, Mona grabs Deborah's hands and says, "Thank you for coming. You're the only Americans who've ever visited us. My family wouldn't like me telling you this: It's terrible for us here. We never know what will happen next. The future will bring more killing and suffering."

With deep emotion, Mona continues, "I envy you. You must have a wonderful life in America. I wish I could be like you—just visit Lebanon and leave, but I can't. This is my home." She swallows back her tears, and says, "Thank you again for coming. It makes us very happy knowing you thought of us." Now fully composed, she looks directly at us and says, "Don't worry. We'll be okay." She smiles and rejoins the family.

Neither Deborah nor I have Mona's self-control. Wiping the tears from her eyes, Deborah whispers to me, "I wish we could take her with us."

Holding hands in the back seat of Mahmoud's car, Deborah and I sit in silence until we reach the outskirts of Beirut. She puts her head on my shoulder; I feel her tears on my cheek. "It's been an amazing day," Deborah says, "but right now I'm overwhelmed by the pain of it all. I keep thinking about Nazha and how much she's suffering, and Mona who's such a beautiful, sensitive girl. She deserves better; they all deserve better. Nothing's changed: Kab Elias is still a place to leave.

"I've also been thinking today about eight-year-old Debbie Risk from Charleston, West Virginia, the girl with the giant imagination who loved to sit hand in hand with Sito at St. George's Syrian Orthodox Church and breathe in the frankincense and myrrh and feel the priest's haunting chants vibrate inside her skinny body. That imaginative girl would fly in her mind to an enchanted village called Kab Elias where you could pick fresh figs and pomegranates straight from the trees surrounding Sito's home.

"I came to Kab Elias," Deborah continues, "for that eight-year-old girl so she could taste the fruit and feel the magic. The pomegranates were hard, but the magic was real. I felt it in their love and hospitality, in their smiles and warmth, and in their pain and loss. But to that eight-year-old girl I have to say, 'Just like Sito, your place is not here in Kab Elias or in Beirut. It's time to move on. Lebanon is not your home.'"

At six thirty, we arrive at the Bedford Hotel. Mahmoud opens the door for Deborah and asks to speak to her in private. After five minutes, she joins me in the hotel lobby.

"What was that about?" I ask.

"He told me he loves me and wants to spend the night with me."

"You're kidding."

"I'm afraid not. He promised me that 'together, we can climb mountains of passion.'"

CHAPTER 19

Beirut to Cyprus: November 8 to November 10

A note awaits Deborah from Khalid: "Please call me immediately. It's an emergency."

Khalid tells Deborah that her best friend, Dasia, a cellist, is in a terrible state. She has until tomorrow to decide whether to accept an offer to join a major Parisian orchestra. It's a once-in-a-lifetime opportunity, but it means leaving her parents, two sisters, and brother. Her father doesn't want her to go; her mother does. For the first time in her life, she may defy her father. For a typical American, it's a no-brainer. Personal freedom and growth trump family loyalty. However, for an unmarried, twenty-one-year-old Muslim girl, this is as hard as it gets.

Khalid wants Deborah to meet with Dasia to help her to decide. "I'm an American. I'm biased toward leaving. It's in my DNA. I left home when I was sixteen and I never looked back. How can I possibly understand her attachment to family?"

"She understands that," Khalid answers. "That's why Dasia wants to speak to you. She wants you to convince her to leave."

"I don't do that. I don't convince people to do what I think they want. If this is what she really wants, I'll help her find the strength to stand by her convictions."

At seven thirty, Dasia meets Deborah at the Bedford where they retreat to our room. Meanwhile, I hustle Riad in a game of gin rummy. He loses four sets in a row, cursing me for cheating a poor Muslim boy out of his hard-earned money—which neither of us expects him to

238

pay. After ninety minutes, Deborah and Dasia come downstairs, hug, and say goodbye. Deborah's eyes are red and moist.

"She's leaving for Paris tomorrow. That girl's so brave. We role-played telling her father. At first, she was terrified—afraid he'll cut her off emotionally and financially. I kept on asking her, 'If he does, what will you do? Can you handle it?' She can and she will. I don't think it will come to that. He'll come around," she says.

"Spending the day in Kab Elias helped me to understand her dilemma. Family loyalty doesn't exist for either of us. Family is what you get away from, not what you hang on to for your sense of belonging. It's not the same for Mario or Mona or Dasia. And it wasn't the same for Sito either.

"Her mother told her, 'God blessed you with talent. You cannot let your family stand in the way of God's will. Your father's my problem, not yours. I will help him.'"

A few hours later, Dasia calls to say a miracle happened. Her father apologized for being so hard on her. "He cried, told me he was proud of me and loved me." Dasia tells Deborah she'll be grateful to her forever.

"Dasia," Deborah says, "my job was easy. You're the one with the courage to follow your heart. You're my hero. Never forget it."

It's now nine thirty, and we retreat for our nightly decompression session. Nothing helps facilitate emotional discharge more effectively than wine, cashews, and cookies made from clarified butter and rosewater. You nibble and process; you sip and share; you savor the sweet and salty flavors while you reflect on personal freedom and family loyalty.

Until . . .

The tracers fly. The bombs burst. And you realize that less than a quarter of a mile from your hotel, the biggest battle in five years has just begun. The flash of a mortar round sounds dangerously close. From an adjacent street, a grenade explodes. Kalashnikov rounds hit the outside walls of the Bedford, ripping chunks of cement from the side of the building. White dust covers the windows and balcony.

It's time to get the hell out of here.

As we run down the stairs to the lobby, we feel the building shake from side to side—or maybe it's the pounding pulse of our hearts. The first person we meet is Mariana, ghost-white and whimpering. She shakes, babbles incoherently that she's too young to die, and asks Deborah to hold her. Deborah puts her arms around Mariana's frail shoulders and talks her down like she's a kid who's just seen a real elephant walk out of her closet. To see someone ten times more scared than you has a strangely soothing effect. Someone needs to hold it together, or we'll all drown in the same cesspool.

The entire Bedford population—the three Germans, Riad, the receptionist, Deborah and I—huddles shoulder to shoulder around one small table. Missing are the two crazies from the second floor. Riad tells us they darted from the hotel thirty minutes ago, armed to the hilt and drugged to the core.

To be an excellent psychologist, you need to walk a thin line between clinical distance and objectivity on the one hand, and compassion and rapport on the other. Tilt in either direction and you fail to create a human-to-human connection, or you so overidentify with your client that you can't remember where you end and the client begins.

I'm in a therapeutic state of mind, and from the way Deborah holds and soothes Mariana, she is too. Call it our default positions when facing extreme anxiety—our flight to health when others' needs are greater than our own. I talk down Gustav, who's blaming Peter for suggesting they sell Mercedes cars in a "fucking war zone." Mariana—who's been sleeping with Peter—takes a momentary hiatus from whimpering and jumps to Peter's defense. "Gustav, you fucker, you wanted this as much as Peter."

In my mind, they're three children, in way over their heads, doing what juveniles do when the shit flies—they blame one another. So, I do what I know to do: I take control. "Listen, you three. We're all in a shit storm here. I don't want to hear you fight for the next few hours. I suggest you do the smart thing and shut up, and let's get through this together. Sounds good?" Confrontation by itself is never sufficient. There's always a risk of a power struggle. So, before any of them can respond, I say, "We're all fucking scared. It could be a long night of fighting. Let's help each other stay calm."

They all pause and look at me like I'm the grown-up who's supposed to tell them what to do. I don't. And then Mariana says to Gustav, "I'm sorry."

And then Gustav says to Peter, "I'm sorry."

And Peter says to Riad, "Riad, can you bring a deck of cards? Let's play poker."

Meanwhile, Riad, the Lebanese connoisseur of American expletives, morphs into his Richard Pryor alter ego and says to Peter, "No problem, *muthafucka*, the house *nigga* will get your cards." We all laugh, which is all Riad needs to launch into more Richard Pryor lines from *Blue Collar*.

So, the three German kids are now happy. Riad's thrilled to have a captive audience. I'm teaching Deborah how to play poker, and the receptionist, Musaf, an AUB English literature major, is reading Hemingway's *The Old Man and the Sea*.

But not for long.

The sound of battle reverberates throughout the lobby, reminding Mariana that she's terrified; Gustaf and Peter, how they have "to get the fuck out of here as soon as possible," even if they have to sell the one remaining Mercedes at cost; Riad, how much he hates "the muthafucking crazies;" Deborah and Michael, how they need to breathe, focus, and talk themselves down from fear; and Musaf, how each new round makes concentrating on the *Old Man*'s struggle so much more difficult.

And, then the poker game begins—seven-card stud, high-low, no limit on our imaginary bets. Peter and I are the competitors in the group. Mariana's clueless. Deborah's a cross between eager to learn and competitive. Riad takes on the persona of an intimidating Black gambler. Gustav's serious about doing it right, and Musaf reads his book. And, so it goes for the next few hours—bad poker, small talk, and Riad's badass imitations that keep us entertained. Even Musaf picks his head "out of the sea" to hear another round of *muthafuckas* from Riad.

Around three a.m. the second-floor crazies storm into the lobby.

As usual, they're dressed in combat fatigues and carry AK-47s with five magazines attached to their chests. However, this time they've accessorized their uniform with multiple strands of gold jewelry that hang from their necks. As they approach our band of seven, I notice their glassy eyes and dilated pupils. Our crazies are high on a cocktail of amphetamines and weed. They stand before our poker table, click their heels in unison, thrust out their right arms, and shout, "Heil Hitler!" They then make a sharp about-face and goose-step across the lobby and up the stairs.

"Fuck them," Riad mutters. "Fucking Nazi criminals. That's stolen jewelry around their necks."

Every limb in Mariana's body shakes in terror. She mumbles something about the Holocaust. Peter leans toward me and tells me that part of her father's family is Jewish and died in the camps.

Deborah overhears Peter and puts her arms around Mariana and rocks her. Mariana rests her head on Deborah's shoulders and sobs. Tears stream down Deborah's cheeks. Gustav's a ghost or he's just seen one. He stares at the ornate chandelier as if the light might explain what his mind can't comprehend. I ask Gustav if he's okay, and he tells me, "No not at all. The 'Heil Hitler' freaked me out and sent me to a dark place. I don't know how to explain it."

I'm too busy focusing on everyone else to take my temperature. But I know I'd like to blow the crazies' fucking brains into a million little pieces and feed them to the sand crabs burrowed deep in the Beirut beaches.

At four a.m., all's quiet. Twelve hours later, we fly to Cyprus. At five thirty p.m., we arrive at our Limassol hotel, shell-shocked yet relieved that the only sounds we hear are the squawking of seagulls outside our window.

In two days, we take the overnight boat to Haifa.

Part 3
Returning

The Rebbe of Kotzk once challenged a newcomer to his court with, "Young man, why have you come here?"

"I have come to discover God," answered the young man.

"Then you have made an unnecessary trip, young man," the Rebbe said. "God is present everywhere. You could have discovered him right at home." "Then why have I come?" the young man asked.

"To discover yourself, young man," the Rebbe of Kotzk answered. "To discover yourself."

—A Hassidic story

CHAPTER 20

Israel:
November 10 to November 16

We're sitting on a terrace balanced at the edge of a wide cliff that scans the Mediterranean coast. Below us, you can hear the waves pounding against the boulders and rock face. By the shore, hidden within the bowels of this cliff are grottos— tunnel-like structures formed over years by the movement of the waves against the soft rock. A cable car runs from the terrace to the grottos where we can wade through this six-hundred-foot maze of caves and tunnels.

The Bible first mentions Rosh HaNikra in the Book of Joshua, where it's described as the northernmost border of the tribes of Israel, and then again in the First Book of Maccabees as one of the places where Shimon HaHashmonai ruled.

I remember Shimon HaHashmonai from my Hebrew school days as one of the heroes in the Hanukkah story who led the Jewish revolt against the Greeks. When it was close to Hanukkah, our teacher, Mrs. Feldman, would have us dress up like Shimon and his fellow warriors. A plastic sword in our hands and a white tunic covering our young bodies, we'd march around the classroom imagining ourselves to be brave Jewish soldiers in a battle to overthrow the loathsome Greeks.

At the table to our right sit two young dark-haired and brown-skinned Israeli soldiers. Their M-16s rest by their legs; their fully loaded magazines are strapped to the butt of their rifles. Behind them sit three Israeli girls, one of whom—the smallest and prettiest—has fair skin and light brown hair that falls halfway between her shoulders and waist. She wears the green khakis and combat boots of the Israeli

Army. Like the guys in front of her, an M-16 lies on the stone floor next to her right foot. All four soldiers don't look older than eighteen or nineteen years old.

Farther to our right sits a table of French tourists. To their right, a handsome, coal black UNIFIL (United Nations Interim Forces in Lebanon) soldier wearing a brown and green camouflage uniform and a cool blue beret leans back on his chair sipping a cappuccino. He's not armed.

Close to the edge of the terrace, we can see ten to twenty miles down the Israeli coast. Neither of us notices any of the ever-present bottles, newspapers, and plastic wrappers that spoil the Italian, Greek, and Lebanese shorelines. Farther south, Haifa, the third largest city of Israel, appears as a blur of mist and buildings.

Approximately three miles from us, where the sandy beach indents to create a horseshoe-shaped cove, surfers sit on their boards searching for their wave. To see them, I need to squint to block the hot midday sun from burning my eyes. We turn from the sun and walk to the eastern edge of the terrace, from where we can see the brown and dusty Galilee plains where Jesus walked barefoot and preached.

In front of us is a tall barbed-wire fence with a sign in Hebrew, Arabic, and English that reads, "Stop, beware Lebanese border. Danger!" Next to the fence, four Israeli soldiers stand guard. If we bolted past this well-fortified border between Israel and Lebanon and rode our bikes straight north, keeping the Mediterranean on our left, we'd be in Beirut by tomorrow eating Ibrahim's delicious cheese pies. So close but so far away.

*   *   *

My mother wanted to visit Israel one more time before she died. A month after she returned home, the breast cancer she'd been battling for nine years killed her. I had just turned nineteen.

My mother knew nothing about Judaism, but she was a relentless fighter for Israel. In her position as the president of Long Island Hadassah, she'd badger politicians through letter and phone campaigns, demanding they support Israel.

During the War, while my father was stationed in India, my mother lived with her parents in Philadelphia. Close to them was a POW camp. My mother called it a country club. I remember her once telling me, "While our people were being gassed, these Nazis hung out in the country club playing soccer and smoking." Beneath her devotion to Israel was a deep-seated paranoia toward the non-Jewish world. She never wanted to live in Israel, but she understood the Jewish people needed a haven.

Three days earlier, on the boat from Cyprus to Haifa, Israel

As we sit on the deck watching the seagulls dive for fish, more memories of Israel surface from some stored file deep within my unconscious mind. I share a memory with Deborah from 1966 when I was an undergraduate student at NYU.

"I never told you this. Maybe it was a month after my mother died. I was smoking weed and playing poker every day until three in the morning. I never went to classes. I was lost—not realizing how much I missed my mother. I had this idea to run away to Israel and work on a kibbutz, or volunteer to be an Israeli soldier. I even got a passport."

"So, why was Israel your place to escape to?"

"That's the question I'm asking myself. Why Israel? Obviously, it held some very special place in my psyche—like a refuge from suffering or some unconscious need to fill the emptiness after my mother's death. But I think there was more. I didn't realize it then, but I needed to discover my Jewish soul."

"So why didn't you go?" Deborah asks.

"Too scared to go alone. Or maybe the time wasn't right to discover the Jew in me."

"Well, maybe that's why you waited to go with me."

* * *

Most American Jews—especially someone like me who grew up in Roslyn Heights, Long Island—only know nominally religious, or anti-religious, or couldn't-care-less religious Ashkenazic—European—Jews. The only religious Jew I knew (barely) was a pretty Orthodox girl I met after high school when I was working as a photographer in the Catskills. She was vacationing at a bungalow colony near South Fallsburg. I saw her in a grocery store. Unlike most girls I knew, she was dressed modestly. She had large blue eyes and blonde hair—more Swedish-looking than Jewish. I struck up a conversation with her and asked her for a date. She told me she'd only date for marriage. So, I said on the spot, "I'll marry you. Now let's go on a date." She laughed and said no.

As Deborah and I walk around Haifa looking for a restaurant, I notice that most of the Israelis look more like her than me. In Israel, the Ashkenazim are the minority, outnumbered by the more Arab-looking Sephardim—Jews from North Africa and the Middle East—and dark-skinned Yemenite and Indian Jews.

From the stares Deborah gets from young Israeli men, I guess they're checking out the hot Israeli girl with Middle Eastern features. I'm surprised to see so many men wearing small multicolored kippot, different in size and style from the black yarmulkes worn by the ultra-religious Ashkenazic Jews. No one wears the floppy silk blue, white, or black yarmulkes we were required to wear inside Temple Beth Sholom.

Speaking of Temple Beth Sholom, I had the honor of being the only kid expelled from Hebrew School. Sometime after my bar mitzvah, my Hebrew-school teacher, Mr. Abrams (not his real name), screamed at me in front of the class for not doing my homework. You don't get away with that.

At the next class, I brought a bag of greasy french fries. When Mr. Abrams was writing Hebrew letters on the blackboard, I threw the fries at him and hit him in the head and back. He turned around, saw it was me, and in a fit of rage, attacked me. The room was on ground level with large open windows. I jumped out; he tried chasing me but was too fat and slow to catch me. For that offense—much to my satisfaction—I received a lifetime ban. If Mr. Abrams had been a Holocaust survivor, my mother would have put me on room arrest with only bread and water for a month. But it turned out she didn't like him either, so I never got punished.

That was the last time I entered a synagogue until that Yom Kippur with Deborah in Vermont.

We stumble upon a small dairy restaurant that serves familiar Ashkenazic cuisine: potato latkes, borscht, cheese blintzes, and onion rolls. Deborah's thrilled because it's vegetarian, but for me, it's a trip down memory lane—Sunday brunch at the local Jewish deli.

The waitress is a sweet, rotund lady in her midfifties with an Eastern European accent. She doesn't just serve; she converses and inquires as well. She wants to know who we are, where we're from, and where we're going. She asks if we're both Jewish. She tells Deborah, "You look Jewish, dear. Are you sure you're not?"

She shares this piece of advice with us about Israel: "Israel and Israelis are complicated. Look beneath the surface and hear the stories.

"You know why native-born Israelis are called Sabras?" she asks. We don't. "Because the sabra's a prickly fruit, hard and tough on the outside, but sweet and soft on the inside."

Not so with the Israeli owner of the youth hostel where we stay our first night. He's hard on the outside and harder on the inside. He doesn't smile, tells us males and females must sleep in separate dormitory rooms, warns us he locks the doors at ten p.m., and adds, "You'll sleep on the street if you're late." Later that evening, he screams at me for using hot water to wash my clothes. "You spoiled Americans think you can get away with anything."

Armed with maps and an Israeli guidebook, we'll ride due north along the coast to Akko and then from there to Nahariya. It's only fifteen miles to Akko and another six to Nahariya. We'll take our time to explore the mostly Arab walled city of Akko.

The Old City juts out like a triangle with two sides facing the Mediterranean. Fishing boats of all sizes and sophistication crowd the harbor. Some return with the morning catch; others leave the dock equipped with nets and poles to try their luck on this warm and bright November morning. On the narrow cobblestone streets, stalls sell a potpourri of Beirut-type Middle Eastern foods such as roasted nuts and dried fruits of all kinds, honey and nut pastries, soft and hard goat cheese, and green and yellow melons with the most alluring fragrances.

If it weren't for the absence of violence and the presence of Jews, you'd think you were in West Beirut, standing among Arabs in traditional garb bargaining with the merchants over the price of tomatoes, which is what the Arab wearing a keffiyeh and a white gown and the religious Jew dressed in a black fedora, black suit, and a white shirt are engaged in at the carts to our right and left. The hand gestures are similar, the languages different—Arabic and Hebrew, respectively. The outcome is the same—a significant discount on the price of tomatoes.

As we stop to buy roasted cashews from an Israeli merchant, I notice a tattooed, dark-skinned woman with fine-boned features, dressed in a long white dress. She bargains in Hebrew with an Arab merchant over the price of potatoes. The center of her forehead displays a prominent star-shaped image. Her entire neck, from front to back, displays a plethora of black snakelike dots, lines, and whorls. I imagine a secret code embedded within this intricate design.

I ask the kippa-wearing, English-speaking merchant who she is. He tells us she's an Ethiopian Jewish woman.

According to most scholars, he explains, the Ethiopian Jews descend from the Tribe of Dan, one of the Twelve Tribes of Israel. Twenty-eight hundred years ago, they emigrated from the Kingdom of Judea with one of King Solomon's sons and settled in the mountainous region of northwestern Ethiopia near the Sudanese border. There they practiced biblical Judaism, as distinguished from the rabbinical Judaism that originated during the Talmudic period approximately two thousand years ago. The merchant then launches into an esoteric lecture on the difference between the Oral Law (the Talmud) and the

Written Law (the Bible).

I sense the nutty aroma of roasted cashews and almonds calling me from my pocket and I can hear my stomach growling. I want to cut this short, but I want to know about the tattoos. So, I interrupt his monologue on Jewish history and ask him.

"The Ethiopian Jews," he tells us, looking rather annoyed at my abrupt intrusion, "adopted this local custom to blend in. Historically, there's been violent prejudice against the Ethiopian Jews from the Ethiopian population."

He finishes his history lesson with a question to me. "Do you know anything about Judaism?" When I say no, he responds by shaking his head in disappointment and says, "You should know something about your own people."

He's right. To learn about *my people* is to learn about myself.

We find a small outdoor restaurant to have a late morning breakfast. At a nearby table, two young Arabs sit with two European girls, a blonde and a brunette. From their accents, I assume the brunette is from Australia and the blonde from a Scandinavian country. One of the Arab men turns to us and invites us to join them.

Ali introduces us to his friend Sulie, the other Arab. Ali's girlfriend is Wendy from Australia, and Sulie is with Katya from Denmark. Ali and Sulie tell us they have engineering degrees from the University of Haifa but are currently unemployed. Wendy and Katya are volunteers at a kibbutz close to Akko.

All four of them ask about our trip. When we tell them about our recent experiences in Lebanon, Sulie and Ali seem pensive.

Ali asks me, "Does everyone blame the Palestinians?"

"Yes," I answer, "along with the Israelis."

"Fuckers," he says. He looks around and whispers, "I have family in a refugee camp in Beirut. I never met them." He tells us that, along with ten thousand other Arabs from Akko, they were driven from their homes by the Jews during "their War of Independence." Ali claims the Jews threatened to massacre "his people" if they didn't leave.

"The Jews were clever. They threatened to drop a nuclear bomb over Akko. The Jews steal our land, drive us out, and we end up with the rats in refugee camps in Lebanon and Jordan. We Arabs pay for the Jewish Holocaust with a Palestinian Holocaust." It's why, he informs us, the Arabs call the 1948 War of Independence *Nakba*—"The Catastrophe."

"The Israelis celebrate. We cry."

Suddenly, an old man waving a cane chases a young guy out of his store. The old man stops, panting heavily, and throws his cane at the fellow. The young man dodges the cane; his glasses fall and break. He picks up the cane and charges. Ali leaps from his chair, grabs the young man, and restrains both of them. He takes the young man by his neck, pulls him to the side, and using his index finger for emphasis, threatens him.

After a few minutes, he returns to the table and tells us the story.

"The young Jew wanted the old guy to sell him something on credit. The old Jew said no. The young one got rough. He hit the old Jew. You don't mess with that old man. He's nasty. I told the young Jew if he ever hits the old man again, I'll kill him."

"Would you really?" Wendy asks.

"Yes. You got to respect old people."

"But they're Jews," Wendy says. "You don't like Jews."

"I don't like Jews that shit on Arabs. And, I don't like Jews that shit on old Jews." He whispers again and says, "It's the Israeli government I hate. We Arabs don't exist. Invisible. If the world wasn't watching, they'd expel all of us. Fucking hypocrites—Nazis."

There's a part of me that wants to shout, "If the Israelis were Nazis, you wouldn't be telling us they are. You'd be in a concentration camp waiting to be exterminated. And, if the Jews were Nazis, you and Sulie wouldn't have received your engineering degrees from an Israeli university. And, if the Jews were Nazis, you couldn't vote . . ."

I don't say any of this. In part, because of Ali's heroic and principled act to protect the old man. And, in part, because after two days in Israel, I'm only beginning to understand how topsy-turvy things are here. Who would expect a young Jew would attack an old Jew, and an

Arab would come to his rescue?

And, because there's a part of me I'm not proud of: I hid behind my therapeutic neutrality and overlooked a disgusting anti-Semitic comment. I need to learn something from Ali. When it's a matter of principle, respond with outrage . . . not understanding.

We continue up the coast and stop at a Holocaust museum south of Nahariya. The exhibit traces Jewish life in Vilna from the eighteenth century through the Nazi era. From 1750 until the Nazi takeover of Poland in 1939, Vilna was the preeminent center for Torah scholarship throughout Europe.

From wooden models of eighteenth- and nineteenth-century yeshivahs (Jewish houses of learning) and synagogues, and photographs depicting the day-to-day life of the community, the exhibit portrays the richness of Jewish life in Vilna up to the time of the German invasion in 1941. The photographs from 1941 until 1943 follow the systematic destruction of Jewish Vilna. The primary focus is on the Vilna Ghetto:

On June 24, 1941, the Germans enter Vilna. The local Lithuanian Christian population greets them as conquering heroes. The Nazis confine the Jews into two overcrowded ghettos, Big Ghetto and Small Ghetto. The Jews suffer from malnutrition, disease, and torture. Yet despite these deplorable conditions, the dynamic intellectual and cultural life continues within the ghetto walls. The Jews of Vilna establish a 45,000-volume library with its own reading rooms, a center for scientific research, and a theater company that puts on original plays and dramatic readings in Yiddish and Hebrew. A Yiddish literary magazine publishes short stories, poems, and essays about ghetto life.

In the summer of 1941, the Germans evacuate the small ghetto and march most of its Jewish population to Ponary where the Nazis push them into pits and massacre them in waves of thousands. There, in the killing fields of Ponary, the Nazi beasts murder over 100,000 people.

In 1942, under the banner "We will not go like sheep to the slaughter," the ghetto members create the first ghetto resistance force for self-defense and sabotage. Many join the local Partisan units and engage in armed attacks against German army units and supply centers. Some remain in the ghetto to fight against the occupying force. By 1942, the Germans crush the Jewish resistance and transport the remaining ghetto population to the death camps. Over 100,000 of the remaining Jews die in the gas chambers of Auschwitz, Bergen-Belsen, and Majdanek, and with them, hundreds of years of Jewish life in Vilna come to a tragic end.

At the end of the exhibit, there's a glass case with an enclosed letter written by an Israeli lieutenant killed in the 1973 Yom Kippur War. He writes to his friend that he feels honored to serve in the Israeli Defense Force (IDF):

I and my fellow Israeli soldiers will never again allow a Jew to die a defenseless death in a gas chamber, nor will we stand idly while any nation persecutes a Jew wherever he or she may be. Our presence in the IDF stands as a negation against another Holocaust.

Both Deborah and I leave the exhibit in silence. She's crying. I'm somewhere between shock, rage, and pride. If I were a Jew from Vilna, I would hope I'd have the courage to fight shoulder to shoulder with Abba Kovner, the leader of the Vilna Resistance and the man who penned, "We will not go like sheep to the slaughter."

I think about this young Israeli lieutenant, a Jew and a soldier with a sense of history and destiny, so prepared to sacrifice his life for *his people.*

His people . . . are my people.

The resistance fighters and the victims, the survivors and the ashes of the Six Million—my people. I've floated for so long, free from family ties, disconnected from my Jewish roots, unaware of an inheritance that is rightfully mine. I glance at Deborah crying, and for the first time, I sense a terrible divide—a crack so wide even love might not be strong enough to bridge. I don't want to think about it, yet there's no power of denial strong enough to erase what I know to be true—what Simone warned us about—owning my Jewish identity is incompatible with being with a non-Jewish woman. Sure, I could live some watered-down Jewish identity and raise our kids with a Hannukah bush, Easter eggs, and matzah, but I'd know in my heart I was living a lie. Maybe Simone's Jewish boyfriend was right. The deeper you dive into your Jewish soul, the more you're faced with terrifying choices. Like this unbearable one: Must I sacrifice my relationship with Deborah for the sake of my Jewish identity?

Deborah gazes at me and says, "We'll figure it out."

How? I wonder.

For now, we get back on our bikes and continue north toward Nahariya, a small coastal town six miles south of the Lebanese border.

German Jews founded Nahariya in 1935. Religiously secular, rule-bound and efficient, and far too German for a significant portion of the Israeli population, the German Jewish immigrants built an aesthetically pleasing and efficient town. Parallel rows of eucalyptus trees line both sides of the streets; canals run from the Mediterranean on the western edge to the town borders on the east. There's no litter in Nahariya—the abundance of trash cans makes certain of it.

Orderliness is the word that comes to mind when describing Nahariya. You can sense the plan behind the layout. The founders had an idea about what a town modeled on the best of German know-how and efficiency should look like—German to the core:

Like my maternal grandfather, an unaffiliated German Jew named Louis Lehnstuhl, who died two years after I was born. From what my mother told me, he was a real Yekke, a German Jew—punctual, precise, and rule-bound. Just like the German Jews who built Nahariya. My people; my mother—straight lines, efficient, never deviate from your principles.

On both sides of the streets and canals, people sit in cafés leisurely drinking coffee and reading newspapers. Scores of bicyclists of all ages ride up and down the roads. Several bicycles carry baskets filled with loaves of bread, fruit, vegetables, and an assortment of other staples. There appear to be far more bicycles than cars, more quiet conversations than disruptive noise.

We find a café with a view of the Mediterranean where we watch the last rays of the sun disappear in the dark blue water. We order apple strudel and a fruit shake made from papaya, mango, bananas, and strawberries. I'm surprised to discover I can order a shrimp salad. Granted, I know little about Judaism, but I do know shrimp is one of those tasty foods that—like its cousins, lobsters, crabs, squid, and clams, along with bacon and ham—observant Jews don't eat. We learn the German Jews, like my grandfather, not only don't care but even eat those forbidden foods as an act of protest against what they consider to be arcane laws from an irrelevant ancient book.

Perhaps they're right, but that didn't help them on Kristallnacht.

We spend an extra day in Nahariya hanging out on the beach, lounging in the cafés, visiting Rosh HaNikra, and planning our trip around Israel. Our next stop is Safed, a walled city perched high in the Galilee hills. The guidebook says that during the sixteenth century, Safed became famous as the center for Jewish mysticism or Kabbalah, a Hebrew word that means *to receive*. I like that. Similar to what Joseph Campbell was referring to: You have to open your heart and mind, let go of your attachments, and like the bumper sticker says, "Let go and let God."

As we're lying on a white sandy beach outside of Nahariya, my mind drifts back to France . . .

The weather's hot and humid. The nonstop, uphill climb is brutal. I'm fighting negative self-talk. Suddenly, I hear a voice in my head repeating the Shema in Hebrew. Shema Yisroel Adonai Eloheinu, Adonai Ehad— Hear, O Israel, the Lord Our God, the Lord Is One. I haven't recited that prayer in over twenty years. From where did it come? From Jacob? I don't have answers. I ride to the sound of the Shema like it's a mantra. The suffering stops, and in its place, I feel joy and freedom. For the rest of the trip, the Shema never returns.

Two days later, at the pass of Col du Lautaret, we're meditating in a quiet spot a hundred and fifty feet above the noisy campsite. It's near sunset; the sky is clear; the temperature is pleasant. We feel that sweet sense of accomplishment, perhaps more like a sense of appreciation for the opportunity and for the gift of strength.

I fall into a deep meditation. Silent. Still. Tears flow down my cheeks. Not tears of sadness—tears of gratitude, tears of release. I experience a profound sense of connection to something far greater than me. Is this God? The Universe? My Higher Power? I have no idea, but what happens next is that, instead of my Sanskrit mantra, I hear a voice from some far- away place within me saying, "I want to serve. I want to serve." The tears pour like rain. I feel light, free, yet grounded as if I'm on a path home.

And, as suddenly as it appeared, this feeling of wholeness disappears. Until now, here on this beach.

I share this with Deborah. She says nothing at first. She just looks at me with her soulful, green meditator's eyes, and then says, "Maybe Israel is home. Perhaps your Jewish soul is waking up from a long slumber."

I want to ask what that means for us, but I stop myself. I'm too afraid of the answer.

We leave Friday morning for the thirty-three-mile trip to Safed. The manager of the campground warned us that it's a steep climb to Safed. The road from Nahariya to Safed is straight up with no switchbacks to soften the slope. Hard going like Greece—steeper by a degree or two, but minus the potholes and crevices every two or three feet. As difficult as it is, we can still enjoy the dark green hills of the Galilee covered with stately pines, cypress, and eucalyptus trees.

Forty years ago, these same small mountains were barren—just soil and rocks with occasional brown nestles and weeds that the goats and sheep fed on. But thanks to kids like me who gave their weekly Keren Ami (Fund for My People) *tzedakah* (charity contribution), hundreds of thousands of trees were planted, each one in the name of someone the donor wished to honor. For all I know, my trees may be among the thousands planted on both sides of the road. I wonder if the great Willie Mays would feel honored to know a ten-year-old boy named Mike Tobin planted a few trees somewhere in Israel in his name. I hope so. It took hours of washing cars, shoveling snow, and mowing lawns to pay for them.

Before we set out, the campground manager also told us we should be mindful of the time, since Shabbat, the Jewish Sabbath, comes in around four thirty in the afternoon. "At one o'clock, stores and restaurants close in Safed. The only place to stop between Nahariya and Safed is in Ma'alot. Just remember it may take you longer than you expect to get to Safed." And, as an afterthought, he says, "You do know about Ma'alot, don't you?"

"No," we tell him. "We never heard of it."

"Six years ago, two Palestinian terrorists murdered twenty-five teenagers in an elementary school there. This is the price we pay to live in our own country."

It's now three p.m. We're a mile and a half from Ma'alot and fifteen miles from Safed. At our current laborious pace, we'll arrive in Safed after dark, when everything's closed. As we approach the entrance to Ma'alot, we ask the guard if there's any lodging in the area. He thinks there's a guesthouse in the town center.

We ride slowly, looking right and left for a sign in English advertising a guesthouse. No luck. Up ahead, a woman stops her late-model Subaru and peers out the window toward us. At the moment our bikes come next to her window, she says to us in an identifiable Midwest accent, "You both look tired and hungry. Why don't you come to my place for lunch?"

We accept, and somewhere between the tuna salad and the Coke, she invites us for dinner, shows us two places for our sleeping mats, and says, "You're welcome to stay as long as you like."

Lyn's an attractive forty-five-year-old divorcee and school psychologist from Cincinnati who came on *Aliyah* a year and a half ago. (The literal translation of *Aliyah*: came up, elevation. Actual meaning: a term used to describe the Jewish immigration process to Israel.) Her nineteen-year-old daughter, Judith, is living with her until she starts a program in hotel management in Haifa. We stay with Lyn for two nights and, except for about eight hours of sleep on Friday and Saturday nights, we talk nonstop.

"Why *Aliyah*?" I ask.

Two things happened simultaneously for Lyn. She ended her four-teen-year marriage to her non-Jewish husband, and she started to take courses on Judaism at Hebrew Union College in Cincinnati. Judith was active in Jewish youth groups, so she encouraged her mother to light candles on Shabbat and to attend services at the Reform Temple.

"About four years ago, I visited Israel for the first time. I came for a month-long kibbutz ulpan (an intensive Hebrew language school). I know it sounds like a cliché, but I fell in love with the country from the first day I was here." She looks to see if her daughter is paying attention and then whispers, "Especially with the Israeli men. Maybe it was sex, not Zionism that brought me to Israel. Or, maybe sex with Israelis is Zionism."

She again looks toward Judith, who says, "Mom, I heard all that. I really don't care who you have sex with. Just not in the apartment while I'm here."

We all laugh, and Lyn picks up where she left off. "I like who I am when I'm here. I'm more free-spirited, not concerned about being po-lite and saying the wrong thing. Israelis aren't like us Americans. They say what they think—sometimes without tact, usually not with malice.

"I'm more at home in Israel than I ever felt in my forty-three years in America."

After meandering around the challenges of adjusting to her new life, she begins to talk about the Ma'alot tragedy.

"Soon after I completed my six-month ulpan, I began to work as a school psychologist in the regional high school in Safed. I had experi-ence in the States working with seriously traumatized Vietnam vets, but nothing prepared me for this."

We tell her we just heard about the massacre of the twenty-five students.

"Actually, twenty-two students were killed and over fifty were wounded. It was a bloodbath. At four a.m., the terrorists entered the building armed with AK-47s, grenades, and plastic explosives. One hundred and two students and their three teachers were sleeping. The teachers escaped; the terrorists forced the students to sit on the floor. They placed explosive charges between them. They demanded the exchange of twenty-three Arab terrorists for the lives of the students. Israel said no. We don't negotiate with terrorists.

"At five that afternoon, an elite counterterrorist unit stormed the building. The terrorists threw grenades at the students and opened fire on them, killing twenty-two. The soldiers killed the two terrorists. Israel retaliated by bombing the terrorists' refugee camp in southern Lebanon.

"This is what I stepped into a year ago. My primary job is to treat the younger siblings of the deceased and the wounded. Sometimes, I work with the entire family, including the survivors and their parents, most of whom are furious.

"Many of the children mimic their parents. Even after six years, coming to terms with their loss is just too painful. I guess it's easier to hate Arabs and blame the government than to mourn your children. Hate and blame keep their kids alive in their hearts. To move on means abandoning your flesh and blood."

To the question, "How do you treat them?" she says, "Like any good psychologist, I listen, accept where they are. When possible, I ask them to bring in photos or other memorabilia about their deceased child or sibling. Then I cry with them. Therapeutic distance makes no sense here. Holding and rocking does."

Lyn's a curious listener and probes us for thousands of details about our trip. For us, it's like weaving multiple strands of silk into an elaborate pattern in which each thread is an intricate part of the whole. Her comments about what she calls our "quest" are worth noting.

"Isn't the purpose of your trip to strip away the fat in order to find the Truth?"

"Yes," I say.

"Well, it seems like the Truth found you or you found the Truth. One thing's for sure: You can't run away anymore. You opened this

Pandora's box the moment you closed your practice and started pedaling east.

"There's a wrinkle in your Jewish roots experience. You've got a partner. Everything you've gone through, she's gone through with you, except for Sweden—a necessary detour for her.

"So, while you're struggling to reclaim your Jewish soul," she tells me, "did you ask yourself what Deborah's experiencing? Is it possible she's also questioning why she's having these encounters with Jewish survivors, with Jew-hating Lebanese, with the destruction of Lebanon? Those same experiences that are awakening your Jewish consciousness. She moved on from Lebanon. On to the Promised Land with you."

She turns to Deborah, whose eyes are moist, and says, "I'm sorry for talking about you in the third person. I know I'm going out on a limb here. What's your reaction to what I'm saying?"

"You're right. My heart's not in Sweden and it's not in Lebanon. So where is it? With Michael? That's not an identity; it's a relationship—a deep one, maybe the catalyst to find myself.

"I'm reluctant to say it's my Jewish soul I'm searching for. I don't know if I'm not ready or it's just too big of a leap right now. To you, these experiences prove I'm Jewish—maybe a reincarnated Jew like Solomon said. I don't deny it, but I'm not there yet. It's a lot to digest. I need time." She glances at me and then says to Lyn, "Michael hasn't said it, but I know that if it's a choice between Judaism and me, he'll choose Judaism. I need to know that if I choose Judaism it's not merely to save our relationship but because this is who I am and who I'm meant to be."

Lyn hugs Deborah and kisses her on her cheeks. She says, "I hope for the sake of the Jewish people, you choose our team. We need players like you."

Before we depart on Sunday, Lyn tells us we should stop at Kibbutz Sasa on the Lebanese border. "It's only eleven miles from here. If they invite you in, you won't regret it."

CHAPTER 21

Israel:
November 16 to November 21

W e arrive at the gated entrance to Sasa on Sunday morning at eleven o'clock. Like every day over the last six days, this morning is radiant. The sun casts a light so pure the only word to describe it is holy.

We tell the guard, a fellow in his late twenties who is carrying a loaded M-16, that we'd like to tour the kibbutz and speak to a member about becoming volunteers. In near perfect English, Moshe tells us he lived in San Francisco for a year, running a falafel stand near the Golden Gate Bridge.

He questions us about our trip, listens to our answers, and then focuses on Lebanon. "Does your Lebanese family blame Israel for their problems?"

"Depends on which family. It's an excellent question; the answer's complicated."

"No problem," he interrupts. "I'm off duty in an hour. You'll tell me then. You're my guests for the day and you can sleep in my room tonight." We tell him we'll think about it.

"There's nothing to think about. Just say yes." He lets us in to explore the grounds.

We're no more than twenty feet inside the kibbutz when a non-Israeli-looking guy with long blond hair approaches us. In response to our questions about life as a volunteer, he tells us he picks and sorts apples six hours per day. Monotonous work. "Because volunteers come and go, the members don't invest in us. They don't invite us into their homes. We don't eat with them. For me, the best thing about being a volunteer is hanging out with the other volunteers and reading."

"If that's the volunteer experience, I don't want it." Deborah agrees with me.

We continue our walking tour on gravel and pebble pathways lined with red, yellow, and pink flowers. Built close to the walkway are small homes and buildings made from beige and pink stone. The windows are shaped in the same arched, Arabesque style we saw among the shattered remains of Beirut. Enclosed within the windows' stone frames, dark brown sashes, like doors, open and close to let the light in or to protect the interiors from the brutal Middle Eastern rays. Well-manicured lawns, with an occasional bench and chair for relaxation or conversation, soften the dramatic effect of the wood, glass, and stone buildings. To punctuate the fact that we're in the heart of the Middle East, twisted old olive trees, their branches ripe with fruit, stand proudly next to their indigenous companions, the cypress and eucalyptus.

As you walk along the outside perimeter of the kibbutz, you can see the forested slopes and peaks of the nearby hills and distant mountain ranges. Israel owns all this green thanks to kids like me who never stopped giving money for trees. Every new sapling symbolized a tree of life and stood as a negation to all the Jewish lives lost during the Holocaust.

The Lebanese side is dead—barren, absent of any green or color that shows proof of life. From a refugee camp close to Sasa, the Ma'alot murderers began their reign of terror—a camp that, we'll soon discover, houses Arabs who once lived on the same land where we now stand.

We check out the dairy barns, where state-of-the-art technology milks fat cows that are calmly waiting in line for their turn on the stainless-steel milking machines. There's no question that Kibbutz Sasa stands as a fine example of Israeli ingenuity and commitment. All you need is to face north toward Lebanon and then pivot 180 degrees toward Kibbutz Sasa to witness a philosophy of despair on the one hand and its counterpoint, a paradigm of hope, on the other.

As we wheel our bikes past the guardhouse, Moshe steps out and asks, "Where are you going?" We tell him we're on our way to Safed. "No, you can't go. I want you to stay with me. You'll eat with me in the

kibbutz dining room and you'll meet my friends. You can leave tomorrow. No way I'm letting you go." So, we don't go.

The dining room has long oak and pine tables with wooden benches
on either side. Members dressed in coveralls and jeans sit with plates
overflowing with fresh food. A buffet table displays an array of yogurts,
wheels of cheese, pastries, loaves of fresh bread, Middle Eastern salads,
mounds of fresh melons, apples, pears, and persimmons, and platters
of sliced and diced vegetables.

One look at Moshe and you can't help but love him. He's got large,
expressive brown eyes; curly black hair that's naturally permed; and
silky, light brown skin. Words leap from his full lips in bursts, like
rounds from a rifle. Enigmatic he's not; what you see is what you get—
a moment of love becomes an expression of sadness that morphs into
anger and then lands at understanding. His mind's a lightning rod for
ideas and opinions that he freely shares, raw and unfiltered. Right now,
we're Moshe's best friends, and so we will remain for the next twelve
hours. He keeps his promise "to give us a day to remember."

"Israel reflects its people," he tells us. "Multicolored, complex, brilliant and stupid, kind and cruel, peaceful and aggressive."

Moshe is an Iraqi Jew. After the War of Independence, his parents
escaped to Israel along with 100,000 Iraqi Jews. A two-thousand-year
Jewish presence ended following the war. The Iraqis hated the idea that
Israel had defeated them, so they torched and ransacked Iraqi Jewish
homes, businesses, and synagogues. A mob of angry Muslims murdered his grandfather.

After his parents arrived in Israel, the Israeli government sent
them to transit camps for new immigrants called *ma'abarot*. "If you
told a pig to live there, he'd tell you to eat shit. The *ma'abarot* are an
ugly, black mark for Israel. I blame the elitist Ashkenazi Jews. They
treated their Sephardi brothers and sisters like they were shit on a shoe.
They packed the traumatized immigrants in the *ma'abarot* like sardines in a tin can, which is where they slept, in tin huts—furnaces in
the summer and freezers in the winter. Proud men, like my father, sat

all day doing nothing.

"The good news is Israel's a much kinder place in 1980 than it was in 1950. We're a young country on the way to becoming amazing if we're not afraid to look in the mirror."

Eventually, they closed the *ma'abarot*. His parents got help from an American Jewish organization and moved to Petach Tikva, a town in the center of the country. "My father won't talk about the past, so what I know—which isn't much—comes from my mother. I grew up under the shadow of their story. No one laughed in our home. The only language my family spoke was silence. I was dying and I had to get out. So I ran away to Kibbutz Sasa."

He tells us a brief story about his experience during the Yom Kippur War. His paratrooper unit fought the Syrians at a place called Tel Saki in the Golan. Close to tears, he tells us, "It was hard—very hard. I thought for sure I wouldn't make it. When you defend your home, you fight with everything you got. Kibbutz Sasa is only forty-five miles from Tel Saki."

Much later, when I do research for this book, I learn that Tel Saki was the battleground for one of the War's fiercest struggles. The Syrians outnumbered Israeli soldiers by one hundred to one. During three days of constant combat, the Israeli soldiers stopped the Syrians from invading the Galilee. Thirty-five Israeli boys died fighting.

During twelve hours of intense conversations, we cover much ground from religion to politics, but it is the history of the kibbutz and the Good Fence that I found most intriguing—more pieces in this crazy, complex puzzle called Israel.

In 1949, a young American *gar'in* (a small community of Jews organized for the purpose of making Aliyah) founded the kibbutz on abandoned Arab land. Before 1948, there was an Arab village here called Sasa. The mukhtar, along with all two thousand villagers, fled to Lebanon during the War of Independence. Most of the surviving villagers, their children, and grandchildren live in the Palestinian refugee camp, Nahr al-Bared, a few kilometers across the border.

When the Haganah's Seventh Brigade entered Sasa, the villagers surrendered without a fight. The Palestinians claim that Israeli soldiers tortured and killed innocent civilians. "Those rumors may or may not be true," Moshe tells us. "If I didn't know personally how cruel some Israelis can be, I'd say it's Palestinian propaganda. I'll assume the truth is somewhere between Palestinian exaggerations and Israeli denials.

"What we can't deny is that the kibbutz museum was once the mosque, and the mukhtar's home is now the communal shower. Many of the original Arab homes were redesigned to fit into the overall plan of the kibbutz. You can say it's ours because we defeated them. You know, all spoils go to the winner. Or, out of fear, they abandoned a village they had lived in for thousands of years. Or, as the Arabs claim, we terrorized simple people and forced them to flee their village.

"Sometimes, when I walk around my kibbutz with its Arab-style buildings, I wonder to myself if Arab ghosts hide there. But that's my crazy imagination. Or, maybe my guilt for being on the imperfect side of what I hope are the good guys. Whatever the true story is, we're here and they're not. You can't change history. You live in your time and build for the future. The Arabs live in the past and dream of a future that will never be."

Late in the evening, after much wine and arak, a licorice whiskey, he tells us about the Good Fence and his work with it. In 1976, a Christian child from a village close to the Israeli border was wounded in a Palestinian attack on her village. On her own, she came to one of the border crossings close to Sasa to seek medical help from Israel. Israel took her in, treated her, and returned her to her village. Word soon spread within the Christian communities bordering Israel. Before long, there were lines of sick and wounded Lebanese Christians in need of medical care. Israel organized clinics and field hospitals to provide medical assistance to their Christian neighbors.

"I know some Arabic, so I visit with the patients and try to make them feel like someone cares. Sometimes, I come as a clown and make the kids laugh. At other times, I sit by the bed of an old person and listen to a story about the way it used to be. They all say the same thing: 'Life was so much better before the Palestinian refugees came to Lebanon.' Israel's a strange and beautiful place where nothing makes sense.

"Unless you believe in miracles and God," he says.

*   *   *

At nearly 3,000 feet, Safed, a small metropolis of approximately thirty thousand Jews and no Arabs, is the highest city in the Galil. In 1948, prior to the War of Independence, the picture was significantly different. Seventeen hundred Jews lived among an Arab population of twelve thousand. In February 1948, an Arab militia attacked the Jewish Quarter where a small band of poorly equipped Jewish fighters repelled the larger Arab forces. Over the next few months, Arab attackers attempted to capture the Jewish Quarter and (as ordered in an intercepted Syrian directive) slaughter its inhabitants.

In April 1948, the moment the British peacekeeping forces evacuated Safed, the Arab Liberation Army attacked the Quarter. Over the next few months, two hundred Jewish fighters held them off until reinforcements arrived. In May, after fierce fighting, the Jewish forces drove the Arab army from Safed along with its twelve thousand Arab residents who fled north to Lebanon and east to Jordan. Hence, "The Catastrophe," if you're a Palestinian. "Israel's garbage," if you're a Lebanese Christian. An "extraordinary victory against overwhelming odds," if you're an Israeli.

Fast-forward thirty-two years and the only citizens walking the narrow stone streets of Safed are Jews—mostly the religious kind. *Hareidim.* Many of the men wear the long black cloaks and black hats that serve as the uniform of the ultrareligious. Some of them have long side curls that fall to their shoulders, and all of them wear four white strings that extend below their coats and jackets.

Their wives cover every strand of hair with scarves, wigs, and hats. Their dresses and skirts fall close to their ankles; their blouses extend to their wrists. It's like time stopped in the 1800s for these ultrareligious Jews. And, for me, it's as if we've traveled back to 1890 to the vanished world of an Eastern European shtetl, the kind of poor village in which my father's father, a religious Jew who died years before I was born, lived, until at the age of twenty he escaped for the better life in the *Golden Medina*—America.

Better, for him, was a relative term. Economically, he thrived—first as a house painter and then as a real estate entrepreneur. Religiously, he suffered. He mourned the loss of his nine children, of whom my father was the youngest, to the *goyishe* glitz of *Amerdica*.

Irrelevant. Old fashioned. "We can't fit in with yarmulkes and *tzitzits*." One by one, they changed their names, took off their yarmulkes, stopped *davening* (praying), refused to speak Yiddish, forgot about Shabbos, and showed up once a year on Yom Kippur at their fancy synagogues where nobody fasted.

"When I stopped keeping Shabbos," my father told me, "Papa sobbed. I can still hear his Yiddish words when he discovered me listening to the radio on Shabbos. *Nu, Motke, nit ir aoykh*—'Nu, Motke, not you too.'"

Forty-eight years after my grandfather's death—the man after whom I'm named—nearly all his grandchildren intermarried. Not one member of his large extended family steps into a shul on Yom Kippur. His vanished world vanished in America.

The last and only time I've seen so many religious Jews in one place was in the summer of 1964 in the Catskills. At the end of June, the ultrareligious from Brooklyn vacate their crowded, hot apartments for the greener, cooler pastures of the Catskill bungalow colonies. Like it was a visit to the zoo—or maybe a museum is a more appropriate analogy—I drove my car through the most ultra of ultraorthodox bungalow colonies where Hasidic Jews spent the summer. To my eighteen-year-old brain, these people were weird, un-American, and definitely not me. I couldn't understand why they'd want to live such a cloistered and restrictive lifestyle.

Now here in Safed, it feels more like being on a safari than a visit to the zoo. In a Jewish country, the ultrareligious appear to be in their natural habitat, roaming the savanna, so to speak, with the other Jews, including this assimilated one with his Lebanese Christian girlfriend. I try out this sentence in my head to see what bells ring: "I am them, they are me, and we are one." A stretch, yes, but nothing like that summer of 1964, when I watched two Yiddish-speaking Hassidic boys throwing a ball like a nerd from the elbow, not the shoulder. Disdain was what I felt then. Now, it's curiosity I feel.

Deborah carries no baggage—neither the anti-Semitic kind, nor the discomfort of a self-hating Jew. For her, the *Haredim* of Safed are merely another culture, no different from the Greeks of Krini or the Muslims of Lebanon. She's intrigued by what she's read. The guidebook says many Jews in Safed follow the mystical traditions of the kabbalah, compiled here four hundred years ago.

We wander the well-worn, twisted alleyways of the Old City, where the sixteenth-century mystic Rabbi Izsak Luria (known as the Arizal) lived, prayed, and taught. With its smooth stone steps and clusters of small homes, Safed reminds me of a cross between the stone-everything village of Krini and the stunning Alpine town of Saint Pierre de Chartreuse, where we ate the most wonderful ice cream sundae.

Only here, the doors to the synagogues and mikvahs—Jewish ritual baths—are painted blue. Blue reminds you of the sky; the sky reminds you of the Heavens (seven according to the Jewish tradition); the Heavens remind you of the Host of Hosts, the Holy One, Blessed Be He—God Himself.

Raise your eyes to the Heavens and know before Whom you stand. God-consciousness in Judaism, as we will also discover later today, is a full-time job. Everything's a gift from above. The Jew's mission and calling: to cultivate an awareness of God's immanence and to express gratitude for His personal guidance and bounty. Nothing less, the Mystics say, than to infuse God-consciousness into every moment of existence. Everything else—a distraction.

We continue our walking tour into that part of the Old City called the Artists' Quarter. Galleries display oils, watercolors, and lithographs of biblical scenes, portraits of wizened rabbis, and landscapes of the rocky Galilee heights that surround Safed.

We pause before a painting. An old Arab, probably a sheik or an imam, leans his back against one side of an ancient olive tree. On the other side of that same tree, a gray-bearded rabbi mirrors the Arab's pose. Both the Arab and the Jew gaze in opposite directions toward the Galilee hills populated by groves of olive trees.

We enter the gallery of a Hassidic artist named Yehoshua, a former leader of the French student uprising in 1968. In the early seventies, he tells us, he felt an emptiness that Marxist philosophy no longer could fill. He explored Buddhism and spent six months at a monastery near Kathmandu.

"After six months of meditation and chanting, I felt something was not right—a kind of dissatisfaction I couldn't explain. I poured my heart out to the Buddhist priest. I remember how he listened so deeply and then said, 'You are Jewish. You should look for truth where you live.' I did. And I discovered that Hasidism spoke to that disquiet."

"How?" Deborah asks.

"Through prayer and study, I learned to love God and to feel His love toward me. I appreciate Buddhist psychology and meditation but, for me, it never brought me to that place of intimacy . . . I walk the hills surrounding Safed and talk to God. Sometimes, I scream out, 'Where are You?' when I don't feel Him in my heart; at other times, I share my pain or thank Him for my many blessings. He rescued me from my emptiness and continues to guide me to my true self."

His art expresses his intimate longing. Deborah says there's something about his art and his story that resonates with her. "God for him is here and now. It's as natural and as real as our relationship. He never stops working on it. You can see it in his face and feel it when he speaks."

I notice tears flowing down her cheeks. I want to reach out to her, but I don't know if the pain that we share is the pain that divides us. I ache at the thought of losing her. I want to embrace her and tell her, "I know that we're meant to be together forever. Our souls are one. If I'm Jewish, you must be Jewish. That's why you dragged me into the synagogue on Yom Kippur. That's why we're here in Israel together—not me alone in Safed and you in Sweden with Niels." But I stop myself. If my thoughts are true, then it can't come from me. She'll have to discover it on her own.

We stop before the blue doors of the Arizal's synagogue. As we're about to enter, a couple in their twenties approach us. On first impression, I picture Avraham playing sax in a smoky jazz club. He talks like it: "Like man, it's so far out. Do you get it? The Boss dropped you right here next to the Holy Ari."

Avraham is lanky with a wispy beard, wears a black hat like the Blues Brothers, Jake and Elwood, a black yarmulke, and tzitzits that extend to his knees. He dresses in jeans, a blue flannel shirt, and Adidas running shoes.

In my mind, while he smokes weed and searches for that perfect note, Nava, his fiancée, twirls, hops, and shakes her tambourine with the Hare Krishnas in downtown Chicago. "Wow, I mean, it's so deep. Like wow. Can't you feel it?"

Nava's sort of cute in a skinny, eyes-open-to the-world, hippie kind of way—definitely not a JAP. She's covered from neck to ankle with a multitudinous array of clashing colors. Bring me back ten years to the corner of Haight and Ashbury, and I'll find Nava with flowers in her long brunette hair.

"I'm confused," I tell them. "Who's the boss, what's so deep, and what is it we're supposed to feel?"

"The Boss," Nava answers, "that's God. He runs the show. You know, HaShem pulls the strings, writes the script, and steers your handlebars."

"Who's HaShem?" Deborah asks.

"That's what we call the Boss," Nava says.

"So, what does the Boss call you?" I ask.

"It's not like that. It's not like he says, 'Hey, Nava, what's up? You good?' No, none of that. You just feel His vibe. No words. Words get in the way. You go way down deep into the silence and you meet Him there."

"Cool," I say because I can't think of any other response. I mean, how do you question the silence?

We discover that Avraham and Nava found God and each other at the Chabad House in Chicago. Avraham tells us Chabad is a form of *Chassidus*—Hasidism—that's very intellectual, which I find more than a bit surprising. "I mean, man, you've got to really dig into the texts. I'm talking about breaking your teeth on some pretty far-out ideas. Check this out: How did HaKadosh Baruch Hu—oh yeah, that's another name we call God—make room for the Creation? I mean, He's everywhere and everything, so how come we're here? Like, how's there space for us? Try to get your head around this. He makes Himself small so there's room for us. I mean, is that not love?"

"That's so beautiful," Nava adds. "We got to do what HaShem does. You know, make space for each other. Let the other feel the love, just like HaShem."

We continue wheeling our bicycles down the path while Avraham keeps up a constant monologue on far-out Kabbalistic ideas about creation, most of which I tune out or let fly over my head. Somewhere in the middle of his monologue about the female aspect of God, a chubby, red-haired munchkin with a colorful kippa pinned to the side of his head pops out a window and says, "So, nu, vat du ve hav hier?" He then switches to a Philadelphian accent and says, "Come inside."

Inside is plastered with photos of the Phillies celebrating their recent World Series victory, their first in franchise history. Jonathan's the roly-poly, nerdy guy who could tell you who played second base on the 1917 Boston Braves but couldn't hit a ball past the pitcher's mound. No field, no hit, but big brain.

A mob of books piled on top of one another like little Leaning Towers of Pisa rise from the floor to a height a miniature man like Jonathan can reach. Two-thirds of the titles are in Hebrew. From their size and thickness, they look like they contain the entirety of Jewish wisdom. One-third are English books about baseball, world history, Jewish history, Zionism, socialism, Marxism, existentialism, Greek philosophy, and psychology.

Considering Safed sits on the Syrian African fault line, the first thing I'd say about Jonathan is he's an optimist. I figure he's got his head in the sand when it comes to geology, or he's got his head so far into one of his one thousand or more books that the only reality he knows is the current page.

To Avraham, Jonathan says, "I hope you're not torturing these good people with your esoteric ramblings about creation."

"They're not ramblings. They're true."

He turns to us and says, "Avraham's been learning for nine months, and he already thinks he's a Torah scholar. He's on a mission to recruit lost Jews. He believes if he recruits enough Jewish souls, he can cash them in for a third-base seat in the Next World. Right, Avraham?"

Avraham mumbles something that sounds like, "Every Jew is responsible for his fellow Jew," and then he and Nava exit.

"What was that all about?" Deborah asks.

"I hate these born-again, bliss-ninny Jews." He pauses, takes a breath, and says, "I know I should be more forgiving." He points to his literary friends, and says, "You want to know what apoplexy is? It's what happens to me the moment those brainless idiots spew out their mindless aphorisms. It's like they've distilled 3,500 years of scholarship into, 'You know, it's like wow, like so, so deep. Can't you just feel the Truth?' What they do to Judaism is what McDonald's does to food—instant gratification with no nutritional value. For those two, Marx got it right. Religion's the opium of the people."

"So, what's the truth, Jonathan?" Deborah asks.

"The truth is . . . I'm hungry. You want to stay and have lunch with me?"

It turns out Jonathan's more than an apoplectic, intellectual elitist. He's also a kind and generous soul who opens his heart, mind, and home to us for three days. For a good portion of those seventy-two hours, Jonathan guides us on an exhilarating tour de force of Jewish wisdom, from the Revelation on Mount Sinai through the Talmudic brilliance of the Rabbinical period, from the spiritual heights of the early twentieth-century scholarly saint Rav Kook to the contemporary Talmudic existentialist, Rav Joseph Soloveitchik.

Like a rabbit on steroids, he hops from pile to pile to extract the exact volume. Then, at a processing speed faster than IBM's Supercomputer, he finds the precise quote in response to a specific question. Doesn't matter whether the query concerns proof of God's existence, the certainty of the Sinai experience, or more specifically for us, "Did we choose or were we led?"

In a single bound, he tells us all three questions are one question with one answer. "I heard this from a brilliant Chabad rabbi:

"Let's say there was a foolproof blood test to find your ideal partner. You both get tested and, bingo, you get your answer—a perfect match. Incredible, no? No, not at all. Why? Because there's no mystery. No challenge. No romance. The certainty of the blood test erases our freedom to choose. When absolute evidence proves God exists, or we have irrefutable testimony that He revealed Himself at Mount Sinai, or we know for sure He will lead Deborah and Michael to my apartment in Safed, then we are nothing more than mechanized creatures following a predetermined script. There's no love without freedom, there's no faith without doubt, and there's no relationship without choosing it—especially with God. He wants us to be grown-ups.

"Judaism is no pablum religion. It challenges you. It demands you look within and search—not alone, but as a partner with God."

On our second to last day in Safed, Jonathan tells us we should meet a potter named Daniel who has a studio in the Artist's Quarter. "His story and yours are similar."

We find Daniel at his wheel, working on a wall hanging depicting the seven biblical species mentioned in Deuteronomy: grapes, olives, wheat, barley, dates, pomegranates, and figs. He's a handsome Englishman in his early thirties with a large colorful kippa, a bushy reddish beard, and long, wavy hair more blazing than the beard. Jonathan told us, "He fits the biblical description of King David and has the personality to match—a poet and a warrior."

"Jonathan told me you wanted to talk to me," he says.

"Actually," I tell him, "Jonathan told us he thought you should talk to us. He said we have a similar story."

Daniel tells us to wait a few minutes while he finishes gluing a stalk of glazed wheat shaped from clay onto one of four veneered squares attached to a white canvas frame. We're not there; he is—with all the focus and precision of Zoltán Varga, the violin maker from Cremona. Jonathan introduced us to the biblical character Hanoch, a simple shoemaker at one with his craft. "With every stitch, he expressed his love and service to God. Kabbalah says that with each movement of his needle, he unified the upper and lower worlds." Like shoemaking for Hanoch, pottery, for Daniel, goes way beyond making beautiful objects. It's his prayer.

"Okay, so Jonathan wants me to enlighten you with words of wisdom? Doesn't he know I'm a potter, not a guru?"

"He says you're a smart guy with a story that will speak to us."

"Fine, tell me about yourselves, and let's see if our experiences intersect."

We give him a fifteen-minute summary of why we left; where we've been; what we've experienced; and what that means for our immediate and long-term future.

"God gave us different circumstances but the same challenge and opportunity: to create an authentic life or run from it. Here's my story. Take what you need from it."

At fifteen, Daniel began pottery and Zen meditation. "Judaism didn't speak to me and I didn't speak to Judaism. Zen Buddhism did." At eighteen, he began art school in London. "It was torture—technique without soul or inspiration. I hated it. There was no Zen in the pottery the art school was teaching; no sense of the stillness and perfection I felt in Japanese ceramics. Three years after I graduated, I went to study in Kyoto, where half the day I practiced Zen meditation and the other I learned ceramics. To the Japanese, there's no difference between sitting in meditation or throwing pots. Both demand total mindfulness, focus, and inner quiet. I stayed there for eighteen months.

"When I returned to my old London Zen Center, there was a new

Roshi. At our first meeting, he asked me if I was Jewish. He then asked, 'Why are you here? Why are you not learning your own traditions?' He gave me the name of an Orthodox rabbi he wanted me to meet, a former Zen practitioner.

"The rabbi talked straight like a Zen master. 'You know nothing about who you are. You travel thousands of miles to find the truth when it lives in your backyard.'"

I start to laugh. I say to him, "The best recruiters for Judaism seem to be the gurus and roshis. We heard a similar story from the artist Yehoshua."

"I know his story. I've heard others like that. For Yehoshua and me, we needed a guru to tell us we're Jews. The Holocaust and anti-Semitism woke you up.

"This rabbi said to me, 'Before you take another trip East, learn about Judaism.' I half-listened to him. I traveled east—to the Middle East—to study Judaism in Jerusalem. I hated it at first. For me, far too textual and rule bound. I missed the simple practice of sitting and meditating. Just being in the present and letting the truth emerge from within. I felt like I was back in art school again—technique without soul. Religion's supposed to bring you closer to God, and I was feeling more distant. I felt trapped. I wanted to be a Jew, but I rejected this lifeless Judaism.

"There was a rabbi at the yeshiva, a convert from Holland, who pointed me in the right direction. 'First mistake you're making,' he told me, 'is you're stripping your past from your experience. The rabbi was correct when he said the truth lies in your backyard. But Zen helped bring you to Jerusalem. It's your unique path—the one God wanted you to travel. If not, you wouldn't be here.'

"He told me, 'Your lack of fire reflects what's wrong with much of contemporary Judaism. It lacks the immediacy of Zen. You need passion to find God. You need to feel truth in your heart and bones. The Roshi knew Judaism is your path for the obvious reason: You're a Jew. He may have understood, as well, that our purpose is to express God's presence in the world. To find God in the moments of our lives.'"

"Do you know," Daniel asks us, "that we make a blessing every time we go to the bathroom?" We tell him no—that we know nothing about Judaism. "You don't think of defecating as a godly miracle. A necessity at best, an embarrassing bodily function for many. To Judaism, it's an opportunity to express gratitude—to awaken in us a sense of wonder and appreciation for God's creation.

"He helped me to find myself in Judaism. In the process, I discovered the Jewish potter. Different from the Zen potter. I don't try to become one with my work, to express my inner stillness through my art. It's simpler than that. I pray before I sit at my wheel that my art will be my service to God. That my hands will be an instrument of the Almighty. God implanted in me the desire, talent, and opportunity to be a potter. This path brought me to Him. My work is my expression of love."

Deborah's brown-green eyes project a fiery energy that matches the power of Daniel's words. I imagine, like me, she feels shaken by his raw energy, by the strength of his vulnerability and openness. God, for him, and for Yehoshua, is a living reality, the Absolute Truth that governs their lives, that informs their moment-to-moment existence. Yet, I don't experience the slightest sense of fanaticism with either of them. The truth burns within each of them; it doesn't destroy or demand disciples. More like: "This is where I was led; this is the truth I follow. It's up to each of us to make our own calculations."

"My advice to you, Michael, is the same the rabbi gave me. 'Go learn. It's your inheritance.'" To Deborah, he says, "I suppose you know you won't have a future with Michael unless you convert. He won't or can't drop out of his own story—a story that seems to be as much about you, Deborah, as it is about Michael. I pray you both find the truth you seek, whether it's together or separately."

We leave in silence. There's nothing to add. We both know where this journey has been leading us. It's not what we expected; it's not what we asked for, but to quote Deborah, "It is what it is." As the expression goes, "Careful what you ask for because you just might get it." So, what we got right now is a choice.

We both know that I won't drop out of my story. Yet, as Daniel and Lyn before him pointed out, it's Deborah's story as well—a story I could entitle *A Jewish Tale of Awakening and Redemption.* But what's Deborah's title? *The Decision—Becoming a Jew by Choice?* Will it end tragically like Simone predicted? If so, we should call it *Identity Vanquishes Love,* a tale about a Jew who chooses Judaism over love and remains in Israel, suffering the pain of losing part of himself while his non-Jewish lover returns brokenhearted to her non-Jewish life.

I feel myself being tossed and spun by a powerful wave—trapped in a whirlpool of white foam, struggling for control, not knowing if this is the end.

I glance at Deborah. We're both crying.

"I'd like to speak to Yehoshua," Deborah says. "I want to go to his studio now."

Yehoshua welcomes us in. He looks deeply at both of us; he feels our pain. I understand why Deborah wants to speak to him. I'm not exactly sure how, but I know he holds the key for her.

"I want to know," Deborah says, "how and where you ask God for guidance. You told us you walk the hills around Safed. Do you scream to God to hear you? Do you whisper? Or do you walk in silence and invite God to join you in your meditation?"

"I do all of that. I let my heart decide. I let my thoughts drift, and when the spirit moves me to speak or shout, I do. Sometimes I'll go for thirty minutes and sometimes for hours. Trust God is there. Whatever emerges for you is God's way of speaking to you." He looks at her with such kindness and compassion and says, "I pray you'll discover what you're looking for. When a beautiful *neshama*—a soul—like you, Deborah, seeks Truth, God won't ignore you. The truth might be joyous or painful. Listen to its voice."

My eyes are moist; rivers of tears flow down Deborah's cheeks.

Yehoshua draws a map of where to walk. This time of the year, the path will be empty. Deborah tells me, "I want to go alone. I'll meet you back at Jonathan's."

I wander in and around the Old City, past the mikvahs and small synagogues with their sky-blue doors; bypassing pairs of Hasidim, their arms clasped behind their backs, their heads leaning forward, engaged in an animated discussion in Yiddish. I overtake a mixed group of nonreligious soldiers. The boys and girls seem more intent on flirting with one another than on listening to their religious tour guide pontificate about the Arizal. I continue past religious mothers pushing double strollers up and down the polished steps of the Jewish Quarter; moving beyond groups of religious stoners, high on a cocktail of hashish spiked with *Chassidus*; and down the steps toward the cemetery where hundreds of holy Kabbalists rest in peace, which is where I stop to think and to pray—a first for me.

I find it hard—no, impossible—to ask God to give Deborah a sign that she has a Jewish soul, to prove to her that conversion is the path He's chosen for her. That plea dies on contact with awareness. I hear Jonathan's words in my head: "God doesn't run a candy store. He's not Santa Claus, and prayers are not requests for presents."

The only prayer that makes sense is this: "Dear God, please help Deborah know her truth, and whatever that truth is, let me accept it. She's faced with a terrible choice. If she chooses to be a Jew, she most likely loses her family. If not, she loses me. Help her discover her deepest desire and grant her the courage to follow her convictions."

My mind meanders over the peaks and valleys of the past six months, from the rats in Belgium to the encounter with Le Clown—our first awakening to the horror of war and the Holocaust, and then on to Paris, a city that breathes life, elegance, and intelligence. I love Simone. I love her wit, her brilliance, her honesty. She understood what I didn't: Jewish is not an adjective; it's an essence.

Martina. A gorgeous woman, inside and out. She showed me how Deborah's a part of me. From the moment I noticed Deborah on the dance floor, I knew she was the missing piece. How can the missing piece go missing? How can it end here? Will I have to accept what I can't understand? Like Abraham, who remained silent when God commanded him to sacrifice his only child, the future of the Jewish people. Clearly, God's logic is not ours. His mathematical calculations and ours differ by magnitudes.

My journey in my mind stops here. To go further is to realize what I already know—I love Deborah. For me, to say goodbye to her means to sacrifice much of my body to save my Jewish soul. For her to say no to our relationship and Judaism, she'd have to know her essence lies elsewhere. But where? With her family, who doesn't get her? In Sweden, where she left? In Paris, whose luster shines less for her? In Lebanon, that's dying? Or, somewhere farther east, like a cave in India where she can be still with God?

I descend farther into the valley down to the Arizal's ancient mikvah, fed by freezing cold natural springs. Before he died, the Arizal promised all those who immersed themselves in these holy waters that their souls would return in love to God. The barriers of ego and fear will dissolve in his mikvah, and we'll emerge free to commune with God.

Two hours later, I meet Deborah at Jonathan's apartment. Her face glows from sun and sweat. I can't pinpoint what looks different about her. Perhaps it's the heightened color in her cheeks that brings out the green in her eyes. Or her damp hair matted on her forehead that gives an impression of her as an athlete at the end of a fierce competition. What speaks most vividly to me are the softness of her lips—lightly closed, serene. I don't know if she found God or God found her, but she seems to have found her answer.

I feel calm. Whatever she's decided, I know it's right for her. And what's right for her must be right for me as well. She suggests we go out to Jonathan's small western-facing balcony. I suppose it's only fitting we should have this conversation as the sun departs—as we transition from one reality to another.

"Please don't ask me what I decided. It's no secret, but I need to tell you in the order in which I arrived at it. At first, I was scared. I was afraid that whatever I decided, it would be wrong. I would disappoint someone. I couldn't find myself in the argument—only you, my parents, and the Lebanese community. I did what Yehoshua suggested:

I called out to God. I shouted for God to help me find myself, to hear my voice among all the nervous chatter. At first, nothing happened. No flashes of lightning, no drum rolls announcing the king. I kept walking and my mind began to notice the varied tones of brown and green on the hills that border the path. If you pay attention, you can see an occasional red or yellow wildflower peering behind a rock or within a grove of olive trees. As my mind quieted, I felt connected to the land, like I belonged here.

"Then, like in a meditation, my mind shifted to our trip, not chronologically but associatively, from impression to impression, as if my deeper self was organizing the material thematically. I thought of Louisa and I cried. Not in sadness, but in awe at her quiet courage. She knew her true self lay beyond the security of her village. Her heart and her feet led to her career as a dancer. Then I thought about Dasia and her decision to find herself in Paris. I cried for Mona, who I know will say goodbye to her loving family. I want to be a woman like them. To decide from my heart, not from fear.

"But the inner journey didn't stop. I revisited our encounters with the Holocaust and anti-Semitism. I started sobbing. Jacob's suffering was my suffering. I felt my chest throb in pain when I pictured Julian's father sitting in his chair, chain-smoking cigarettes, every moment a nightmare of memories and flashbacks. I could hear Solomon describe the destruction of the Salonica Jewish community. It was so real to me, I wondered if I am one of those non-Jews who possesses the soul of a murdered Jew. I didn't try to think about anything. Pictures and thoughts kept emerging from the trip and from our six years together.

"I heard a question in my mind. Why is it I've always felt this affinity to Jews and to the Jewish religion? I remained in the synagogue, understood nothing, yet felt like I had a profound experience. There's no rational explanation for this. I never had that experience in a church. My mind was slowly compiling an argument. I didn't ask it to. I didn't ask God to reveal my Jewish soul. All I said was please guide me to the truth.

"Then I thought of us and I sobbed. I stopped walking and found a large rock to sit on. Not to meditate, but to let my feelings and thoughts go in whatever direction they needed. I kept hearing myself say, 'Your life and Michael's are one. He knew it from the moment he saw you. You realized it when you tripped together that first time. You fought it, but you knew. You didn't go this far to turn back. Find the courage of Louisa, of Dasia, of Mona and do what you must."

She stops, fixes her eyes on mine, and says, "My place is with you. Like what Jonathan told us about Ruth, the first convert to Judaism. 'Your people are my people. Where you go, I go.' Tomorrow, we ride to Jerusalem to begin our new life together."

The Epilogue

I believe in the sun even when it's
   not shining.

I believe in love even when feeling
   it not.

I believe in God even when He
   is silent.

—Zvi Kolitz, *Yosl Rakover Speaks to God*

November 1980 to July 2021

*O*ne week after her decision to convert, Deborah enrolls in an in-tensive program about Judaism. I attend a separate program for men. Ten months later, she immerses herself in the mikvah, chooses the Hebrew name Devorah Ariella, and officially becomes a Bat Yisrael, a daughter of Israel.

Her parents disown her.

One week later, a day before Yom Kippur, her father is diagnosed with a deadly form of leukemia. Betty Mae summons her now re-owned Jewish daughter to return to Charleston, West Virginia, to care for her father. While I remain in Jerusalem, Deborah—the responsible oldest daughter—lovingly offers emotional and physical support to her dying father who, days prior to his diagnosis, rejected his Jewish daughter.

In January 1982, Deborah and I stand under the chuppah—the Jewish marriage canopy—and become husband and wife. Two months later, at age sixty-two, her father dies. Soon after that, we move to Brookline, Massachusetts, a close suburb of Boston. I'm hired to be the clinical direc-tor of a private mental health clinic outside of Boston. Deborah opens a private practice. In October 1982, Deborah gives birth to the first of our four children, Elisheva.

Over the next few years, we add two more children, Shayna and Aaron. Our practices grow, we purchase our first home, and we become an integral part of the Brookline Jewish community. Once again, we achieve the Jewish American dream. And once again, I feel trapped, stuck in the same place I left five years earlier.

I know how to read the signs of emptiness and longing. My place is no *longer in a comfortable suburb of Boston.*

It's in Israel. Deborah agrees.

In October 1986, two weeks after the Boston Red Sox blow the seven-game World Series to the New York Mets, our family of five makes Aliyah to Israel. I'm forty years old. Nine months later, we buy our home in Efrat, twelve miles from Jerusalem, in a region called Gush Etzion. In April 1988, our fourth child, Ilana, joins our family. A few months later, we open our psychology practice in the center of Jerusalem. The practice flourishes.

In 1992, The March of the Living asks Deborah to accompany a group of university students on a trip to the concentration camps of Poland. Her role: to provide psychological support to the emotionally overwhelmed students. In Auschwitz, she stands before an oven and sobs uncontrollably. She assumes it's a cathartic reaction from days of listening to horrific stories from survivors and from witnessing the ovens, the gas chambers, and the barracks where the near dead like Jacob clung to life.

The following year, she accompanies another group of students. As in the previous year, they spend days witnessing the intact Nazi extermination apparatus: the gas chambers and the ovens where the Nazis cooked the bodies until they became the ash that fertilized the commandant's rose garden. Once again, she stands before the same oven and sobs uncontrollably. From a place deep inside of her, she knows why. Not in a way that you can prove empirically, but in that same knowing she felt walking the hills around Safed.

Over the next twenty-six years, we build a beautiful life in Israel. Our children develop into the best of their parents and beyond. For two people from fractured families, we learned important lessons in parenting: Do the opposite of what my father and her parents did. We build a close and loving family. Our children marry, have children, and develop their respective careers. Despite the periodic danger from direct participation in the ongoing drama of Jewish and Israeli history, our lives are dramatically undramatic. The family grows to seventeen grandchildren.

We live a blessed life, filled with love, financial security, and a deep sense of purpose. The love and connection between Deborah and me grow through the years. Throughout our forty-four years together I continue to be in awe of her intelligence, her kindness, and her moral compass that never deviates from true north.

Yet all things change.

In 2018, after we return from our fourth trip to Nepal, where we trekked to the Everest Base Camp, we notice something's different about Deborah. It begins with forgetting names of grandchildren. We dismiss it as the normal cognitive challenges of your average sixty-eight-year-old.

Then, one day, the whole family gathers together at a restaurant. A female friend of Deborah's—someone she's known for thirty-two years—approaches the table to say hello to all of us. I notice Deborah looks confused; our oldest daughter, Elisheva, does as well. "Imma, do you know who she is?"

Deborah answers, "No, should I?"

Two weeks later, in November 2018, following extensive neurological testing, Deborah's diagnosed with Alzheimer's disease, an illness she shouldn't have. She has no family history, no genetic markers, and one month before her diagnosis, she climbed 19,000 feet.

But so much for what should be—the journey of life has a mind of its own. Sometimes angels wait around the bend to guide you home, and sometimes, terrifying challenges demand you dig into yourself and find your truth. And sometimes, there are questions for which there are no good answers.

It is now July 2021. Day by day, the only woman I've ever loved fades away. Our children suffer the loss of their brilliant, loving mother; our grandchildren don't understand what's happening to their mama.

And Deborah slips into a world without memories . . .

Memories I preserve and share so all will know the extraordinary woman I've loved from that day in June 1974 when our eyes met on the Antioch dance floor.

That woman who shows me how to listen to the silence . . .

Acknowledgments

This book was written with love and driven by an inner necessity to release a story that I and others felt had to be told.

Riding the Edge would not exist if not for the love, support, and critique of my dear friend, Danny Chertoff, who insisted—no, demanded—that I write it. I feel blessed to have a soul mate that believes in me to my core.

Kudos also go to another close soul mate, Daniel Ratzersdorfer, who for years encouraged me to write this story.

The first very partial draft of this book began in 1988. The original believer in this story was my agent at the time, Deborah Harris. In 2007, I took my manuscript out of mothballs and added a few more chapters, much of which I rejected for the 2020 version. Along the way, I need to mention the input I received from Sara Eisen, who helped me become a more competent writer.

There are many friends and family who have been extremely supportive during this process of writing. I want to draw special attention to Toby Klein Greenwald, who has been my collaborator and partner on a number of writing projects and was an early believer in this book.

A big shout out goes to my dear friends Lynda and Ruby Wolbromsky for their support and encouragement.

When I searched for an editor, I had three criteria: 1) The editor couldn't know me; 2) The editor had expertise in memoir writing; 3) The editor was an excellent writer. Marion Roach Smith filled all three categories. I sent her a fat, first draft of 575 pages. She found the story within the noise and taught me how to wield a literary scalpel. As it must, the Truth is often ruthless. Thank you, Marion, for being the ideal Zen editor.

Myriam Miller, my second editor, possesses an eagle eye for detail, structure, and flow. She was both a fierce critic when necessary and a passionate believer in the story and its message. I thank her for her zealous commitment to quality.

James Buchanan, my Greenleaf Book Group editor, added the final touch this book needed. He discovered the loose threads and the dots that didn't connect and taught me how to find the whole amid the thousands of details.

A thank you goes to my talented graphic artist, Gal Weizman, who designed the beautiful book cover.

I am blessed to have four wonderful children, Elisheva, Shayna, Aaron, and Ilana, and seventeen grandchildren. Throughout this process of writing, my loving family has been there by my side, literally and figuratively. They—better than anyone—understood the need to write this story.

My father once told me, some forty-five years ago, that the first smart thing I did was "convincing" Deborah to be my girlfriend. He gave her all the credit for turning his "lost son" into a "mensch." He was probably right. This book would never have come to fruition if it weren't for her. She taught me how to love. I hope I found the words to express it.

Reader's Guide

1. "The journey toward self-knowledge begins from confusion and doubt." What part did confusion and doubt play in driving Michael and Deborah on their journey?

2. How does the fact that Deborah has had mostly Jewish friends in her life and Michael has had mostly non-Jewish friends foreshadow what happens to them on their journey?

3. In chapter 1, Michael says, "But back then when the river flowed by itself, I couldn't imagine that a gentle ripple contains a raging force and that the other side of the moon holds no light." How does this eloquent statement describe Michael's journey?

4. Michael asks his clients, "You're watching an instant replay of your life. What would you do differently? What choices would you have made or not made?" Turning this back on Michael, what choices do you think he might have wanted to change in his life? And then, making it personal, in your own life, what might you have done differently or what alternative choices do you wish you had made and why?

5. Regarding riding bike in the cold rain in Belgium: "Intense experiences like this force you to dig into yourself, to discover a level of mental toughness and resilience you didn't know you had." When in your life did you "dig into" something tough and come out on the other side more tough and resilient?

6. How do you think Michael and Deborah's habit of daily meditation helped them on their bike odyssey? Have you tried meditation and found it to be helpful in your life?

7. Michael and Deborah's journey is enriched by the people they take the time to meet along the way. Which relationship do you think is the most meaningful to Michael? Which one is the most meaningful to Deborah? Describe a time that you took a risk to get to know someone new. Did it turn out well or not?

8. Many stories seem to have a theme or at least allude to the fact that people go to Paris to "find themselves." Why do you think that is? Did Michael and Deborah "find themselves" in Paris?

9. In the days before Deborah leaves for Sweden, Michael is frightened but chooses to make the most of each moment, choosing "love over fear." Is he successful in this conscious choice? How has this lesson exhibited itself in your own life OR how could this lesson change the way you feel about a difficult circumstance?

10. Sweden was a turning point in the odyssey, a fundamental test of love, loyalty and trust. What impact do you think it had on the trip and on Michael and Deborah's relationship?

11. Were you surprised that Michael did not press Deborah to tell him what happened in Sweden? Do you think he handled it well? If you were him, would you have wanted to know what happened between Deborah and Niels?

12. Were you able to predict how this around-the-world bike tour/ soul-searching trip would end? What hints along the way led you to predict the ending?

13. Which experiences/conversations were especially important in Michael's journey toward acceptance of his Judaism?

14. Why do you think Deborah is so drawn to meet her Lebanese family even though she needs to face danger to do so?

15. In chapter 18: "We find our truth by leaving the family. Not by staying glued to it. It's how we learn to breathe on our own. Deborah's Kab Elias cousins find their sense of belonging within the family. It's their respirator." Which side do you tend to lean toward? Do you need to leave the family to find yourself, or do you find yourself within your family?

16. What thoughts and emotions arise in you regarding Michael and Deborah's interaction with Deborah's Lebanese family? What do you admire in these people?

17. Food is a major theme in Michael and Deborah's journey. What stands out to you as a food that sounds especially good or especially bad? Do you feel inspired to up your game, culinary wise?

18. What do you think Michael would have done had Deborah decided to not convert to Judaism?

19. The author says in the note to readers: "I share this story with you in the hope that the lessons we learned will inspire each of you to love with more passion, to take more risks for the truth, and to give of yourself to others as others gave to us." After finishing this book, do you feel inspired to love more, to risk to find truth more, or to give more of yourself? How might that look in your life?

20. In chapter 21, Deborah's conversation with the artist Yehoshua: "I want to know how and where you ask God for guidance. Do you scream to God to hear you? Do you whisper? Or do you walk in silence and invite God to join you in your meditation?" "I do all of that. I let my heart decide. I let my thoughts drift, and when the spirit moves me to speak or shout, I do. Sometimes I'll go for thirty minutes and sometimes for hours. Trust God is there." Do you find parallels in your own spiritual journey? Is your style more to scream, whisper, or be silent when conversing with God? Or is the whole idea of attempting to converse with God one that doesn't resonate with you?

Author Q&A

1. Your writing style is so beautiful. What kind of a writing routine do you have?

"The inspired kind. When the writing fire rages inside me, I write. I have no choice.

I have many daily routines: meditation, exercise, prayer, reading, to name a few, but writing is not one of them. Until *Riding the Edge,* I never had a compelling inner necessity to write. Writing this book had nothing to do with will, drive, discipline, or motivation. I wrote because I had to, because there was an inexplicable force in me demanding that this story be told.

Perhaps the catalyst was when my beloved wife, Deborah, was diagnosed with Alzheimer's Disease. I wanted our children, grandchildren, extended families and friends to remember this extraordinary woman as she was before this soul-destroying illness stole her life.

Writing this book was an act of love and truth. Every moment I sat recreating our journey was an experience of exquisite pleasure tempered by the knowledge that I'd give it all up in a heartbeat to get my wife back. I suspect the writing was an escape from the pain of losing my soul mate and life partner.

I didn't anticipate the impact this story would have on so many people beyond my circle of influence. There's a Talmudic statement that says, "What comes from the heart, penetrates the heart." This book came from my heart. Love was the fuel that ignited the creativity and commitment to complete my *love song to Deborah.*

Before I forget, thank you for your lovely words. A writer never tires from hearing praise."

2. What kind of physical preparation did you do to prepare for this 1980 bicycling adventure?

"I was a daily, long distance runner and competitive marathoner prior to the bicycle trip. I hadn't ridden a bicycle since I was a kid. Deborah was in decent shape from yoga and aerobics but was not an endurance athlete and she had very little experience as a bicyclist. We started slowly so she could acclimatize to the challenges of long-distance bicycling. By the end of the trip, she snarled at eighteen-degree slopes and soared down twisted mountain passes like a crazy road warrior."

3. Did you do any other multiple-day bicycle adventures after this one in 1980?

"No, I continued to run marathons for many years, and I became a competitive master's runner. Deborah became a serious yogi, and, along with her practice as a psychologist, taught yoga. In our sixties, we both fell in love with high altitude trekking and have trekked multiple times in the Himalayas and the Alps."

4. Do you have any other books in the works?

"Yes. One is a crazy idea about doing a sequel to this book in which we ride across America on electric bikes – both of us in our seventies, she with Alzheimer's, and me with a body that – let's say – 'aches in places where I used to play.' (Leonard Cohen) It will be an FU to Alzheimer's, aging, and giving up. And a big yes to rediscovering the wounded soul of America and its better angels.

The second idea is a novel that's based on a real story about someone I knew when I was in my mid-twenties. The story takes place in war torn Vietnam, in Europe prior and during World War II, and in Israel during the War of Independence."

5. What kind of advice do you have for up-and-coming writers who wish to be published?

"Find your passion, give it a voice, and put it to writing. Just do it. Whatever you first write will most likely be cringe worthy but just write and tell your inner critic to 'f' off. By the tenth revision your manuscript will begin to take shape and by the twentieth you'll have something you might feel proud of."

6. When you look back at the Michael Tobin of 1980, how are you a different person now than you were then?

"I still have a fire inside me to grow and to explore. So, the same restless spirit still exists in me. On the other hand, children, grandchildren, my long and loving relationship with Deborah, and her subsequent diagnosis of Alzheimer's Disease have all contributed to turning me into a kinder, more generous, and more compassionate version of the Michael Tobin of 1980.

I'm no longer so crazy that I'd soar hands-free down a mountain at fifty miles per hour. I'm more aware now that bones break, brains stop functioning, and pee doesn't always flow. In other words, my limitations remind me to be less arrogant."

7. Did Deborah know you were/would be writing this book? Did she have any part in helping you recall the adventure of 1980?

"Deborah was very involved with me during the process of writing. As soon as I completed a chapter, I would read it to her. She didn't remember any details from our trip, but I could tell she was emotionally moved by the story. Prior to Alzheimer's, Deborah was one of those rare souls who knew what you felt and could speak to your truth. Sadly, along with her memory, Alzheimer's has robbed Deborah of a large chunk of her emotional intelligence. Yet, on a number of occasions she did what she rarely does anymore, she cried while I read to her."

8. Food is a major theme in this book. How did culinary adventures play a part in your life, post-1980? Did any of your children become foodies also?

"I love to eat, and I love to cook gourmet meals. My kids often call me up for recipes, most of which I make up. We've travelled a great deal to India and Nepal. I'm wild about Indian food. Nepalese cuisine is a poor imitation of Indian cuisine. My son has learned how to cure meats from some of his Israeli Druse friends who know the fine art of aging and tenderizing steak and lamb. Sadly though, some of my children still put ketchup on their steaks. May God forgive them."

9. Tell us more about your four children. What kind of careers did they choose? Where did they choose to settle? And the big question, is Judaism a big part of their lives, or did they have to go through a searching process like you did in order to embrace their religion/ identity?

"Our four children, Elisheva, 38, a psychologist; Shayna, 36, a wedding gown designer; Aaron, 34, a building developer; and Ilana 32, a special education teacher, are all married with children. We moved to Israel when Elisheva was four, Shayna was two, and Aaron was five months old. Ilana was born in Israel. My children are all fluent English speakers, but their native tongue is Hebrew.

Unlike Deborah and I who went through a major transformation to discover Judaism, our children have grown up as Israelis and as Jews. None of them are particularly religious but all of them are committed to keeping the Jewish holidays and many of the family rituals. We are fortunate that our children all live close to us and we're frequently in one another's homes."

10. The subtitle of your book is "A Love Song to Deborah." What does Deborah think about the subtitle?

"I struggled with the subtitle for months until in a moment of deep contemplation I heard a voice in my head say, 'A Love Song to Deborah.' I immediately cried and I knew it had to be this. This epiphany occurred on August 23, 2020. The pre-Alzheimer's Deborah would have sobbed, on that day Deborah said, 'Oh, that's nice.'"

11. What was Deborah's relationship with her mother like after her father passed away?

"Since you're asking me, I'd say, 'psychologically challenging.' Betty Mae, more or less, came to terms with Deborah's conversion and even visited us a number of times in Israel before she passed away nine years ago. Nevertheless, she remained Betty Mae: controlling, manipulative, and self-absorbed. She and I had a number of run-ins over the years, but, by and large, we managed to get along. I could—but won't—write a book about the complexity of Deborah's relationship with her mother. On the other hand, how can I not forgive Betty Mae? She gave me an extraordinary gift."

12. Did you find peace regarding your own relationship with your parents? How did you describe your mother to your own children, since they never got to meet?

"My mother died when I was nineteen so neither Deborah nor my children knew her. However, every year on the anniversary of her death I gather the family together and tell anecdotes about her life. My children know how much I admire her and how much she's influenced my life.

My father moved to Israel with his new wife in 1982, four years before we did. He died in 1999. So, all four of our children grew up with their Zadie (grandfather) as part of their lives. They were all at his bedside when he passed away. Some of my children have fond memories of him, others less so.

My relationship with my father remained complicated. He was the most mercurial person I've known. He had his periods of being a delightfully engaging and loving individual and his times of being painfully angry and critical. That, too, is a book that will never be written. At this stage in my life, I focus more on what I gained from him than where he failed as a father."

13. What books or authors motivated and inspired you in your journey as an author?

"For much of my life I've been an avid reader. The authors who had the strongest influence on me are Hermann Hesse, Nikos Kazantzakis, and Fyodor Dostoyevsky. From studying Peter Matthiessen's, *The Snow Leopard,* I learned how to write about nature. And from meditating on Ernest Becker's, *The Denial of Death,* I learned a great deal about human psychology and the necessity to live life like your life depended on it."

14. You say that your original manuscript had over 500 pages. What kind of additional details/stories were included in that version?

"Mostly my meanderings about philosophy, psychology, love, God and the meaning of it all. Simple stuff like that. I sort of fancied myself as being able to write something akin to *Zen and the Art of Motorcycle Maintenance* but funnier, more literary, and significantly less focused on my personal battle with sanity. I deleted it all (but saved it) since it distracted from the story. Although, IMHO, an interesting diversion, nevertheless."

15. Was writing about this 1980 adventure cathartic, painful, or some of each?

"All of the above. It was like reliving the whole journey all over again but from the perspective of forty years. Fortunately, since I had kept all my journal entries, letters, maps, and photos, I could recreate the whole trip. What I didn't have were verbatim transcripts of dialogue. Therefore, I wrote dialogue as I imagined it would have happened based on who the individuals were. The whole process of writing was thrilling—like the journey itself."

16 What do you hope readers take away from reading this book?

"Exactly as I wrote in the beginning of the book: "I share this story with you in the hope that the lessons we learned will inspire each of you to love with more passion, to take more risks for the truth, and to give of yourself to others as others gave to us." The caveat is this: Whatever the reader takes away is fine. An author doesn't get to tell the reader what his experience should be."

17. Tell us about the process of writing *Riding the Edge*. Did you have the whole book outlined before you wrote it?

"I had all the chapters outlined before I wrote. I also had all the maps organized by days and routes. However, writing this book, like the journey itself, had a life of its own over which I had no control. I found myself understanding my relationship with Deborah in new and deeper ways and I discovered lessons from our numerous serendipitous encounters which I hadn't realized previously."

18. What was your favorite part of this book to write?

"Truthfully, I loved every part and relived every encounter and place as I wrote about them.

I must say of all the characters in the book (excluding Deborah) I had the strongest affinity to Simone. I truly loved her for her quirkiness, her brilliance, her insight, her pain, and her friendship. I regret that after numerous attempts to contact her, including three subsequent trips to Paris, we never found her."

—

Made in the USA
Las Vegas, NV
05 November 2021